THE LIFE OF ST. GEMMA GALGANI

by her Spiritual Director
VENERABLE FR. GERMANUS
of
ST. STANISLAUS, PASSIONIST

Translated by
THE REVEREND A.M. O'SULLIVAN, O.S.B.

With an Introduction by
THE RIGHT REVEREND FR. ABBOT AIDAN GASQUET,
O.S.B.

Passionist Nuns
1151 Donaldson Highway
Erlanger, KY 41018-1000

Nihil Obstat

H.S. BOWDEN,
Censor Deputatus

Imprimatur

✠ EDM. CAN. SURMONT
Vic. gen.

WESTMONASTERII, *die 18 Decembris 1913.*

Visa relatione Censoris a Nobis deputati, librum cui titulus "Life of Gemma Galgani" anglica lingua a R.P.D. Adalberto O'Sullivan Monacho Congr. Nostrae conscriptum, imprimi permittimus, si üs ad quos pertinet, ita videbitur.

D. MAURUS M. SERAFINI, O.S.B.
Ab. Gen. Cong. Cas. P.O.

D. ISIDORUS M. SAIN, O.S.B.
a Secretis

ROMAE, 3 Decembris, 1913

Passionist Nuns
1151 Donaldson Highway
Erlanger, KY 41018-1000

1999

Dedication
To Our Lady, Mother of Holy Hope

Translator's Preface

by Fr. A.M. O'Sullivan, O.S.B.

I WANT to say something that will help to spread a knowledge of the Servant of God, Gemma Galgani, and don't quite know how to put it briefly.

This something has nothing to do directly with the translation of her Biography. It starts from a conviction that the facts of this wonderful yet comparatively hidden life being recent, are emphatically on that account calculated to do more good than if they were of a remote period.

Having tried unsuccessfully to find someone who would undertake to do this Life into English, I was induced to attempt it, because kind and capable friends were ready to help me. Impelling motives were my devotion to this Seraphic Virgin of Lucca, my desire to meet the wish of the Author, Father Germanus of St. Stanislaus, whom I greatly esteemed, and my veneration for the Apostolic Institute of the Passionists to which he belonged; also my hope that the story of this Servant of God would do as much good among English readers as it was already doing among others.

The lives of Saints are generally of past history, and considered by many to be almost necessarily of that very elastic period "the Middle Ages." They are looked upon also by many as out of reach of ordinary mortals, and merely as interesting subjects, to be preserved in a sort of moral museum—encased in the annals of the Church to be looked at; perhaps also to color more vividly the supposed truths of fiction. We know how false such ideas are. We have Saints with us today as in the past; but it is true that their lives do not come to be known immediately. Their whole aim is to imitate Him who is meek and humble of Heart, and to live up to the teachings of the Gospel as opposed to the maxims and ways of the world; their choice is always to be unknown and totally forgotten. Another marked characteristic of the lives of God's faithful Servants is, that while here denying themselves and carrying their cross, they are always strengthened and consoled by the Church in this warfare which is the lot of man, whereas no sooner have they triumphed in the battlefield and gone to their reward, than the Church becomes silent with regard to their virtues. She then awaits the manifestation of their heroism sooner or later by the body of the faithful, who in their turn invariably come to observe, to inquire, to be moved to devotion, and loudly and universally to call on her to examine and pronounce on such holy lives.

The greatest value, I think, attaches to this Life from the exceptional fact that it is not of past history. This young girl has been with us quite lately; indeed, so recently that we all might have known her. Add to this another fact that enhances the preciousness of this biography: the great saints whom we know to have received some of the extraordinary favors, vouchsafed by Heaven to this humble virgin, were either Religious or were living in the world singular lives that attracted public attention and curiosity. Gemma Galgani did not belong to either class, but lived an uneventful commonplace life.

Behold this unassuming girl: of few years, but reaching the old age of a spotless life; a little child of the weaker sex, yet already stronger than all the powers of darkness. Then we have in her a talented girl also of striking candor, always consistent in her words and actions, of perfectly uniform temperament, and at the same time full of active energy, and ready to sacrifice herself for others. She scrupulously avoided all singularity, so that none could be detected in her, except her rare attractiveness and an indescribable majesty of bearing. She strove to hide her heavenly endowments from all, and partly succeeded. God, however, effected the ends He had in view during her life through her ingenuous simplicity, and spoke, while she was silent, through her angelic grace and dignity which riveted the attention of beholders and illuminated their minds. In a word, Gemma was an ideal. According to a distinguished writer all the Saints of the Catholic Church are ideal men and women. She, like them, charmed and satisfied everyone, leaving nothing to be desired.

But it is her most wonderful supernatural endowments which specially signalize this child of heaven as a messenger of light and encouragement to this generation. Indeed, it may be claimed that no other Servant of God of whom anything is known has been found to have received so many of those extraordinary and exceptional gifts which even among the Saints are reserved to a chosen few. These marvels, owing no doubt to the fervent prayers and unceasing watchfulness of this angelic girl, have only become generally known since her death; and observe here again, that, precisely because of their recent occurrence, they have all been verified beyond a shadow of doubt. They have likewise, through the testimony of countless witnesses still living, brought with them the most unanswerable refutation of most of the empty assertions of modern scientists regarding such supernatural matters. This innocent girl is a proof, standing in our midst, of the Infinite Mercy and Love lavished by our Savior on His creatures in the Incarnation, and another instance of His intimate personal dealings with His faithful Servants.

The pages of this Life are to many as rays of light and gifts of grace. That some will not reverence the miraculous works of God in His faithful Servant goes without saying. The votaries of atheistic science, ignoring the First Cause, build on an unsettled foundation, and refusing to raise their minds to the supernatural, they necessarily remain grovelling in sense. They cannot, because they will not, understand; for pride will never yield to Eternal Truth. Of such it is written: "The sensual man perceiveth not these things that are of the Spirit of God; for it is foolishness to him and he cannot understand."

We await with reverent submission the infallible judgment of Holy Mother Church, for whom alone it is to pronounce on the sanctity of her children, and are full of hope that she will soon proclaim the sanctity of Gemma Galgani. We are emboldened in this by the widespread and rapidly increasing devotion to this child of benediction, and by the numerous miracles that are being wrought through her intercession.

It is my humble and trustful prayer that this angelic virgin may take under her spiritual patronage all those who have helped to continue the Mission she had on earth by helping to spread the knowledge of her Life.

Preface

WHEN about to write the first edition of this wonderful life of the Servant of God, Gemma Galgani, discouraging and perplexing thoughts beset me. That was not because of the difficulty I found in the undertaking; it was owing to the distorted line of thought and reasoning so often met with when discussing supernatural things. Who does not know how, today, the Christian sentiment has become enervated and the faith has grown cold? Shameless theories and absurd doctrines have become a sort of gospel. Nay, one must scarcely speak of God even with bated breath, and eternal good is willingly renounced for the sake of temporal pleasures. Society at large has returned in mind and heart to Neopaganism, and, what is worse, those who propound and practice perverse theories are looked up to as possessed of gifted minds, and as restorers of the human race; hence they are gladly listened to and followed without inquiry.

In the midst of such sad realities what credit, I asked myself, would be given to the wonderful things that marked at every stage the life of this humble Christian maiden?

This question has since been satisfactorily answered by facts; and I will now merely say, that I began to write the Life with the conviction that at least most of those who would have the patience to read this Life through, and not be content with glancing at detached passages, would remain convinced of the genuineness and truth of what was stated in it. They would find fresh motives of edification and greater strength of faith. They would have proofs that our Lord has not ceased to lavish love on His poor creatures, and that in the midst of the general corruption of the world there ever exist chosen souls who by the fragrance of spotless and holy lives restore our fallen nature.

Most of the fears I expressed in my Preface to the first Edition have been dispelled. The Biography has pleased the public. It was sought for and read with avidity. One after another new edition was called for, and in little more than two years 23,000 copies had gone. The demand continues, the volume is read with unabated interest, and what is more important, the effect for good has been extraordinary. It seems as if God wished to be glorified in His faithful Servant and, making her merits prevail for the good of souls, has thrown around her a halo of singular attractiveness. On being merely named she becomes admired, and on hearing of her virtues, listeners feel stimulated to imitate her.

I have by me hundreds of letters from persons of every class: lay and clerical. The Holy Father, Pius X., several Cardinals, countless Bishops, all, in a word, unite in expressing their great admiration of this Angelic girl, and in their devotion to her.

The Catholic Press, becoming aware of this general manifestation, so singular in the case of a humble maiden lately gone from us after a short and hidden life, has been profoundly impressed, and has spoken of it in eloquent terms. Italian papers have continued a chain of praise, and many foreign journals are following their example. From France and Germany, from Russia, Poland, England and Spain, from India and America, etc., applications have come for leave to translate the Life of Gemma Galgani. Those who obtained this leave set immediately to work; Portuguese, German, and Polish editions are already in circulation, and others will soon follow.

Those whose applications to translate the Life were forestalled have nevertheless expressed their devotion to the Virgin of Lucca by writing charming articles about her in numberless periodicals.

It is noteworthy, that no special effort whatever has been made through advertisement, reviews, or otherwise, either to push the sale of this Biography or to excite the marvelous widespread devotion to the Servant of God that has arisen so universally. The movement has been entirely spontaneous, having its origin merely in the minds of individuals.

I have been enabled to improve the sixth edition, because of the time allowed me for ample study of all the documents already in my possession; also because of the new and fuller information that I have received regarding the Life of this humble maiden, and finally through the chronological ordering of the chapters.

Although the task of writing this Life is difficult and laborious, it is rendered less so by the abundance of matter at my disposal, and the extraordinary beauty and limpidity of the soul it portrays.

To very few biographers indeed, if any, has such an abundance of riches fallen. There has not been the least need to look up bygones, or consult remote traditions in order to describe the life of this Angelic girl.

I have no need to present to my readers, instead of historic Truths, the mere impressions of witnesses, who may not always be the most reliable. I myself am in this case the witness. In fact the greater and better part of the mystic life of this virgin has passed, so to say, before my eyes. Hence in all truth I may say in the words of St. John: "We come to make known to you what we ourselves have seen and heard, and our hands have touched." And in this my position has not been that of an ordinary observer who in like circumstances might have seen and tested what was only exterior. My dealings with her have been most intimate as her confessor and spiritual director, in which capacity nothing in the main can have escaped me of the secret mysteries of her soul.

I will add, that after God had entrusted the direction of this child's conscience to me by ways that were indeed extraordinary, I subjected her to a most rigid examination for a considerable time. Having thus made myself well assured of the quality of her spiritual disposition, and of the unmistakable truth of the divine action in her soul, I set myself to study and observe her attentively in all her movements so that nothing might escape me. Seeing that she avoided speaking of anything that concerned herself—the usual way with Saints—I frequently contrived to put to her artful questions on various topics;

and she with the candor of a little child, though in her profound humility fearing to err, always answered me to the point as well in conversation as by letter. I continued to collect her answers and compare them one with another, the earlier ones with the more recent, examining them when needed on the principles of mystic science. Thus I became daily more convinced that heavenly grace, so multiform, as St. Paul says, in its effects, and yet so consistent because divine, was actively working in her soul.

God was pleased in a wonderful way to co-operate with my efforts to obtain information. He so disposed things that the dear child should be taken into the house of a pious lady in Lucca, who loved her as if she were her own daughter, and venerated her as a Saint. As this lady also was far advanced in God's ways, she was, more than any other, in a position to value the great virtues of this chosen soul. By keeping Gemma continually near her she was able easily to follow with attentive eyes the effects of grace in her adopted child, and to note the most minute circumstances of its wonderful manifestations. As I could not always be near Gemma a happy thought struck me; it was to enjoin on her through my authority as her director, that, in order to avoid all deceit of the enemy, she should manifest regularly to her Mamma, as she affectionately called this lady, all her inner experiences, without concealing anything. The latter would then be able to report everything to me faithfully, and I should be better able to give advice and direction. By these means, seconded by the rare ingenuousness of the child, I was able in a short time to collect so much information that if I were to publish all it would fill several volumes.

With a view to render this poor work of mine still more useful, I shall not be satisfied with cursorily relating particulars of the life of the Servant of God. I shall make it a subject of study, confronting every fact with the most approved mystic doctrines, and writing only what I know to be true. This method will serve to prove the genuineness of all that is stated, and will afford directors of souls a certain practical guidance in this divine science. All are aware how abstruse this science is, and how difficult to be understood by means of theories. Hence, not a few will be grateful to me for having set it forth in its practical application to a Soul whom God had destined to pass through all its ways.

Notwithstanding what has been said, I do not pretend to be able to please everybody, and am well aware that if men of mind and thought are satisfied with what is reasonably related, it is not so with those whose aim is to fish in muddy waters. The latter not being able to refute directly what they are unwilling to accept, give vent very often to personalities against the unfortunate writer who has dared to put the distasteful doctrine before them. And who will assure us, they say, that he has not been deluded by excessive credulity? May he not be an impulsive fantastic or mistaken writer? He asserts without proving his statements. Can we hold to his words or to those of his heroine, whose revelations are often the only proof of what he says about her? Good heavens! But let me answer: If a historian, in order to gain the confidence of the public, were obliged to prove with positive arguments that he is truly a right-minded man and incapable of the least error, who would dare to take his pen in hand to write? And besides, it is assuredly a ridiculous pretension to demand that one who declares himself an ocular witness of what he narrates should step by step prove its truth as a condition of credibility. With how much greater force must not this be said when it is a question, as in the present case, not merely of stating historical facts but of describing the internal action of grace in a soul? As a matter of fact, only two persons can here give true evidence, the soul herself, by revealing what passes within her to her director, and the director who examines those secrets of conscience, in order to be well informed regarding them. But what kind of evidence would they look for in this matter with a view to make certain of the truth? The most they could expect would be renewed proofs from exterior manifestation, for holiness is not so confined to the inmost soul as not to let its beauty be evident in exterior actions. I shall not fail from time to time to bring such renewed proofs before my readers, together with abundant corroboration by witnesses most worthy of belief.

My work is to write a biography, and a biography is a collection of lines like those of a portrait the result of which when put together must be either failure, if correspondence be wanting between them and the prototype, or a true picture, if the individual they depict cannot be mistaken for any other person. The painter of this likeness may easily be at fault in some unimportant details, since it is human to err; or, not having been able to see all the minute accessories. It must not be wondered at should he draw a little from the less carefully made statements of other people. But the fact remains that a picture, to be true, must faithfully represent and must be drawn from, the original. That my biography, or portrait, truly represents, and has been carefully drawn from the original, is proved by countless facts and living witnesses. Hence those who without having seen or known the original despise it because they imagine they detect in it some inaccuracy, give proofs of deficient judgment or of prejudiced minds.

"But instead of a humble child," they say, you are presenting us with a Saint of the first order fit to stand side by side with a Teresa, a Mary Magdalene, a Veronica Juliana. And I answer: Why not? Is there anything repugnant in the fact that a humble child of our own time should be as highly favored by heaven as were, three centuries ago, the above named Saints? Certainly, judging from outward appearance, no one would have imagined such things of Gemma Galgani. But who can claim to have known her intimately and to have dealt with her familiarly, so as to arrogate to himself the right to say: "you have excessively exaggerated the lines of your portrait." With much more reason could I in all truth retort: It is you who are in fault; you seek to lessen the power of the Omnipotent, Who precisely from the most despised and contemptible of the world is wont to raise up His most glorious Saints. The Church of Christ was and ever will be the fruitful Mother of Saints. Blessed indeed are those who can glory in having had one in their midst! And wretched indeed they, who ignoring the gifts of God, render themselves guilty of that ingratitude with which our Lord reproached the Nazarenes when He said: Non est propheta sine honore, nisi in patria sua et in domo sua: *"A prophet is not without honor, save in his own country, and in his own house."*

May God be glorified in all things, as He will always be glorified in His Saints! *Qui glorificatur in conspectu sanctorum suorum.*

PROTEST OF THE AUTHOR
OF THE LIFE OF GEMMA GALGANI

In humble deference to the Decrees of the Holy See I protest and declare most explicitly, that I do not wish any other than human faith or significance to be attributed to my words or statements regarding the Servant of God, Gemma Galgani. Not intending therefore in any way to forestall the infallible judgment of the Church, whose alone it is to pronounce in matters of virtue and Sanctity, I submit myself and this book unreservedly to its censure.

Introduction

by Fr. Abbot Aidan Gasquet, O.S.B.

AT THE Beatification of Blessed Gabriel of the Addolorata in 1908, to many of us, who had the privilege of being at the function in St. Peter's, the most interesting figure amongst those present was certainly the Passionist, Father Germano di S. Stanislao. Not only had the result of the process for Canonization depended in great measure upon the zeal, work, and prudence of this holy priest, but he had also given us an account of the Saint's wonderful and saintly life.

The same Padre Germano di S. Stanislao, who only died a few months ago, is also the author of the Life of the Servant of God, Gemma Galgani, which is here translated for the benefit of English readers.

Gemma had the advantage of having as her chief director in the spiritual life this saintly Passionist Father, evidently so well-skilled in the science of the Saints. It is fortunate indeed that he was spared to complete the life of this holy soul, for no one could have given the particulars so fully, or with such authority, or have won the confidence of the reader to credit the marvels he has to relate as the author who writes with such transparent honesty, calm common sense, and perfect knowledge. He hoped, as he says, that he might be allowed to live long enough to see his spiritual daughter, Gemma Galgani, beatified. This has not been granted to him, but by this Life he has written he will have made it morally certain at no long delayed date, and his prayers in the other world will no doubt hasten the consummation of his pious wish expressed in this.

The story of Gemma Galgani will well repay perusal, for though it is merely the narrative of the life of a young girl born in a village near to the city of Lucca in our own times, it would, I think, be hard to find another such wonderful record of the dealings of Almighty God with a soul, that had given itself entirely to the leadings of His Divine Grace. To us, who live in this most materialistic age of reason alone, when the very name of God is being expunged from the school books of the young, and the dealings of His Providence with the world He has created are explained away as ridiculous and childish fables, and when the supernatural is being constantly denied altogether, or held up to so-called criticism is declared to be at best doubtful, it is useful and refreshing to have a book like this to read, which brings before us God very near indeed to our world, and in a way that can be spoken to and attested by those that have witnessed the marvels here recorded. Personally, I do not know of the life of any saint in any age of the Church which has brought home the Supernatural to my mind more plainly and fully than Father Germano's story of the Life of Gemma Galgani.

In the atmosphere in which we are called upon to live in this twentieth century, God and the things of God are apt to appear a long way off from our lives, if indeed they appear at all. Belief in the Supernatural World, which our Faith teaches us is all round about, and even any real sense of the presence of God Himself, "in Whom we live, move, and have our being," is often weakened and obscured, if not altogether obliterated by the general skepticism and infidelity of a world which claims to make the bodily senses the sole evidence of all that is real. In the middle ages, whatever may be thought of the general ignorance of the times, about which nothing need here be said, it is impossible to deny that the sense of the Supernatural was very real and universal. Heaven, in those simple days, as someone has well said, "was hardly even next door," and the Spiritual World merged almost without distinction into the world of sense, so that the one formed the acknowledged complement of the other. There was too much credulity perhaps, and some little tendency to superstition, but the Faith itself was very real and true and earnest, and there was a "bloom," so to say, upon it in those simple times, which alas! in these prosaic days of gloomy skepticism is scarcely to be recognized, and which it is hardly possible to preserve. In the "Ages of Faith," as Cardinal Newman has somewhere written, there was a kind of life in regard to God, which was almost Arcadian in its simplicity, and which reminds us of the days of the patriarchs of old, who sowed their fields and tended their herds and their sheep, and the Angels of God visited them.

We are apt to think, I fancy, that these days are no more, and that in the mists of doubt and distrust engendered by the spirit of this materialistic age of ours, not to speak of the breathless condition, which allows no time for sober thought, caused by the ever quickening pace with which we hurry along the path of life, lest we should be left behind, God's presence has withdrawn itself farther from a world that has less and less to do with Him.

In regard to ourselves too, who have to live our lives in these latter days, we seem to imagine that His arm is shortened, and the marvels of His dealings with our human souls no longer appear, as they did in the simpler and more peaceful ages of Faith.

Every now and then, however, we are startled into recognizing as a fact that God is with us still, and that it is mere folly to suppose that the days of His miracles have passed away. At one time, perhaps it is the fact of some miraculous cure at some chosen shrine or other, which manifests His power and His presence and stirs our failing Faith; at another, it may be some personal leading of His Grace which it is impossible to doubt, which comes to our help and shows His leading hand; at another, it is perchance some evident proof of His Providential care over us; at another, it is the answer to some heartfelt prayer, which proves to us at least that He is not far off from us.

The life here printed I look upon as one of those helps which are given to us from time to time to assist our Faith, and to bring God nearer to our souls. It is quite impossible, at least so it seems to me, for any Catholic to read the following pages without deep feelings of thankfulness that Almighty God has manifested Himself in such a truly marvelous way in the person of this saintly girl even in these our own days. The story of this simple maiden must be read to be fully understood; but in its main lines it is as follows: Gemma Galgani, the daughter of a fairly well-to-do chemist in the village of Camigliano, near Lucca, in Tuscany, was one of several children, most of whom died young. She was born on the 12th of March 1878, and had the great advantage of having a truly saintly mother, as well as a father who was an excellent Catholic of the old school. The surroundings of the child were thus those of an ordinary Christian household of middle-class people. From her earliest years Gemma was attracted in an extraordinary way to things of a spiritual nature, and her mother, by every means in her power, encouraged these sentiments. In fact she of set purpose instructed her how to walk in the way of the supernatural life, teaching her to realize from childhood the sacred presence of God and of His holy Angels, and to yearn after the personal love of our Divine Lord with all the ardor of her pure heart. The child responded to these early lessons of her mother, who, however, died of consumption when Gemma was but seven years old. But even at this early age the child had already experienced at the time of her Confirmation, which took place May 26, 1885, the beginnings of that direct and personal leading of the Holy Spirit, which continued all through her life and brought her whilst young in years to tread the higher paths of the Spiritual life. She herself describes this "leading" as "a voice at my heart" which "said to me" so and so. Throughout her whole life she could have no doubt both as to the reality of the voices which spoke so clearly to her soul nor as to their meaning. It was as clear and certain as if the voices were external. Generally it was Our Blessed Lord Himself Who thus manifested His desires and commands to her, for with the eyes of her soul she saw as well as heard Him. Those with whom she lived, who were nearest to her and most intimate with her, as well as her Spiritual director, had likewise no more doubt than she had, as to the honesty and reality of these manifestations. Later on in her life when she was frequently unconscious in her ecstasy, many intimate friends were witnesses without her knowledge of what at least she answered in the conversations she had with Our Lord; and these replies were so clear that from them it was possible to judge of the nature of the communications. She also, at the bidding of her director, wrote down a great deal of what was told her during these spiritual "locutions," as they are called in this Life.

Another manifestation of the supernatural world allowed to this simple girl was the constant visible presence of her Guardian Angel. He watched over her at all times, conversed with her, and often showed her what to do in order best to please her Divine Master, which was her great and in fact her only desire. From the time of her First Communion, as she told her Confessor, she experienced "an ardent desire to know in detail all the life and sufferings of Jesus," and it may be said that the memory of Our Lord's Passion was constantly in her mind during the rest of her life, and was the perpetual subject of her meditations and her prayers.

It must be borne in mind that during all the time she was the recipient of the remarkable Supernatural favors from God, which characterized her brief existence in this world, Gemma always retained the simplicity and docility of a child. Her surroundings, as I have said, were at first those of an ordinary fairly well-to-do home, in which she took her share with the rest in carrying out the domestic duties of the household. After her father's death, when the family was reduced to poverty, and she had been adopted, really on account of her piety, by a devout lady, she found herself among a number of children, in a small house, which left her even less privacy than she had enjoyed in her former home, since she had often to share her room with one or other of the daughters of the house. Here, too, she took her share of the domestic duties. It was in this way that some, at least, of the marvels wrought by God's grace in her later years were known so well to others, many of whom must still be living. We have also the absolute testimony of those who know Gemma, that so far from obtruding these favors or publishing them abroad, she did everything that was possible to hide all knowledge of them from others. She was ever modest, simple, humble, and a model of obedience in everything and to all. She lived as the others lived, and worked with the rest of the household, and she did as the rest were wont to do in every way, and was much loved and respected by all.

The account of her exalted gift of prayer given by her spiritual director in Chapter 24 of this Life is very instructive and interesting. She began the exercise of ordinary meditation under her mother's guidance whilst quite a small child of under seven years, and from the first she applied herself to it at fixed hours of the day with obvious pleasure. The morning while at church and the evening before going to bed were sacred times of mental prayer, but besides these she devoted every other spare moment she could get in the day to this holy occupation, which was really her greatest delight. At first she followed out the rules for preparation, etc., for her mental prayer, which are laid down by most spiritual writers, and which are necessary for some souls and are useful to many others. Quickly, however, she found that these ordinary helps to mental prayer did not assist her, but on the contrary were calculated to hinder her from entering upon that intimate communing of her spirit with God, which is of course the real end of all such prayer of the soul. She apparently had no difficulty whatever in regulating her thoughts, and required no artificial aids to bring God's presence before her mind. No sooner had she set herself to pray, then the world seemed to vanish from her imagination, and, as her biographer states, "she remained free to treat with God as if the earth no longer existed." The whole account of her state of prayer will well repay study, for her gift of contemplation was such that it will be difficult to find examples of it in the lives of many Saints.

The statement as to her method of prayer, which she wrote down at the bidding of her spiritual director is worth quoting from here:

"When I place myself to meditate," she says, "I use no effort, my soul immediately feels itself absorbed in the immense greatness of God, now lost at one point, now at another. But first I begin by making my soul reflect that being made to the image and likeness of God, He alone has to be its end. Then in a moment it seems that my soul flies away to God, loses the weight of the body and I, finding myself in the presence of Jesus, lose myself totally in Him. I feel that I love the heavenly Lover of His creatures, the more I think of Him the more I come to know how sweet and amiable He is."

But all these great spiritual favors were but the preparation of what was to come. The favorite, and indeed almost constant subject of thought and prayer with Gemma was Our Lord's sacred Passion. Often she begged of Our Blessed Lord to be allowed to share those sufferings with Him, or at least to be permitted to feel physically something of what He had to bear in the hours of His Passion and at the time of His death. Some few years before her own death, in 1903, her longing was partly satisfied by the reception of the Stigmata in her hands, feet and side. These wounds opened and poured forth copious streams of blood every week for some years, during the period between each Thursday to Friday night. They then closed of themselves in such a way that by Saturday all trace of anything beyond a white mark in the flesh had disappeared. Besides these marks of the Crucifixion, at various times Gemma received other tokens of her participation in the torments which Our Lord endured. For example on July 19, 1900, whilst in an ecstasy the vision of Christ wounded and bleeding came so clearly before her that she begged Him to let her suffer yet more of His Agony and bodily pains, upon which He took the Crown of Thorns from His own Head and pressed it upon hers. From that time, on the Fridays, she bore also the marks of the thorns. Her forehead was frequently seen by many witnesses to be encircled with punctures, such as the actual thorns would have made, and more strangely still, the whole of her head was found to be pierced in various places as it would have been had the crown been made in the shape of an entire cap, as the revelations of some saints have indeed described it.

Besides these marks of the Passion, Gemma was permitted on many occasions to suffer a sweat of blood like Our Savior underwent in His Agony in the Garden. This phenomenon, which naturally could not be hidden from those who lived with her, is testified to by many witnesses, and the fact cannot reasonably be called in question. She also had on her left shoulder the open wound, which according to some revelations, although it is not recorded in Holy Scripture, Our Blessed Lord received from carrying the Cross to Calvary. With this also came the bruised knees, which must have been caused by His repeated falls.

But perhaps the most extraordinary marks of Our Lord's sufferings, which the saintly girl bore on her flesh, were those of the terrible scourging at the Pillar. These marks on her body are described by many witnesses as fearful to behold: great gashes appeared in the flesh of her body, on her legs and arms as if they had really been torn open, in places even to the very bone, by the loaded whips of the soldiers as in the case of Our Lord.

Sufficient has been here said to show that the life of this saintly maiden, here made accessible to English readers, is no ordinary one, although it is the story of a young girl of our own time. A perusal of its pages cannot but make Catholics realize the fact that God is really nearer to us than, in the midst of our usual absorbing occupations in this rationalistic age, we have perhaps thought possible. Of course those who are not of the "Household of the Faith" will probably be skeptical about the whole account, and the words "fraud" and "hysteria" will be taken by many to explain satisfactorily the strange phenomena here recorded. I would beg anyone into whose hands this volume may come who may think this an adequate explanation, to read the Appendixes before passing a definite judgment. In these this precise question is discussed by the author of the life, who had the best knowledge of the holy maiden that it is possible for anyone to have.

Catholics, who believe that God is ever with the world He has created, and that even in our materialistic age His arm is not shortened, however much our vision may be restricted by our surroundings, may well thank Him for this manifestation of the power of His Grace in the Life of Gemma Galgani, which brings so clearly before us the fact that the Supernatural world is as sure, as real, and as near to us as the world of which our senses tell us. God is indeed "wonderful in His Saints."

Contents

THE LIFE OF
ST. GEMMA GALGANI

"Together, let us visit Jesus Crucified. Let us look at him; he is lifted up on the cross. If Jesus is nailed there, let us not complain if we must stand at his feet."

—Words of St. Gemma Galgani

Chapter 1

1878-1886: St. Gemma's Birth and Early Education. First Flowers of Virtue. Her Mother's Death.

CAMIGLIANO, a village in Tuscany near Lucca, was the birthplace of the angelic girl whose life I am about to write.

She was born on the 12th of March 1878. Her parents were Henry Galgani, a chemist, descended we are told from the family of the Blessed John Leonardi, and Aurelia of the noble house of Landi, both good Catholics of the old school and honored citizens. They had eight children, five boys and three girls. All of them, except three who are still living, died in their youth.

According to the custom of truly Christian parents, these good people were careful that their children should be baptized as soon as possible; and so Gemma, fourth child and eldest daughter, the day after her birth was baptized in the Parish Church of St. Michael in Camigliano by the Rector, D. Peter Quilici.

The name given her in baptism seemed providential, for she was destined to give luster to her family by the splendor of her virtues, and to shine as a brilliant gem in the Church of God. The parents of this child of benediction were no doubt moved in a special way to give her this name, for we are told that her mother, just before she was born, was full of joy; and her father also, as soon as he saw her, was impressed with feelings of special gladness. Not having experienced such feelings at the birth of any other of their children, it was natural for them to look on her as a specially precious gift, and call her Gemma. It is certain that so they regarded her as long as they lived. In their eyes Gemma was always the first among all her brothers and sisters. Her father was often heard to exclaim: "I have only two children, Gemma and Gino." Gino, though her elder by some years, yet tried to copy the virtues of his little sister, and thus came to have the second place in his father's affections. He was an angel of purity and innocence. When he died he was aspiring to the Priesthood, and had already received minor orders.

Signor Galgani, soon after Gemma's birth, in order to provide efficiently for the education of his children, took his family permanently to Lucca.

When two years old Gemma was sent with her brothers and sisters to a private half-boarding school for little boys and girls of the best families. It was kept by two excellent ladies of Lucca, Emilia and Helen Vallini. She continued to go to that school for five years. Her good mistresses some years later in a written report expressed their admiration of her as follows:

"Dear Gemma was only two years old when confided to us. From that early age she gave evidence of ripe intelligence and seemed to have already attained the use of reason. She was serious, thoughtful, wise in everything, and differed from all her companions. She was never seen to cry nor to quarrel; her countenance was always calm and sweet. Whether petted or blamed, it was all the same, her only reply was a modest smile, and her bearing was one of imperturbable composure. Her disposition was vivacious and ardent, yet during her whole time with us we were never obliged to punish her; for in the small faults that necessarily attach to that tender age the slightest reproof was enough for her and she at once obeyed. She had two brothers and two sisters at school with her. She was never seen at variance with them, and invariably yielded the best of everything to them, depriving herself of it. At the school dinner Gemma was always satisfied, and the smile that played on her lips was her only complaint or approval. She learned at once all the prayers that are daily said by children, although, if repeated together, they would occupy half an hour. When five years old she read the Office of Our Lady, and of the Dead, from the Breviary as easily and quickly as a grown person. This was owing to the special diligence of the Angelic child, from her knowing that the Breviary was a network of Divine Praise. She was assiduous at her studies, and quickly learned all that was taught her, even things that were superior to her tender years. Gemma was greatly loved in the school, specially by the little girls who always longed to be with her."

Having lately visited the Signore Vallini in Lucca, I heard their full confirmation of the above report. It ended thus: "We also wish to say that we owe to this innocent and virtuous child a great favor we received from God. While she was attending our school a very malignant type of whooping cough invaded Lucca and all our family were attacked by it. We felt that we ought not to keep the five children while it lasted; but having consulted the Parish Priest, he advised us not to abandon them because their Mother was lying ill and in danger of death. We took his advice, and on dear Gemma praying at our request the epidemic ceased, and not one of our pupils remained affected by it.

(Signed) EMILIA and HELEN VALLINI."

Gemma's father followed attentively her rapid progress in virtue and learning. He blessed God for it, and at the same time his tender love for her increased.

He used to take her with him for walks. Whatever he gave her or got for her he insisted should be of the best. On the days of school vacation he delighted to have her near him, and when he came indoors his first question was sure to be: "Where is Gemma?" Upon this the servants invariably pointed to the little room where she spent her time alone in study, or in work, or in prayer.

Without doubt such partiality on the part of a father was not praiseworthy, and it was specially displeasing to Gemma, whose singular rectitude of mind and heart was manifest to all from her very infancy. There was not a shadow of jealousy on the part of her brothers or sisters, so great was their love for her, yet her father's partiality caused her bitter grief. She often complained to him of it, protesting that she was unworthy of such attentions, and declaring how much she disliked them. And when she could not prevent them she poured out her grief in abundant tears.

It occasionally happened that this affectionate father, taking his little one on his knee, would attempt to kiss her, but in this he never succeeded. Angel in human form that she was, though most ardent in her affection, she showed even at that early age an intense dislike to all that savored of sense; and using all her strength to get away from her father's caresses she used to say, "Papa, don't touch me," and on his answering, "But surely I am your father," her reply was, "Yes, Papa, but I don't want to be touched by anyone;" and he, not to sadden her, would let her go, and, far from being displeased, ended by mingling his tears with hers and withdrew in astonishment at angelic tendencies like these in so young a child. Gemma in her turn attributed these victories to her tears, and, being always on her guard, she knew how to hold them in reserve, and used them successfully when needed.

On one occasion a youth, her first cousin, attempted to touch her, and paid dearly for it. He was on horseback at the door of their house, and, having forgotten something, called out to Gemma to bring it to him. She answered at once, and in an instant brought him what he wanted—she was then seven years of age. Touched by the graceful way in which that little service was rendered him, the youth, to show his gratitude to his dear little cousin, put out his hand when leaving to pat her on the cheek. But Gemma immediately repelled his action with such force that, losing his balance, he fell from the saddle, and was injured by the fall.

Gemma's love for her mother was quite different from that which she bore her father and the other members of her family, although it was not less true and strong. Aurelia Galgani was not only a good Christian, but a Saint, and a most perfect model to all Catholic mothers. Her prayer was continual. Every morning she partook of the Bread of Life with sentiments of vivid faith, allowing no obstacle to prevent her going to church, even when suffering from fever. From this divine Food she drew strength and spirit for the perfect fulfillment of her duties. She loved all her children, but above all Gemma, in whom she, better than anyone else, was able to recognize the gifts of God. Grace had begun very early indeed to operate in the soul of the child. Its workings became evident in her perfect and condescending dispositions; in her love of retirement and silence; in her abhorrence of vanity and pleasure-seeking; and in a certain dignity of bearing that certainly was not that of a child. Hence her mother, well-aware of her own duty, and far from indulging in useless demonstrations of affection, set herself, with the utmost care, to cultivate in her child's soul those precious germs of all virtues. Here we see a mother becoming the spiritual directress of her daughter, and Gemma, in her turn, full of gratitude to our Lord for having given her such a mother, was ever mindful of the assiduous and unceasing care thus lavished on her. She used to declare that it was to her mother she owed her knowledge of God and her love of virtue.

This saintly mother used often to take her Gemma in her arms, and teach her holy things, mingling tears with her words. "I begged of Jesus," she said to her, "to give me a daughter. He has indeed consoled me, but too late! I am failing and soon must leave thee; make good use of thy Mother's instructions." And then she would explain to her the truths of our holy Faith, the preciousness of the soul, the deformity of sin, the happiness of belonging entirely to God, and the vanity of the world. At other times she used to show her the Image of our crucified Lord and say to her, "Look, Gemma, how this dear Jesus died on the cross for us;" and adapting herself to the capacity of the child, she studied how to make her understand the mystery of the love of God, and how every Christian is obliged to correspond thereto. She taught her how to pray, and habitually said prayers with her, in the morning, as soon as she rose, in the evening before going to rest, and very often in the course of the day.

All know how tiresome it is for children to listen to sermons and recite vocal prayers, owing to their difficulty of giving fixed attention to anything, and to their eagerness for novelties. But it was not so with Gemma. She found her whole delight in those first lessons of piety, and consequently she never tired of hearing sermons and praying; and when her mother got tired, or had to stop in order to attend to her home duties, Gemma following her closely used to say: "Mamma, tell me a little more about Jesus."

The nearer this good mother felt herself drawing to her end, the greater became her zeal and ardor in the religious education of her children. Every Saturday she took them with her to the church, or, if not able to go, got someone else to take them. She arranged for the elder ones to go to Confession, although some of them, including Gemma, were not yet seven years of age. She thus accustomed them while young to frequent this salutary Sacrament. She herself prepared them for it, and when it was Gemma's turn, this devout mother used to weep on seeing her gravity and attention, and the great sorrow she displayed for her little faults.

On one occasion she said: "Gemma, if I could take you when Jesus calls me would you be glad of it?" "Where?" answered the child. "To Paradise, with Jesus and His angels." At these words the heart of the little one was filled with great joy, and from that moment there was kindled within her so great a desire to go to heaven, that it never left her. Indeed it so increased with her years as to consume her whole being. This we shall see in the progress of her story. She herself once said to me, "It was indeed my Mother who from my earliest years instilled into me this longing for heaven." Then, alluding to my having forbidden her to ask to die, she added with indescribable simplicity: "And now, after sixteen years, if I still desire Paradise and long to go there, I get good scoldings for it. To Mamma, I answered, `Yes'; and because she so often spoke to me of Paradise, I wished never to be separated from her, and never left her room."

Signora Galgani's disease was consumption, and for five years it had been wasting her away. No sooner had the doctors ascertained its nature than a strict prohibition was issued forbidding any of the children to approach their poor sick mother's bed. Gemma was bitterly afflicted at finding herself thus in an instant separated from her whom she doubly loved as a mother and as a spiritual guide. "And now," she would say in tears, "away from Mamma, who will urge me to pray and to love Jesus?" She begged and implored, and with great difficulty obtained that in her case at least some exception might be made. We can form some idea of how this fervent child availed herself of such a permission. She so took advantage of it, that thinking over it afterwards, she felt deeply grieved, believing that she had disobeyed and allowed herself to be led by caprice. She herself tells us how she was employed by that bedside: "I drew near to her and knelt by her pillow, and we prayed." Sublime instinct in a little girl, not yet seven years of age!

Meanwhile the day of final separation was drawing nigh. The sick mother grew daily worse, although outwardly the imminent danger was not visible. Even at that last stage she showed herself ever solicitous for the spiritual good of her children. Gemma, though of such tender years, was more than well fit to receive the Sacrament of Confirmation; and, "now," thought her devout mother, "I cannot do better than entrust this dear child to the Holy Spirit before I die; when the last hour is near I shall know to Whom I have left her." Gemma meanwhile had been preparing herself to worthily receive this Sacrament; and not content with that, she brought a Mistress of the Christian Doctrine to the house every evening in order to add greater perfection to her own work. When all was ready, on the first occasion that offered itself, the child was accompanied to the Basilica of St. Michael in Foro, where the Archbishop, Monsignor Nicholas Ghilardi, was giving Confirmation. It was May 26, 1885. From particulars that escaped from Gemma later on, we shall be able to form some idea of the exceptional communications she received from the Holy Spirit in that Sacrament. It is well that she herself should tell us in all her candor what happened on the occasion.

When the ceremony was over, those who accompanied Gemma wished to remain to hear another Mass in thanksgiving, and she gladly availed herself of the opportunity in order to pray for her sick mother. "I heard Holy Mass," she said, "as well as I could, praying for Mamma, when all of a sudden, a voice at my heart said to me: 'Wilt thou give me Mamma?' 'Yes,' I answered, 'but provided Thou takest me also.' 'No,' replied the voice, 'give Me unreservedly thy mother. Thou hast to wait for the present with thy father. I will take thee to Heaven later.' I was obliged to answer 'Yes,' and when Mass was over I ran home. Oh! the ways of God!" This, if we are not mistaken, was the first heavenly locution to Gemma. Many others followed which we propose to relate in their order. The circumstance of the sacramental descent of the Holy Spirit in that innocent soul is of itself a good reason for believing that He was the author of that locution, the truth of which moreover was corroborated by what followed.

Gemma had made the sacrifice to God of what she held most dear in the world; the merit of it was secured to her in heaven. She came home from the church and found her mother dying. She knelt and prayed by her bedside, shedding bitter tears, declaring at the same time that she would not leave till all was over as she wished to hear Mamma's last words. But her father could not bear to leave her there, through fear that she would die before her mother. He made her a sign to leave, and directed that she should go with her Aunt Helen Landi to San Gennaro and there remain till he recalled her. She had nourished a constant hope to be able to keep close to her mother, and go with her to Paradise. She had only just resigned that hope at the foot of the Altar, and now again generously obeying her father's will she left at once. Meanwhile her mother rallied a little but soon relapsed, and on the 19th of September 1886, died the death of a saint in the thirty-ninth year of her age. The sad news was taken immediately to Gemma, while still in her Aunt's house, and admirable beyond words was the resignation with which she received it. But we can well imagine what must have been the poignant grief of such a separation.

Thus, O my God, dost Thou will to try souls most dear to Thee, even in their tenderest years.

Chapter 2

1886-1887: At S. Gennaro With An Aunt. Returns to Lucca. Is Sent to School. Her First Communion.

ALTHOUGH her Aunt Helen, by whom Gemma had been received, was good and pious, yet she could not be compared to her mother. This child who found pleasure only in practices of devotion soon became aware of the great void that was created around her, first by her separation from her mother, and then by her death. "Then indeed," she said to me, "I had to weep over the time when Mamma let me pray so much." She wished to go to church early in the morning, but found no one at that hour to accompany her. She longed to remain alone in some solitary place to commune with God, and they would not leave her in peace even for a moment. Her extreme humility made her look on herself as a great sinner, and therefore in need of frequent confession; nor in this was she gratified, as all knew well what a paragon of innocence she was. There was no one in the absence of her spiritual director to speak to her of Jesus; yet this was the only nourishment she relished. Owing to these and other privations, the poor child had to undergo pains like those of death. But God soon came to shorten her martyrdom.

Gemma's Aunt Helen Landi loved her angelic little niece most tenderly, because of her staid and ingenuous manner, her rare modesty, and her illuminated piety, so rare in a child of her age. She accordingly took steps to keep the precious child permanently with her. Gemma's brother, Gino, at the same time felt her absence unbearable and implored of his father to bring her home. Signor Galgani too was more than anxious to have his beloved child with him. Hence in his desolation after his terrible bereavement, having thought seriously over what had to be done with regard to his children, who were scattered here and there, and having their religious instruction and education more at heart than anything else, he resolved to recall them all around him. That was about Christmas of the same year, 1886.

This affectionate father had not the heart to separate himself from Gemma, by placing her at a boarding school. He therefore determined to send her as a half-boarder to finish her education at the renowned Establishment in Lucca, managed by the Sisters of St. Zita, and commonly known as the Guerra Institute, from the name of its Foundress. It was a happy thought of her father to confide his daughter to such excellent teachers, who, together with literature and the arts, impart abundant religious instruction to their pupils, and ground them in solid Christian piety.

The great joy felt by Gemma at this determination of her father is quite manifest from the following words to her director: "I began to go to the school of the Sisters; I was in Paradise!" And she had good reason to say so. For having mistresses consecrated to God by profession, with many pious practices between the hours of study and work and recreation, she, who from her earliest years had been accustomed to live rather in Heaven than on earth, had certainly found her true center. Very soon indeed her new teachers and companions were struck by her rare dispositions and drawn to admire and love her. She on her side strove to pass things off, in order to keep hidden from the gaze of others. But she did not succeed in preventing the candor of her soul from radiating through her whole person. This was particularly visible in her eyes. Hence one of the Religious said to her on a particular occasion: "Gemma, Gemma, if I did not read you through your eyes I should not know you." Although she was in years among the youngest in her class, yet so great was the reverence with which she inspired the others, that all looked up to her as the first among them. We shall have more to say later on about Gemma's School life; here we must speak particularly about her First Communion which she expressed her desire to make at once on going to the Sister's School. That great act was to be the crowning one of Gemma's life. Long before this time the innocent child, pierced through the heart by the arrow of Divine Love, was being consumed by her longing to be united with Jesus in the Adorable Sacrament of the Altar. Her mother, a saint indeed, had instilled into her a knowledge and foretaste of its sweetness; and, in order to excite within her more and more a craving for the Bread of Life, she very often took her before the Tabernacle, whence Our Savior continually sends His Divine Rays into the hearts that long for Him, and, more particularly, into guileless souls.

Gemma was then nine years old, and already at that early age her heart panted for Jesus. She longed to have Him, and repeatedly with tears besought her Confessor, her father, and her school teachers to give Him to her. The prevailing custom, however, was against her; the more so, because she looked much younger than she really was, owing to her small and delicate frame, so that, at nine years of age, she appeared to be scarcely six. But she repeated her entreaties: "Give me Jesus," she would say, "and you will see how good I shall be. I shall be quite changed. I won't commit any more sin. Give Him to me, I so long for Him, and I cannot live without Him." Her confessor, the Rev. John Volpi, later on Bishop of Arezzo, gave way at last to her repeated entreaties, so unusual in a child of her age. He assured her father of her great worthiness, and said: "If we do not want our Gemma to die of longing, we must allow her to go to Communion."

Let those describe who can, the joy of this angelic child at the granting of her desire. After having, with overflowing heart, thanked Our Lord and His Blessed Mother for the favor, she directed her thoughts to the perfect performance of the great act and at once determined to make her preparation in the Convent, where, after a course of spiritual exercises in quiet and solitude, she would be better able to attend to the great object in view. Her father, however, was much opposed to this plan, as he did not wish to be separated from his beloved child even for a day. But she so wept and implored that, at last, he yielded to her wishes. The reader will be glad if I give Gemma's own words of what happened: "He gave me his consent in the evening," she said, "and early next morning I went to the Convent, and remained there ten days. During that time I saw none of our family. But, oh! how happy I was! What a paradise! Immediately on entering the Convent enclosure, I ran to the chapel to thank Jesus, and with all the earnestness I could command, implored of Him to prepare me well for my Holy Communion. Then I felt, rising in my heart, an ardent desire to know in detail all the life and sufferings of Jesus." We have seen already how her pious mother initiated Gemma from her earliest years in meditation on the Passion, and the Religious in the school taught her to continue it. But who had told this child how our Savior's Passion allies itself so intimately with the mystery of the Blessed Eucharist, that the way to realize and possess the one is by means of the other? Without doubt that same Holy Spirit Who, even in her tender years, had so divinely enlightened and inflamed her soul, was again her Teacher. "I made known," she continues, "my ardent desire to know about Jesus to my mistress, and she began to explain it to me, day by day, choosing for this purpose an hour when the other children were in bed. One evening, when she was telling me something of the Crucifixion, Crowning with Thorns, and all the sufferings of Jesus, her explanation was so true to life, and caused me such pain of heart, that I had to remain in bed all the following day. The mistress, in consequence, stopped her instructions, but I continued to attend the sermons. Every day that good preacher used to say: 'Whoever feeds on Jesus shall live of His Life.' These words filled me with the greatest consolation, and I went on reasoning thus to myself: 'When Jesus, then, comes to me I shall no longer live in myself because He will live in me!' And I almost died with longing to be able to say those words: 'Jesus lives in me!' Sometimes I passed the whole night meditating on them, all inflamed with desire. I prepared for my general Confession, and made it at three intervals to the Rev. Dom Volpi, and finished it on the Saturday, vigil of the happy day!" That was the 19th of June 1887, to which day the solemnity of the Feast of the Sacred Heart of Jesus had been transferred from the previous Friday.

On the same Saturday Gemma wrote to her father, and, drawing her ideas from the depth of a heart overflowing with holy affections, she composed the following short letter—short, indeed, because one who feels deeply can say but little:

"DEAR PAPA: *Today is the vigil of the day of my First Communion; a day for me of infinite contentment. I write these lines only to assure you of my love, and to move you to pray to Jesus, in order that the first time He comes to dwell in me, He may find me disposed to receive all the graces He has prepared for me. I beg your pardon for all my disobedience and all the pain I have ever given you, and I beg of you this evening to forget them all. I ask you to bless me—Your most loving daughter—*GEMMA."

At length the day so longed for dawned. She wrote as follows to her spiritual director: *"The Sunday came at last. I rose quickly. I ran to Jesus for the first time. My longings were finally gratified. I then understood the promise of Jesus: 'He that eateth Me, the same also shall live by Me.' My father, it is impossible to explain what then passed between Jesus and me. He made Himself felt, oh so strongly, in my soul. I then understood how the delights of Heaven are not like those of the earth. I felt seized with a desire to make that union with my God everlasting. I felt more detached from the world, and more than ever disposed to recollection."*

Words like these cannot indeed be spoken by one who has to invent them. Art cannot rise to such a height, or give expression to thoughts so full of the fire of heavenly love.

Before leaving the retreat of the spiritual exercises, the holy child wrote down the following resolutions:

1. I will confess my sins and receive Holy Communion each time, as if it were to be the last.

2. *I will often visit Jesus in the Blessed Sacrament, particularly when afflicted.*

3. *I will prepare for every Feast of Our Blessed Lady by some mortification, and every evening I will ask my Heavenly Mother's blessing.*

4. *I will endeavor to keep always in the presence of God.*

5. *Every time the clock strikes I will repeat three times: My Jesus, mercy!*

She desired to add many other resolutions, but was prevented by her mistress, who came to her while she was writing. She desired her not to add more to what she had written, for fear that, by taking too much on herself, she might injure her health. For it was certain that, gifted as she was with the greatest firmness of character, and with such extraordinary fervor, whatever she promised Our Lord she would fulfill with all the energy of her soul.

The happy impression made on Gemma's heart by her First Communion never left her. "The dear child," says one of her mistresses, "spoke of that great event with inexpressible joy, and in the hours of recreation often returned to the subject of the spiritual consolation experienced in those happy moments. During the spiritual exercises that are always preparatory to the First Communion of our children, her joy was at its height, and she used to take part in them, as if she also was then about to make her First Communion." She used also every year to commemorate that great day with special devotion, and called it her Feast Day. Let anyone who wishes to know in what this devotion consisted, simply read the letter that, on one of these Feast Days, in June 1901, she wrote to her spiritual director. It has two parts. The first was written while she was in ecstasy, witnessed by several members of her family, and is a sort of introduction:

MY FATHER: *I don't know if you are aware that the Feast of the Sacred Heart of Jesus is also my Feast Day. Yesterday, father, I passed a day of Paradise! I remained all the time with Jesus. I spoke always with Jesus. I was happy with Jesus, and I wept too with Jesus. Interior recollection kept me more than ordinarily united with my beloved Jesus. O freezing thoughts of the world, away from me! I wish to remain always with Jesus, and Jesus only!"* Then turning to herself, as was her custom, to humble herself after such an outburst of love, she continued: *"My Jesus, and Thou still bearest with me? The more I think of my baseness, the more I lose myself in astonishment, and find nothing to bring me peace, until I fly to Thy infinite mercy. My Jesus, Mercy!"*

She came out of the ecstasy, and remark with what ease she then continues her letter: *"Father, where are my thoughts taking me? To my beautiful First Communion Day! Yesterday, the Feast of the Heart of Jesus, I felt again the joy of the happy day of my First Communion. Yesterday again I tasted Paradise. But what is it to taste it for one day only, when, later, we are to taste its delights for ever! Truly, the day of my First Communion was the day on which I found my heart most truly burning with love of Jesus. And how happy I was, when, with Jesus in my heart, I was able to exclaim: 'O, my God, Thy Heart is mine! That, surely, which constitutes Thy Beatitude can make also mine! What more, then, is wanting to happiness? Nothing!'"* Then returning, as usual, to her work of self-humiliation, she adds: *"O father, father! But all days are not alike. I pass many in which I feel ashamed of myself. Oh! how many times have I not listened to the deceits of the world! Oh! that Jesus would come quickly, and take my heart away, and take possession of it Himself. If He does not wish me to turn back, and to rob Him of it by my sins! O my God"* (and here again she became rapt in ecstasy as she wrote) *"I would make a bundle of all my wicked inclinations, and hand it to Thee, in order that Thou mightest consume it in the furnace of Thy Love. But, my God, if I am not able to do everything at once, I will at least make it my object to destroy all my passions. And I promise Thee never to approach Thy*

Holy Table, if I have not previously been victorious in something over myself."

I should never end, were I to quote all those passages in which she returns with always fresh eloquence to the subject of her First Communion. However, those few words of hers that I have put before my readers may be enough to make them understand the large heart that was within this child's bosom, and the great heights to which this angel of the earth soared, when only nine years of age.

At her Confirmation God spoke to her heart, and, asking her for the sacrifice of her greatest treasure on earth, her mother, detached her from every earthly affection. In Holy Communion He made her taste the sweetness of the Bread of Life, and, inviting her to perfect union with His Divine Majesty, He thus disposed her to suffer those hard trials by which the love of God is exalted and purified.

Thrice happy child! to whom it was given so soon to know the mysteries of the Kingdom of God, that are hidden from the greater part of mankind; and to taste the sweetness of the heavenly manna of the Blessed Eucharist, given by Him Who has said: "He who shall eat My Flesh, and drink My Blood, shall have eternal life."

Chapter 3

1888-1894: At School Her Character and Virtues Develop and Become Better Known.

WE HAVE seen with what fervor Gemma performed the solemn act of her first Communion. Immediately after it she resumed her school duties and with her wonted diligence, piety, and engaging ways, became daily more dear to her mistresses and companions. "She was the soul of the school." These are the words of another mistress: "Nothing was done without her during the whole time she was with us. All her companions bore her the greatest affection, and wished to associate her in their festivities, and in everything they did. And all this notwithstanding that her disposition was reserved, her words concise, and her action resolute, even sometimes apparently rude."

No doubt one would occasionally so conclude from external appearances. It could not however be said with truth that such was her disposition. She spoke little, through fear, as she often quite ingenuously told me, that, yielding to her natural impulses, she might transgress and offend God. And as she knew well how to master self so as to make that which was the fruit of virtue appear in her to be natural, it happened that a friend seeing her so serious and unwilling to speak, accused her of haughtiness and pride, and she smiling answered: "What could pride have to do in the matter? I am not even thinking of it. I don't answer because I don't know what to say. I don't know if I should answer rightly or wrongly, so I keep silent and there is an end to it."

When she was a little older, remembering to have been accused of pride, she observed with her inimitable candor and humility: "Yes, truly I was guilty of that sin, but Jesus knows if I was aware of it. I have often gone to the Mistresses, to my companions, and to the

Mother Superior to ask them to forgive my pride. Then in the evening and often during the night I wept on account of it. Still I did not know it." Oh! Humble pride!

A marked feature of Gemma's disposition was her vivacity, and whoever observed her closely and attentively could easily see that she was of a sanguine temperament and all impetuosity. For this reason, if it were not for the violence that she continually did herself, she would have been, as indeed was said of her by some, a perfect madcap; and with mental gifts so prompt and piercing she would have been able to domineer over others. How often did I not myself behold her suppressing the first risings of that mental fire, and for that purpose using even muscular exertion! And how often have I not been filled with wonder at seeing virtues so generous, so constant and so prompt in a mere child! Others have the same to say about her. "She was of vivacious temperament," says one, "but quiet, for she always conquered herself." She never lost her temper, never argued, and when others contended with her, or even abused her, her way of answering was with an amiable glance, followed by a smile so sweet that not rarely her adversary was forced to throw her arms around her neck, and hug her affectionately. "Occasionally," observes another, "it happened that someone, attributing a disorder in the house to Gemma, scolded her angrily for it. Then she, having listened in silence, whether right or wrong, used to say: 'Don't get angry. Don't let it trouble you. You will see, I will be good, and won't do it again.'" So great was the command this angel had of herself.

As to her apparent rudeness, that came from her natural and characteristic candor and sincerity. With her, yes was yes, and no was no, white was white, and black was black. There were no double meanings, no folds in that heart. As she felt within her, so she spoke and so she acted, without seeking any middle terms, whatever her aim might be, no matter with whom she might be speaking. That which passes in the world as ceremony was unknown to her. Accordingly, content with the observance of the essential rules of civility, she did not wish to be informed of any others. She spoke openly to all, and could not imagine how such sincerity could displease anyone. When this candid child wished to hold a long conversation, a thing which seldom happened, it was so interesting that one could remain listening and talking to her for any length of time without feeling tired. This sometimes happened at the school, where all the pupils loved Gemma so dearly. And when she fell ill and had to leave school there was general grief among her companions.

In like manner because of her singular reserve in conversation and her constant inner thoughts some imagined her timid and others pronounced her dull. Gemma however paid not the least attention to opinions and remarks, and when forced to answer them she would modestly say: "Am I obliged to try to please people? I am certainly stupid, and what harm if others think me so? It does not matter in the least to me." On one occasion when ill she was visited by a doctor; and he, seeing her so modest and collected and averse to being touched, took her to be an oddity. Accordingly when the visit was over he ventured to make her some propositions based on worldly maxims, with a view to convince her of mistaken views. Gemma, who up to then remained silent, rose to the occasion, and with such promptness and force of reason attacked one by one and demolished his feeble arguments, that the learned gentleman found himself silenced, to his great confusion, and to the wonder of all who were present. I myself, more than once, wished to try the experiment by proposing to her a variety of sophisms; but I had always to acknowledge myself worsted by her answers, so animated, wise and conclusive were they.

Let me return to the School, and to the Religious. In a long attestation of Sister Julia Sestini, from which some of the particulars so far noted have been taken, I find also the following words, showing the admiration in which Gemma was held by her teachers:

"With regard to her mistresses, including the Reverend Mother Superior, Mother Guerra, who was her mistress in her finishing

course in 1891-1892, they all esteemed and loved her greatly. By reason of my office I had occasion to be with her more than the other Sisters, and was constantly struck by her solid piety and childlike candor. Nay, from the very first days that I knew her, she impressed me as being a soul most dear to God, yet hidden from the world. I noticed later when urging the children to the practice of a little mental prayer in the morning, and examination of conscience in the evening, that she, who was already advanced in these exercises, took them always more to heart than her companions. But I never could get her to tell me how much time she devoted to them, and only from a few curt answers she gave when questioned on the subject was it made evident that she employed much time in meditation. Gemma longed to hear the Word of God, and showed the greatest satisfaction on the days when the priest, the Rev. Raphael Cianetti, came to explain the Catechism. The same may be said with regard to the sermons that were preached in the Institute on various Feasts of the year. She had resolved to become a Saint, like the Ven. Bartholomea Capitanio, and reminding her of this I often said to her: 'Gemma, remember that you have to become a truly precious jewel.'"

As there cannot be true sanctity unless it is acquired at the foot of the Cross, God put into Gemma's soul an ardent desire to know this mystery of the Redemption. To this end she applied to her mistress, and besought her so often to explain this great mystery to her, that the Sister consented to do so on the days on which her disciple should get the maximum of good marks both in lessons and work. "What better reward than this?" said Gemma to herself, and setting to work with redoubled diligence she succeeded from that day in almost always gaining the highest number of marks and thus very often secured the desired instruction. "How many times," she said to me when talking over these things, "did not the thought of the love of Jesus, in suffering so much for us who are so ungrateful, force the Mistress and me to weep together!" The good Religious also taught her how to practice some little mortifications, in order to compensate Jesus for her many backslidings. She spoke to her of various instruments of penance, whereupon the fervent child procured some and fitted them for herself; but, notwithstanding all she said and did, she was not allowed to use them. Meanwhile under the guidance of the same Religious, she made up for the refusal by a rigid mortification of her eyes, her tongue, and her senses; and particularly of her will. In this exercise she became truly admirable during the rest of her life, as we shall see.

Things went on in this way until March 1888, when God was pleased to call to Himself this pious Mistress, Sister Camilla Vagliensi, a religious of rare holiness of life. Then Gemma was placed under the direction of another equally virtuous teacher, Sister Julia Sestini, who was gifted with a singular spirit of prayer. "Under this Mistress," said Gemma to me, "I too began to have a great desire for prayer. Every evening immediately on coming home from school, I shut myself in my room and said the whole Rosary on my knees. Also several times during the night I rose for about a quarter of an hour and recommended my soul and its needs to Jesus."

This Angelic child, persevering in her good dispositions and full of fervor, continued during the whole of that year (1888) to attend the same school, and began to take her younger sister, Angiolina with her. The Gospel words, written of Our Blessed Savior, could well be applied to her: she continued to grow in wisdom and grace before God and man.

But the way of the just on earth is often strewn with thorns, and it rarely happens that Our Lord does not subject His chosen ones, even while young, to suffering, thus preparing them step by step for great spiritual battles with the powers of darkness—battles too, of sympathy, love, union. We have seen that it was so with Gemma when seven years of age. A hundred times more severe was the trial awaiting her, that of spiritual desolation called by ascetic writers the inner martyrdom. Previously she had many consolations, heavenly attractions and incentives to the perfect exercise of every virtue. Now instead weariness, sadness, repugnance to prayer. No longer that abhorrence of all that savored of the world. Her Jesus is no longer to be found, and those loving meetings with Him of the past seem now but a dream. This trial was not of a few days but lasted nearly a year. Yet for her it was not lost time, no, it was a great gain, for feeling herself as it were abandoned by her God Whom she so loved, she sought with greater earnestness to find Him, detaching her affections more from earthly things, frequenting Holy Communion with renewed ardor and striving at greater perfection in the practice of virtue. She strove to establish in her heart that horror of sin which increased with her years, and a greater sorrow for those venialities of the past that appeared to her great faults.

The members of her family not knowing that God was leading her to the most exalted sanctity showed their displeasure at the evident change in her exterior. They wanted her to seek amusement, and hindered her going out early in the morning and so often to the church. In the evening they wished her to join them in their walks dressed like her sisters, and in other ways pained her greatly.

But God came to her aid, through the death of her grandfather and Uncle Maurice in 1890. This caused two of her aunts, her father's sisters, to come from S. Gennaro to live with him and his family. These aunts were both devout women and very fond of their brother's children. They came at a most opportune time, inasmuch as some members of the household, not understanding the extraordinary change wrought in Gemma by her First Communion, had begun to put repeated obstacles in her way. But, when her good aunts came to live with them, Gemma found herself entrusted to them, and thus emancipated. She went with them every morning to hear Mass before going to school, and, in the evening, to visit the Blessed Sacrament. With them she used to pray and talk about holy things. In a word, it seemed to her almost as if she had returned to those happy days when her mother was alive. Thenceforth, she never omitted her

Communions. At first, she approached the Holy Table three times a week, as her confessor objected to her going more frequently. Later on, she went to Holy Communion every day; and, as she grew in the spiritual life, she herself with candid simplicity thus puts it: "Jesus made His presence felt in my poor soul more and more. He said so many things to me, and often made me feel the greatest consolations."

Gemma, now thirteen years of age (1891), has already surmounted heights of virtue that others are scarcely able to reach after long years of assiduous labor. Yet all she had done seemed to her but little, and like the Apostle, not looking back but keeping her eyes fixed on the perfection to which she felt called by God, she labored with great energy at her spiritual advancement.

About this time the Sisters of St. Zita were having their biennial course of Spiritual Exercises in which the externs among their pupils took part. "I saw," said Gemma, "that Jesus sent me this opportunity of acquiring a better knowledge of myself, and in order to purify my soul and please Him more." And in her little book of notes she wrote: "Exercises of 1891 in which Gemma must change and give herself all to God." Later when referring to the same Exercises she wrote as follows: "I remember the preacher's sermon on sin. Then indeed I came to know that I deserved to be despised by all. I saw my ingratitude to God, and beheld myself covered with sins. We then made the meditation on Hell. I recognized how I deserved it, and resolved to make also during the day repeated acts of contrition." Here it would appear that she was already accustomed to make those acts frequently during the night, and she added that after the meditation on the humility, sweetness, obedience, and patience of Jesus, she made the following resolutions:

1. To make every day a Visit to Jesus in the Blessed Sacrament, speaking to Him more with my heart than with my tongue.

2. I will make every effort never to speak of indifferent things, but often of the things of heaven.

Let no one think that on account of her lengthened prayer and assiduous attention to spiritual things, Gemma was led to neglect her school duties. On the contrary, she was most diligent, and at the yearly examination carried off the highest prizes. In the scholastic year 1893-1894 she won the great Gold Prize for religious knowledge, which is given only to those pupils who in the whole course of the year have always had the highest number of marks: ten—in the lessons of Christian Doctrine. At the school exhibitions the Sisters sometimes succeeded in overcoming this humble child's great repugnance to display, and made her exhibit compositions, verses, exercises in French, arithmetic, etc. This is a proof of her ability and proficiency in such studies. We are even told that her own family, seeing her so intent on her books, often reproved her saying: "What need of so much study? You know so much already, and yet it does not satisfy you."

Another great loss for the poor child was pending. Her brother Gino, whom we have already mentioned, having fallen a victim to the disease of which his mother died, was at the point of death. Gemma and he loved each other tenderly. They were two souls in one, seeing and feeling alike, especially in all that regarded piety. Hence they became inseparable in this last extremity. The devout youth, the moment he became aware that his sister was in the house, wished to have her at his bedside. She saw clearly the danger of contagion, but regardless of her own life, she remained close by his pillow day and night, serving and comforting him, and suggesting holy thoughts to prepare him for eternity. This innocent youth died an enviable death, in September 1894, and soon after Gemma fell ill of a dangerous complaint that kept her in bed for three months.

Nothing could exceed the anxiety of her family about her. "I cannot give an idea," she said, "of the care they all lavished on me, especially Babbo whom I often saw crying and begging of God that he, rather than I, might die." It would seem that Heaven heard his prayer. Within two years he died. As God willed it she recovered, but her sickness left her so weak and shaken that it was found necessary to forbid her to study. With her usual resignation to the Will of God and to her father's wish that she should leave school, she calmly returned to the solitude of her home, being then in her fifteenth year.

In this way God is wont to chequer the lives of His Elect between roses and thorns. There is no consolation coming from Him whose sweetness is not soon followed by the bitterness of some cross. Blessed are they, who like Gemma know how to accept both consolations and crosses—roses and thorns—with equal resignation and courage!

CHAPTER 4

1894-1897: St. Gemma's Life at Home. Her Heroic Patience in Great Trials.

HAVING left school, Gemma devoted herself earnestly to domestic affairs, and to her little brothers and sisters. She fulfilled all her duties with the greatest exactness, and when she noticed any defect in others she attributed it to her own fault and negligence.

The good example she gave at home could not escape being noticed and admired by all, even by strangers, and up to this day it is talked of. Among others, there was a servant in the house, named Peter Maggi, who often accompanied Gemma when she went out of doors. In order to express his astonishment at the virtues of his little mistress, he used to say that they were more than he could tell about, "because Gemma stood alone and there was no one like her."

She also excited the admiration of others by her singular love of the poor, and she humbly tells us in her obligatory statement, that this charity towards the poor was the only good thing left in her in the midst of so many defects and spiritual miseries. "Whenever I left the house," she says, "I always wanted money from Papa, and, if he sometimes refused to give it me, I besought him to let me take bread, flour and other things. It was God's will that I should meet poor people, because three or four met me every time I went out of doors. To those that came to the house I gave linen and all that I could lay my hands on. I was then forbidden to do this by my confessor. Papa gave me no more money. I could not take anything more from the house, and every time I went out I seemed to meet none but the poor. They all ran to me and I could not give them anything. This was a grief that often made me cry, and it was for this reason that I resolved not to go out of the house any more."

She was not, however, able to keep this resolution. Her father, knowing her ardent nature and the need she had of exercise, obliged her to go out. Another reason was, that her brothers and sisters in the absence of anyone else might have her as a sure guide and companion in their recreations. Then Gemma obeyed, and, scarcely out of the house, through certain by-ways known to her, they reached the country where they could enjoy the benefit of the open air and be out of the bustle and noise of the town. But, even this innocent recreation, accepted only through obedience and spent amid so many precautions, was destined to be embittered by the devil. A young man, an officer in the army, having seen Gemma, took to following her. She did not notice this, but she was told of it, and was intensely pained thereat. She thereupon resolved not to leave the house, except to go to the adjoining church of St. Fridian, and succeeded in gaining her father's leave to act thus.

This devout child had within the domestic walls attained to the highest degrees of virtue and fervor. She believed, however, that she had no such gifts, and, consequently was continually striving to acquire them. "Gemma," she used repeatedly to say, "you must change, and give yourself all to Jesus."

She knew how to draw inspiration for renewed fervor from everything; from the church solemnities, from the beauties of nature, from the changes of the seasons, and from the very games in which she sometimes took part. Thus, in one of these games, having been the largest winner, "This," she said, "is a sign that God wills great sanctity in me, and I too will it." The year, 1896, was near its end, and the thought of the coming New Year served as an incitement to new desires of a yet more holy life. Rising from a meditation she took the book of memoranda in which she used to note her resolutions, and wrote as follows:

"In this new year I purpose to begin a new life. I know not what is going to happen to me during this year. I abandon myself to Thee, O my God! All my hopes and my affections shall be for Thee. I feel my

weakness, O Jesus! but I rely on Thy assistance, and I resolve to live differently, that is, nearer to Thee."

Her daily routine did not change much. She rose early and said her usual prayers, then went to Church for Holy Mass and Communion. Every day she visited the Blessed Sacrament. In the evening she added to other devout practices that of meditation, and said the Rosary on her knees. During the night she rose at different times for about a quarter of an hour, in order to recommend as she used to say, "her poor soul" to Jesus. We know from herself that at this time Our Savior used to communicate with her soul by strong impulses of love and vivid intellectual light, "clear lights" she called them. So that in the midst of temporal affairs, and touching, as it were, the earth with her feet, she ranged in celestial spheres. Heavenly objects so engaged her mind that although engaged in distracting occupations she never lost sight of the supernatural.

Such inner concentration did not hinder in any way the exact fulfillment of her exterior duties. On the contrary, it impelled her to do everything with the greatest diligence and precision because she saw how in this way she greatly pleased her Lord.

It was God's will to detach the heart of this child more and more from all earthly things so as to unite her entirely to Himself. Grace was always at hand and she always corresponded.

About the end of 1895 she had received from a relative the present of a gold watch together with a cross and chain of the same precious metal. In order to please the donor she thought it well to wear these ornaments at least once on going out of doors. But what happened? On her return, when divesting herself of these trinkets, she beheld her Guardian Angel, who looking at her with severity, said: "The precious ornaments that adorn the spouse of a Crucified King cannot be other than the thorns and the Cross," and disappeared. Imagine the impression that such an apparition and such significant words must have made on the mind of this child of heaven. Nothing more was needed. She cast from her both the chain and watch, and knowing that she wore a ring, she took that off also. Then prostrate on her face in tears, she made the following resolution: "O Jesus, for Thy love, and to please Thee alone, I promise never more to wear, and not even to speak of, things that savor of vanity." She kept that promise during her whole life.

This is the first intimation we have of Gemma's intercourse with the Angelic spirits which was afterwards so frequent and even daily, as we shall see. Indeed not only the Angel, but the Lord of Angels favored this blessed child with loving visits. So she herself tells her director: "Jesus came to me despite my sinfulness, and told me so many things. I don't know why He did not appear angry with me— once only He seemed displeased." This must have been to try her rather than because of any voluntary fault that she had committed. At eighteen years of age she was found worthy, not only to hear the voice of Jesus, but to gaze at and talk to Him. She had then begun that supernatural life which by degrees rendered her so holy. Not that holiness consists in such extraordinary favors, as many Servants of God who never received them have been raised to the Altars of the Church. But such gifts may be taken as a sure sign of sanctity.

Now what wonder that Gemma being thus gifted should spurn the miserable things of this life, and ardently long for Paradise? Listen to her words: "From the moment Mamma inspired me with a desire for Paradise I have always longed for it, and if God left it to me, my choice would be to die and fly to Heaven. Whenever I had fever and felt ill, it gave me consolation. And when I recovered from my sickness it grieved me. Once after Holy Communion I asked Jesus why He did not take me to Paradise. "Because my child," He answered, "I will give thee many occasions of greater merit in this life through thy increased longing for Heaven, whilst bearing patiently the pains of earth."

The love of God increased without measure in this young girl's heart, as did her ceaseless ardent yearnings, until it took the form of an all-engrossing desire of suffering. About that time, in 1896, she thus expressed herself: I began to feel another strong desire, an insatiable longing for suffering and to be able to share my Savior's pains. In the midst of my countless sins I every day besought Jesus to let me suffer much. "Yes my Jesus," I used to pray, "I wish to suffer, and to suffer greatly for Thee."

Her prayer and meditation were continual. "On one occasion," these were her words, "I was seized with such intense grief on beholding the Crucifix that I fainted and fell, whereupon Papa, who happened to be at home, began to upbraid me, saying that I injured my health by staying so much indoors and by going out early in the morning. I replied that what hurt me was to be away from Jesus in the Blessed Sacrament. Then I hid myself in my room and it was the first time that I gave vent to my grief with Jesus alone." This shows how up to that time, in her eighteenth year, she had always suppressed the pain caused her by such trials. "Then," she continues, "I said to Jesus: 'O Jesus, I wish to follow Thee at any cost, at the cost of every pain. I wish to follow Thee fervently. No, my Jesus, I will never again, as hitherto, displease Thee by my tepidity. No! I will not offend Thee.' These words were dictated by my heart in that moment of grief and of hope, alone with my Jesus."

Our Lord, meanwhile, by these generous dispositions, was steadily preparing this faithful servant for great things. Gemma had a presentiment of this, and with the presentiment an ardent desire. "In the midst of my very many sins," these are her words, "I asked of Jesus that I might suffer, and suffer much. 'Yes! my Jesus,' I used to say to Him, 'I wish to suffer, and to suffer, O so much, for Thee!'" Not, indeed, that suffering was new to her, the reverse was the fact. For, being chosen by Jesus from her infancy, she had always to undergo many trials, as she herself confessed to her director: "I can say with truth that, since mamma's death, I have not passed a day without suffering some little thing for Jesus." But now that she was no longer a child, Our Lord clenched His Divine Hand and dealt His heaviest blows.

The first of these strokes was a foot ailment, a necrosis that caused her excruciating pain. This fervent child at first did not think that her ailment deserved consideration, and bore it with generous patience. Meanwhile, because of this want of care, the diseased foot became inflamed, the caries spread, and a surgeon had to be called in. Horrified on seeing the gangrenous state of the foot, he declared that amputation would probably be necessary. First, however, he wished to operate on the diseased part, and, having come to the carious bone, he began to scrape and probe it deeply. The sufferer would not take chloroform and bore the torture bravely. All around her were shuddering with horror, while she alone remained indifferent and immovable. A slight, involuntary groan, it is true, escaped her at the most painful part of the operation, but, gazing at the image of her Jesus crucified, she became calm immediately and besought Him to pardon her weakness. "Thus," as she put it, "in response to her earnest entreaty to send her some suffering, Jesus consoled her." Still, He held other and greater pains in the bitter chalice of His Passion, of which His faithful servant was to taste, when cured of that first corporal suffering.

Henry Galgani, Gemma's father, was a man of the old stamp—good, simple, charitable—and, as he knew not how to deceive anyone, so he could not believe that anyone would deceive him. His great good-nature became known, and not a few managed to turn it to their own account. From all sides they were coming to Henry Galgani; some to borrow money; others to ask his signature to bills and securities. His tenants defrauded him in the produce of his lands and in the payment of their rents. Add to all this, long continued sickness in his family, particularly the maladies of his wife and two sons which ended in death. Then came a hundred other reverses, all helping to eat up his rich family property. When at last the bills that he had incautiously signed, fell due, his bankruptcy was complete. All his property, movable and immovable, was seized, and his large family left to languish in a state of deplorable misery. Very soon afterwards he fell ill with a cancer in his throat, of which he died in a short time, aged fifty-seven, leaving his dear children orphans. His death no sooner became known to his creditors than bailiffs and other officials were sent to close the pharmacy and seize the few articles of furniture that still remained in the house. Thus, nothing was left. Does it not seem here as if the story of holy Job was passing before our eyes? Let us hear what Gemma has to say about it:

"We entered on the year, 1897, I alone, without heart," (she used these words to hide what in her was heroic virtue) "remained unmoved by so many misfortunes. That which most grieved the others" (note: the others, not herself) "after Papa's fatal illness, was to be left without means. I understood one morning the greatness of the sacrifice that Jesus required at once, and I shed many tears. But Jesus, during those days of sorrow made Himself all the more sensibly present in my soul; and, even from seeing Papa so resigned to die, I drew such strength that I bore this bitter separation with great tranquillity. The day he died Jesus forbade me to give way to useless grief, and I spent it in prayer, fully resigned to the most Holy Will of God, Who then became my earthly and heavenly father. After Papa's death on the 11th of November, 1897, we were left without anything, and had not even the means of supporting life." Gemma was then nineteen years and eight months old.

CHAPTER 5

1897-1899: St. Gemma's Dangerous Illness and Miraculous Recovery.

ALL SIGNOR GALGANI'S property had gone, and his seven children, and two sisters, Helen and Elisa, had no means of living or any hope save in Divine Providence.

In these great sufferings some of the children's aunts came in part to their assistance. Gemma was invited to stay with her aunt Carolina Lencioni of Camaiore, who being rich, was able to treat her as in her prosperous days at home. But, as she had not grieved over the extreme penury of Lucca, neither did she rejoice at the opulence of Camaiore. Her only delight, as before, was to work in the house, to pray, and to remain alone with Jesus. Tribulation had thoroughly purified her soul, so that in her aunt's house her life was more heavenly than earthly.

Yet Crosses were not wanting. When at home she was at liberty to give full attention to her practices of devotion. But at Camaiore, as at S. Gennaro, she found that she could not do as she liked. She regretted not being able to lend herself to all the ways of society, and whenever she did so remorse followed. What was to be done? She could not consult her Confessor, who knew her whole life, he being at a distance, and she could not bring herself to open her mind to others. Her suffering was all the more acute, because in the midst of her perplexities she could not receive the Bread of Angels as often as she desired. In her anguish she turned to Jesus. But He, to try the virtue of His Servant, seemed not to heed her and left her in desolation. The saintly child however did all in her power to please Him. Like St. Catherine of Siena she made an Altar in her heart, before which in ceaseless palpitations of love she adored the Majesty of God. She also, when able, accompanied by her cousin, visited Jesus in His Sacrament in the near Abbey Church of Camaiore. When obliged to go for walks they invariably ended there, and there too remaining as long as allowed her before an ancient image of the Blessed Virgin, she prayed in tears for the repose of her father's soul.

Soon, however, the enemy came to disturb this repose. Gemma was gifted with no ordinary beauty. She was of dignified bearing, gentle and graceful; and, although she dressed in the simplest way, without any ornament, she still appeared to the best advantage. Her eyes were known to be remarkably brilliant, but it was not easy to see them, for she managed with wonderful tact to keep them lowered. The piety and modesty manifested in her whole person, far from diminishing her gracefulness, rendered her more attractive. It happened at Camaiore that a youth of a leading family in the district, seeing her, fell in love with her, and without further preliminaries asked the honor of her hand from her Aunt. What better opportunity of attaining worldly happiness than this could have offered itself to Gemma? But he asked in vain! Not only did she refuse to listen to the proposal, she determined immediately to leave the place, in order to avoid all pressure.

But how effect her purpose? She knew that her Aunt would not listen to her reasons, so she had recourse to God in prayer, and He came to her aid. Just then she began to feel very ill, suffering from pains in her head and back, and on this pretext she besought her Aunt to send her back to Lucca.

She knew that she would be going to face hunger and want, but did not hesitate on this account, and so insisted with her aunt, that she succeeded in returning to her own home, to find it, as she had left it, in desolation.

Great grief was expressed in the Lencioni family at her leaving, and even her uncle Dominic, though a most unemotional man, shed tears.

But her trials did not end here. Shortly after her return to Lucca, this child of heaven began to feel worse, developing a curvature of the spine. An alarming attack of meningitis set in, together with a total loss of hearing. Large abscesses formed in her head, one of which seemed to make its way down through her chest and settled in her side. Then her hair fell off, and, finally, her limbs became paralyzed. This sweet girl kept her sufferings secret as long as possible. She feared that, if she were to make them known, she would have to undergo a medical examination. Indeed, although for a long time she had felt pain where her side was affected, she did not even once look at or touch the sore part to ascertain what the ailment might be. And now was she to let herself be inspected and touched by the doctor? Her agony of mind was great. She would have suffered all the acute pains of her ailment ten times over, rather than submit to a medical examination. She was, however, obliged to yield to obedience, and made a sacrifice of her will to God. A consultation of learned medical men was held, and from the first it became evident that hers was a very serious case of spine disease, and probably incurable. They however wished to try some remedies, but they failed, and she grew worse.

Thus passed days and nights without any other comfort than what she drew from prayer and resignation to the Divine Will. Occasionally Our Lord consoled her through her good Angel, who once addressed her thus: "If Jesus afflicts thee corporally He always does so in order to purify thee more and more; be good." She herself wrote of this and added: "Oh! how often in my long sickness did He not soothe my heart with consoling words!" Here observe how her familiarity with her Angel kept increasing. She was then in her twentieth year.

She took greatly to heart the anxieties of her friends on her account, and was chided for it by Our Lord. She tells us of it: "One morning they brought me Holy Communion and Jesus making His presence felt, reproached me greatly with my weakness of soul: 'Either it is the result,' He said, 'of thy sinful self-love, or because of thy excessive embarrassment at needing the help of others.'" Taught and consoled by these words, Gemma sought nothing more, and during her whole sickness remained indifferent to all that happened to her.

The account of her great sufferings got about, and many persons visited her in order to witness such great patience in a young girl. She received them all sweetly and thanked them with an assurance that she was equally satisfied either to die or continue suffering as might be pleasing to God.

One of her visitors brought her the life of Venerable Gabriel of the Dolours, who has since been beatified. Gemma up to then had not heard of him, nor did she at first seem to take to him although all her friends had begun to invoke him fervently in her behalf. One day, about the same time, she felt oppressed by the blackest melancholy which turned out to be a temptation of the Enemy. Having first by his arts thoroughly upset the innocent girl, behold, casting off the mask, he appeared to her and said: "If thou wilt be guided by me, I will take thee out of this suffering and cure thee perfectly, giving thee not only health, but every pleasure thou desirest." This is the first time that we find Gemma in open conflict with the devil. We don't know if the temptation was one of real apparition, or, as would seem from her own words, one of mere suggestion. However, it did not succeed. Although this Angelic girl was only a novice in such encounters, she quickly saw through it. A violent general agitation and disturbance of thought, such as she had never before experienced, beset her, and revealed the presence of the evil spirit. The thought of Blessed Gabriel then came to her mind. She invoked him with confidence and, to check the temptation, declared aloud: "First the soul, then the body!" The tempter returned to the assault a second time, and again Gemma invoked Blessed Gabriel, and making the sign of the Cross, returned to her peace of mind and to greater union with God.

Having thus experienced the power of Bl. Gabriel's protection, she became devoted to him, and sought the volume of his Life which she had put aside. "That same evening," she said, "I began to read the Life of Brother Gabriel. I read it over and over and grew in admiration of his virtues and his ways. My devotion to him increased. At night I did not sleep without having his picture under my pillow and after that I began to see him near me. I don't know how to explain this, but I felt his presence. At all times and in every action Brother Gabriel came to my mind."

That lady came back for her book; but how different was Gemma's feeling when returning it to what she felt on receiving it! This time her heart was moved and tears came to her eyes. "That Saint of God," said she, in allusion to her returning the life, "wished soon to repay my little sacrifice, and appeared to me in sleep all clothed in white. I did not recognize him at first. He saw it, and opening the white garment he showed himself clothed as a Passionist. Then I quickly knew him, but remained silent, whereupon he asked me why I cried at parting with his Life. I don't know what I answered but he rejoined: "Be good and I will come back to thee."

Blessed Gabriel's visit left Gemma's soul in great peace and sweetness, and greatly increased her longing for heaven, so that she was often heard to say: "Yes, to Jesus! Let us go off with Jesus, to remain with Jesus." But that was not His will, and she, repressing that yearning of her heart, remained tranquil on her bed of pain, awaiting resignedly that God's will alone might be done in her. She lay always in the same position, except when occasionally moved by some kind hand, as without help she could not stir. Besides those of her family, the good Nursing Sisters of St. Camillus de Lellis frequently called to see her, moved not only by the charity of their Institute, but by the profound veneration they felt for the dear invalid. Occasionally they brought some of their novices with them, persuaded that, in presence of the rare virtue of which Gemma gave proof on her bed of pain, they would be greatly edified. Several others came to see her for the same reason.

Thus a whole year passed by and that breath of life had not yet ceased to palpitate. The misery of the family increased, owing to the debts incurred for doctors and medicine, and there was no one to be found who would lend a farthing. Without doubt, if the kind persons who came to visit poor Gemma had known the extreme poverty of the family, they would have remedied it in some way; but the poor sufferers shrank from making known their want. At last things came to such a pass that they were not able to provide the commonest restoratives for their sick Gemma.

On the Vigil of the Immaculate Conception, 1898, the Sisters of St. Camillus came to pay Gemma one of their customary visits. While they were with her she felt strongly moved to imitate their example, and believing the inspiration to be from God, she resolved to promise Our Lady that if cured she would join them. She felt greatly consoled, as she told me afterwards, at her resolution, and manifested it to Sister Leonilda, who promised on her recovery to receive her. Full of joy in the midst of her many pains, Gemma mentioned her resolution to her Confessor who came that day to hear her confession, and he quite approved of it. "He gave me his permission," she said, "at once; more than that, he gave me another consolation—leave to make the Vow of Virginity, that before then I had not been able to obtain; and that same evening we made it for ever."

In this connection I will give Gemma's own account of what happened preparatory to this solemn act: "I had been begging of my confessor," she said, "for a long time to allow me to make a vow of virginity, and asked this favor of him for many years, but I did not know what it meant. However, according to the idea I had formed of it, there was no beautiful gift that would be more dear to Jesus. It was impossible to get this leave, but instead of the vow of virginity, he let me make that of purity. Then on Christmas night, 1897, I made this first vow to Jesus. I remember that Jesus was very pleased at it. My joy, too, was so great that I passed the night and the following day in paradise."

It was but a short time before his death when that holy prelate, her Confessor, thinking well to set aside all reserve, allowed his spiritual child to make the Vow of Virginity.

Gemma had at last reached the climax of her desires, and could say with good reason that she was all for Jesus and Him only. A sweet calm took possession of her soul that evening, and with ardent desire she looked forward to her Communion of the morrow, in which, united with Jesus, she would promise her heavenly Mother to enter Religion. With these thoughts in her mind a placid sleep came over her aching members, when lo! Blessed Gabriel appears and thus addresses her: "Gemma, make your vow to be a Religious freely and with good heart, but add nothing to it;" and he meant by these words that she was not to bind herself to enter any particular Order, as she was to be a Religious differently from others, that is, mystically to be transformed in Jesus. The simple girl did not understand his words and asked why she should not add anything more to her vow; but his only reply was in two words: "My Sister!" accompanied by a tender look and a smile. Gemma, describing this scene, said: "I knew nothing of all this, and to thank him kissed his habit. He then took the heart worn as a badge by the Passionists, gave it me to kiss, and placed it on my breast outside the coverlet, after which, having again repeated the words: 'My Sister!' he disappeared." When the morning came Gemma received Communion, pronounced her Vow, and remained absorbed in heavenly delights.

In this way pains and consolations kept coming in turns, the strength of the dear invalid was growing less, while her malady grew daily worse. The Doctors, wishing to make a last attempt at her case, undertook to operate on the abscess in her side, and cauterized her repeatedly along the spine, etc. This was on the 4th of January 1899. During all these torturing operations this admirable patient refused to take chloroform, preferring to remain guardian of her own body, rather than accept any alleviation of pain.

Every attempt proved useless and she continued to grow worse until the 20th of the same month when another tumor manifested itself on her head, causing her violent spasmodic pains. The Doctors were again called, and thought of operating on the tumors on her head; but finding the patient in such a weak state, they abandoned the idea, and, being unable to do more, they pronounced her case to be hopeless. On the 2nd of February, by their advice, she received the Holy Viaticum, as she was not expected to live till midnight. She did not die, but she did not grow better. The disease continued its course slowly, consuming an organism already half wasted.

But the time had nearly come for the reward of such heroic patience. Gemma was not going to die, as our Lord willed to be greatly glorified in her before taking her to Himself in Paradise. Nothing less than a miracle was needed to cure such a terrible malady, and God wrought this miracle in a most extraordinary way. It will be well for Gemma herself to relate how it happened: "They were making triduums and novenas for my recovery. I, alone, feeling myself reinvigorated by so many precious words heard from the life of Jesus, remained indifferent. Just then one of my old mistresses, who was very ill, came to see me for the last time, to say good-bye until we should meet in Heaven. She then begged of me to make a novena by myself to Blessed Margaret Mary Alacoque, and assured me that she would obtain me the grace, either of a perfect cure or of going straight to Heaven at my death. To please her, I began it on the 23rd of February 1899. It was nearly midnight when I became aware of the rattling of a rosary, felt a hand on my forehead, and heard a voice repeating nine times in succession the *Pater*, *Ave* and *Gloria*. However, I scarcely answered through exhaustion. The same voice asked me: 'Do you wish to recover? Pray with faith every evening to the Most Sacred Heart of Jesus. I will come to you until the Novena is ended, and we will pray together to this Most Sacred Heart.' It was the Passionist, Blessed Gabriel of the Dolours; and, as promised, he continued to come every evening. He placed his hand on my forehead and we recited the *Paters* together, and he made me add three *Glorias* to Blessed Margaret Mary. The Novena ended exactly on the First Friday of March. I called my confessor and made my confession. In the morning early, still confined to bed, I received Holy Communion. Oh! what happy moments I passed with Jesus! He, too, said to me— 'Gemma, dost thou wish to recover?' My emotion was so great that I could not reply. I answered with my heart: 'Jesus, whatever Thou willest.' Poor Jesus! The grace was granted me. I was cured. It was only a little after two o'clock, then I got up. Those around me were crying with joy. I, too, felt happy, not on account of my recovery, but because Jesus had chosen me for His child. In fact, before leaving me that morning, He said impressively to my soul: 'My child, the gift thou has received this morning shall be followed by many others still greater. I will be always with thee and act as thy Father, and she shall be thy Mother,' He said, pointing to Our Lady of Dolours. 'Paternal help shall never be wanting to those who place themselves in My hands. Nothing therefore, shalt thou lack, even though I Myself have deprived thee of every consolation and help in this world.'"

Indeed just at that time the misery in the Galgani home, instead of becoming less, had increased to such a degree that, when the Aunts in the country omitted to send help, it became necessary to live on occasional small alms brought by a charitable person. How often were not those poor children obliged to go to bed without supper after having had at midday only a miserably small repast of dry bread! And how often had not our Gemma, for her only food during the day, a little wine that a poor woman brought her! "This is enough for me," she used to say; "I am now in good health and have no need of more. If there be anything in the house, give it to my brothers and sisters." And she did with so little because in the morning she had been fully satisfied with the food of the angels—with Jesus in His Sacrament.

Blessed loss! Blessed gain! The rest of this life will convince us of this, and prove it by facts.

CHAPTER 6

March, April, May 1899: Restored to Health St. Gemma
Tries to Enter Religion. Is Not Received.

GEMMA'S cure was as perfect as it was instantaneous—the Sacred Heart of Jesus being its author, Blessed Margaret Mary the intercessor, and Blessed Gabriel of the Dolours the instrument. Having left her bed and her room, all on fire with celestial love and tempered like steel from the furnace, the first thought of this angel in human form was to return to her religious practices and to consider what Our Lord, who had given her health and life, required at her hands. "From that day forward," she tells us, "I began to feel it impossible to live unless I went every day to Jesus."

And having longed for years to enter the cloister she thought the time to effect her wish had come. She made it known to her family and they having no doubt of the genuineness of her vocation put no obstacle in the way. They were the more condescending because the accomplishment of her desire seemed remote. Gemma however did not think so, but imagined that she could fly at once to the desired solitude of the Convent, there to remain with Jesus.

Towards the end of her serious illness three different vocations called for her consideration. The Sisters of St. Camillus had suggested to ask Our Lady to cure her on the condition of her entering their Congregation. Blessed Gabriel appearing to her had often called her Sister, and placed on her breast the badge of the Passionists. Then a mysterious voice had invited her to become a Visitandine. This last invitation seemed to draw her more than the others because of her gratitude to Blessed Margaret Mary, through whose intercession she had been cured. Hence, six days after her marvelous recovery she wrote these words: "I long to fly off at once to where Bl. Margaret Mary wishes! Oh! how ill at ease I feel in the world! Ever since I rose from my bed an inexplicable aversion to everything has taken hold of me."

Meanwhile that wonderful cure got noised in Lucca and many were talking of it. The Visitandines wanted to know all about it from Gemma herself. They received her most cordially and showed their pleasure at the prospect of having her some day as their Sister among their number. Gemma thought she knew when that day would be from that voice which, on her rising from her bed of sickness, had said to her: "Renew all thy promises to Jesus, and add that in the month consecrated to Him (June) thou also wilt go to consecrate thyself to Him." Thinking that this voice invited her definitely to the Visitation she poured out her soul in desires to enter there, and felt it hard to defer this step any longer. "Now," she said, "it is the 9th of March. Who will send me on to the 1st of June?" Those good Religious, to shorten, as it were, the time and please her, promised to receive her into their house to make a course of Spiritual Exercises about the beginning of May, and that a month later they would admit her as Postulant. During the first thirty days of this time of expectation, Our Lord filled the heart of His Servant with ineffable consolations.

It may be said that about this time Gemma began to lead that heavenly and singular life which finds a parallel in very few lives of the greatest saints. Before then she had abundant mental light, locutions, sweetest consolations and heavenly apparitions. But these things happened at varying intervals. Now for the first time began her almost uninterrupted series of Divine Communications that were of the most exalted kind—vivid lights, sublime attractions, strongest impulses. To these she corresponded faithfully and rose rapidly to the highest perfection. Her union with God was intimate. So fixedly did she gaze on Him, that she knew not how to think of aught else. This accounts for her entire abandonment in Him, and her unalterable uniformity to the Divine Will, bringing with it calm and contentment in the midst of the hardest trials. In a word Gemma now lives only for God—He is the object of every desire and aspiration, He alone pleases her, and in Him her soul reposes. I shall have occasion to speak more at length of this happy state always becoming more perfect in the charming existence we are studying. Here I merely notice its beginning as contemporaneous with her miraculous recovery.

Holy Week was drawing nigh. Gemma was awaiting it with anxiety in order then to give full vent to the impulses of her heart towards Jesus Crucified. With a view to relate with exactness what happened to her in that Great Week, I will mention her practice of the "Holy Hour," during which in the latter years of her life the most wonderful marvels of Divine Love were verified in her. When she was ill her school-mistress, Sister Julia, visited her and, to encourage her to suffer her great pains, spoke of the weekly devotion of the Holy Hour every Thursday evening, in honor of the beginning of Our Savior's bitter Passion. Gemma, wholly captivated by what she heard, though weak in body, yet animated by fervor, resolved to practice the devotion even while confined to bed. She asked anxiously for the manual entitled, "An hour of prayer with Jesus agonizing in Gethsemani," and the Sister brought it to her. It was composed by the foundress of the Institute of St. Zita, and consisted of four meditations on the Passion, followed by prayers and offerings. Gemma looked on it as a treasure, and from that moment promised the Heart of Jesus that on recovering her health she would never fail to keep the Holy Hour every Thursday. On Holy Thursday of the same year, with her Confessor's leave, she began this pious exercise, and in order to prepare well for it she prefaced it by a General Confession of her whole life. This shows the idea she had formed of the Holy Hour. Although ignoring the end for which God had ordained such a preparation for such an exercise, we shall see what that end was. Meanwhile let us hear Gemma's own account of what passed:

I began for the first time to make the holy hour out of bed. I had promised the Sacred Heart of Jesus that if I were cured I would make it every Thursday without fail." (And she never omitted it while she lived.) "I felt so full of sorrow for my sins that I passed a time of continual martyrdom. In the midst of this immense grief however, one comfort was left me—that of tears. I spent the whole hour praying and weeping, and sat down. My grief lasted a little while longer and then I felt my whole being rapt in recollection. Then, all of a sudden, I lost the use of my senses. I was able with difficulty to stand up and lock the room door. Where was I? I found myself before Jesus Crucified. He was bleeding all over. I lowered my eyes at once, and the sight filled me with pain. I made the Sign of the Cross and immediately my anguish was succeeded by tranquillity of spirit; but I continued to feel even a greater sorrow for my sins than before, and I had not courage to lift my eyes to look at Jesus. I prostrated myself with my forehead to the ground and there remained for several hours. I came to myself with the Wounds of Jesus so deeply impressed on my mind that they have never since left it."

The vision vanished and Gemma, thirsting with love for her Jesus Crucified, and with desire to contemplate His ineffable pains, yearned for the dawn of Good Friday, so as to be able to take part in the *Three hours' Agony.* But those around her thought it imprudent to let her go to Church owing to their well-grounded fear, lest the intensity of her faith and love might cause her heart to break on that occasion. She felt the prohibition keenly and tears came to her eyes; yet she mastered her feelings, and "doing violence to myself," she said, "I made this first sacrifice to Jesus, and He, so generous to me, rewarded me for it." Being unwilling to lose the fruit of the desired exercise she shut herself in her room and then began the *Three Hours* alone. But why say alone? She had scarcely retired when her Angel Guardian came by her side. He reproved her for having shed those tears a little while before and gave her wise advice about the generosity of sacrifice that God wished to find in her. After that they prayed together, the Angel helped Gemma to keep devout company with Jesus in his pains and with His sorrowful Mother, and, thus aided, many and great heavenly communications were vouchsafed to her during the loving contemplation. Later in her account of it to her director she said:

"This was the first time," thus she ended her manifestation, "and the first Friday that Jesus made Himself felt so forcibly in my soul. And although I did not receive Him corporally from the hands of the priest (which was impossible on Good Friday), yet of His own accord He came and communicated Himself to me. But this union was so strong that I remained as it were stupefied. Oh! Jesus spoke so forcibly!"

Such great favors, whilst indeed filling the soul of this chosen child with consolations, overwhelmed her at the same time with confusion and fear. She deemed herself unworthy of them, she wished that no one should become aware of them, and it needed the authority of the Angel Guardian to induce her to manifest to her confessor the visions we have just mentioned.

She tells us herself of the salutary effects—two ardent impulses produced in her by the vision of Christ sweating blood. "The first," she said, "was to love Him, and love Him to sacrifice; the second was a great desire to suffer something for Him, seeing that He had suffered so much for me." Not knowing how to gratify these yearnings she turned to Jesus asking Him to teach her how to love Him, and He gratified her. This is how it happened: "I was full of anxiety," she writes, "at not knowing how to love; but Jesus in His infinite goodness was not ashamed to come and be my Master." It was an April evening of the same year, 1899. Gemma was alone in her room, with her thoughts and affections centered in Jesus Crucified and intent on making her usual evening prayers, "when all of a sudden," thus she continues, "I felt myself rapt in recollection, and I found myself for the second time before Jesus Crucified, Who said to me: 'Look My child, and learn how to love'" (and He showed her His five open wounds). "Look at this Cross, these Thorns, these Nails, these livid marks and lacerations. These Wounds are all works of Love—of Infinite Love. See to what extent I have loved thee.'" At this sight the tender-hearted girl felt such intense grief that, unable to bear it, she fell fainting to the ground, and there remained for hours immersed in an ocean of sorrow and love.

In spite of all this, it seemed as if grace had not yet found this holy soul sufficiently purified to be capable of receiving the great gift in store for her. Gemma had to prepare herself for it by a course of spiritual exercises. She realized it and hastened to shut herself up in the Convent of the Visitandines at Lucca, where a Retreat was to begin on the 1st of May.

The time was drawing nigh, Gemma counted the days—she counted the moments—that must pass before she entered the Convent, there to be all and alone with Jesus. He in His turn was by His grace working out the perfection of that chosen soul so as to fit her for the great gift she was to receive.

At last the 1st of May arrived. Gemma's heart was full of joy, and at eight in the evening she hastened to the sacred cloister where upon entering she said she seemed to be in Paradise, and as if almost foreseeing what was to be accomplished in her within a month, she went into the exercises of the holy retreat with unwonted fervor. She forbade her relatives to visit her so as to be undisturbed, "for," as she put it, "those days all belonged to Jesus."

It will be interesting to know how she did those exercises, as they gave, so to say, a finishing stroke to the operation of a great grace in her soul. The Sisters wished not only to have Gemma with them for a while, they also counted on her joining their Congregation. They knew she possessed nothing, but had the reputation of great virtue, and would therefore be a great gain for them. They arranged with her Confessor for her not to go through the exercises like other externs, but according to the Horary of the Community. She accordingly joined the Religious in choir, at meditation and work; also in the Refectory, and at other duties as if she were already a Novice. She would rather have remained alone and hidden, passing those days unobserved; yet, knowing that obedience and denial of her own will were more pleasing to God, she raised no difficulty, but cheerfully submitted to the rule of the Novitiate. Those good Sisters intended thereby to try Gemma's vocation. They also desired to be edified by her example because of what they heard of her from her Confessor, Mgr. Volpi, who was their great Protector. They all became enamored of Gemma and loaded her with marks of their esteem.

From what this Angelic girl wrote afterwards, we learn, at least in part, that during those days of retreat she was the recipient of many lights and heavenly communications: "Jesus," she said, "regardless of my misery consoled me, and made me feel Him always in my soul." These words in her mouth meant that all Heaven poured itself into that soul. She felt she was in Paradise, and yet the Rule observed by those Religious did not come up to the promptings of her fervor. Her desire was to treat with God alone and to do great penance for the love of Jesus. That life appeared to her to be too easy, and this sentiment seemed to be an inspiration of grace. "Very often," she narrates, "at intervals Jesus said in my heart: 'My child! a more austere rule is requisite for thee." Still she willingly remained in the Convent, and trembled at the thought of returning to her home. She was also continually importuning her Confessor to use his influence so that she might remain where she was and not return to the world. The Archbishop's approval was sought, and here began difficulties. That holy Prelate, Mgr. Ghilardi, although he had heard of Gemma did not know her. He had doubts of her perfect recovery from the effects of her long dangerous illness.

This difficulty was removed, but still the Archbishop, inspired no doubt by God, remained firm. He would not allow Gemma to enter the Novitiate in June, as was intended, and only permitted her remaining in the Convent till the 20th of May that she might have the consolation of being present at the Profession of some Novices.

This religious ceremony caused her great joy, while little knowing what was going to happen to herself. "Jesus," she said, "caused me to be affected more than usual. I cried and cried a great deal"—tears no doubt of love and sorrow. She remained alone and apart during the ceremony, entirely absorbed in contemplation. While all others were concerned about the newly professed, Gemma was forgotten and left in the chapel without breakfast or dinner. But that was nothing in her estimation. The great trial came the same evening when she was told that she had to leave the Convent next day. Her grief was extreme, and only suppressed by her heroic resignation to the Will of God. "At five o'clock on the morning of the 21st of May," these are her words, "I had to go. I asked the Mother Superior's blessing as I wept, and having said good-bye to the Nuns I left. My God, what grief!"

Thus plunged in sorrow she returned to her home, which seemed so altered in the course of twenty days that she could no longer adapt herself to it. Occupations, persons, subjects of conversation—all were changed, yet knowing that such was the Divine Will she entered on all her duties as before with equal earnestness. She felt that her exterior occupation did not hinder her attending to heavenly things. And, therefore, suppressing her soul's yearnings and setting aside her disappointments, she was all attention to the wants of her Aunts, of her little brother and her younger sister. While serving them punctually she encouraged them by her example to bear with patience their hard trials that were being daily multiplied.

Among her other practices, after her days in the Convent, she renewed that of going frequently with her little Sister Julia on Holy days of obligation to pray at the tomb of their parents. Having heard Mass, and received Holy Communion she went with this beloved companion straight to the Cemetery, which was some distance from the city, and there remained a great part of the day. They often waited for the gates to be opened after midday, and hence a poor woman who lived close by, seeing the two young girls standing on the road in silence and recollection, regardless of the cold rain or sun invited them to take shelter and rest in her house. So charmed was she with them that she made them promise to come always to rest and have something to eat with her. They did so with gratitude. But it sometimes happened that this charitable hostess was not at home, and so they remained fasting all day, stopping on their way home at some church for Benediction of the Blessed Sacrament. Thus those two angels sanctified the Festival.

The Salesian Nuns had not abandoned the idea of receiving Gemma. And she, although feeling in her heart that their life was not her ideal, would gladly have joined them. She was unaware that the Consecration for the Feast of the Sacred Heart, of which Our Lord spoke to her, was not that of the Religious Profession, but quite another. Gemma, mistaking His words, continued to long for it, with perfect resignation, but still with intense fervor. She went daily to the Convent begging to be received and still difficulties presented themselves. At first the Sisters in their desire to have her waived all obstacles; but at length they too began to hesitate. Gemma quickly perceived the change but was not disturbed by it. She took counsel with God, Who at last gave her clearly to understand the mystery of her consecration, at least as far as it concerned the Visitation. Thereupon contented and resigned she ceased from taking further steps and awaited in her home whatever God might will in her regard.

Oh! how truly great, O my God, and how ineffable are the ways by which Thou leadest Thy Elect!

CHAPTER 7

1899: The Servant of God
Receives the Stigmata.

FROM every page of this story the reader has been able to see that Gemma's chief thought, the ardent incessant desire of her heart, was to become like Jesus, and as the Son of God is the Man of Sorrows, that was enough for her: *Jesum et hunc Crucifixum*. The Mysteries of the magnificence that faith shows us in our Savior did not seem to move her much. "Ah! my Beloved," she kept repeating with the Spouse in the Canticles, "is for me a bundle of myrrh. I don't want to see anything else in Him since He has not wished anything else for Himself. Let whoever wishes it contemplate Him on Mount Tabor; I will contemplate Him on Calvary with my dear Mother Addolorata." She did not even seem to make account of the images of our Lord; and in fact she did not wish to keep any by her through devotion except those that represented Him Crucified. "O Mamma," we have heard her say to her Mother when quite little, "tell me of the Passion of Jesus." And to her school-mistresses: "Sisters, explain to me some point in the sorrowful Mysteries of Jesus." And we have seen the saintly child so moved at this explanation, that, for fear of seeing her faint and get ill, those good religious had to stop the devout exercises. This ardent desire kept on increasing until it had effected the perfect transformation of this chosen virgin into Christ Crucified. God Himself is about to show to heaven and earth by wonderful means that Gemma is truly crucified with Jesus.

When Gemma had left the Convent a mysterious voice seemed to say to her: "Rise, take courage, abandon thyself without reserve to Jesus, love Him with all thy being, offer no obstacle to His designs, and thou shalt see the great strides He will cause thee to make in little time without thy knowing how. Fear nothing, for the Heart of Jesus is the throne of Mercy, where the miserable are the most readily received." Comforted by these words the Servant of God, turning to an image of the Sacred Heart exclaimed: "O my Jesus how greatly I wish to love Thee! but I don't know how." And the same Voice replied: "Dost thou wish to love Jesus always? Never cease even for a moment to suffer for Him. The cross is the throne of true lovers; the cross is the patrimony of the elect in this life."

At last one day after Holy Communion, she hears Jesus say to her: "Gemma, courage! I await thee on Calvary, on that Mount whither thy course is directed." To that noble appointment He had directed those numberless contradictions, those torturing pains, those spiritual exercises in the Convent, that extraordinary contrition for her sins, and that General Confession made with such compunction, of which matters we have already spoken.

It was the 8th of June 1899. After Communion our Lord let His Servant know that the same evening He would give her a very great grace. She ran at once to tell her confessor of it. She wished to receive again from him the absolution from all her sins. Then with her soul overflowing with unaccustomed joy and peace and her mind full of engrossing thoughts she went home. Now let us hear what happened from her own lips: "We were on the Vigil of the Feast of the Sacred Heart, Thursday evening. All of a sudden, more quickly than usual, I felt a piercing sorrow for my sins; but I felt it so intensely that I have never since experienced anything like it. That sorrow, I might say, almost brought me to death's door. Next I felt all the powers of my soul in recollection. My intellect knew nothing but my sins and my offenses against God. My memory recalled them all, and set before me all the torments that Jesus had endured to save me. My will moved me to detest them all and willingly suffer everything to expiate them. A world of thoughts turned in my mind and they were thoughts of grief, love, fear, hope, encouragement.

This recollection was quickly followed by a rapture out of my senses, and I found myself in the presence of my dear heavenly Mother who had my Angel Guardian on her right. He spoke first, telling me to repeat the act of contrition, and when I had done so my Holy Mother said: 'My child, in the name of Jesus may all thy sins be forgiven thee.' Then she added: 'My Son Jesus loves thee beyond measure, and wishes to give thee a grace. Wilt thou know how to render thyself worthy of it?' My misery did not know what to answer. Then she added: 'I will be a mother to thee. Wilt thou be a true child?' She opened her mantle and covered me with it. At that moment Jesus appeared with all His Wounds open, but from those Wounds there no longer came forth blood, but flames of fire. In an instant those flames came to touch my hands, my feet and my heart. I felt as if I were dying, and should have fallen to the ground had not my Mother held me up, while all the time I remained beneath her mantle. I had to remain several hours in that position. Finally she kissed my forehead, all vanished, and I found myself kneeling. But I still felt great pain in my hands, feet and heart. I rose to go to bed, and became aware that blood was flowing from those parts where I felt pain. I covered them as well as I could, and then helped by my Angel I was able to get into bed. In the morning I found it difficult to go to Holy Communion, and I put on a pair of gloves to hide my hands. I could not remain standing and felt every moment that I should die. Those pains did not leave me until three o'clock on Friday—Feast of the Sacred Heart of Jesus."

This wonderful event took place at No. 3 Via del Biscione, in St. Fridian's Parish where Gemma was then living with her family. We note this fact because we believe that some day this house will become a Sanctuary like the Verna where St. Francis received the Stigmata.

Gemma, thus divinely adorned, was from that day forward able to say: *Nemo mihi molestus sit. Ego enim Stigmata Domini Jesu in corpore meo porto*: Let no man molest me, for I bear the marks of the Lord Jesus in my body.

Nothing could exceed Gemma's pain and perplexity at finding herself marked externally with the signs of our Redemption. She wished to keep it all hidden, but she was in the midst of the world, surrounded by inquisitive people, obliged to go out of doors at least twice a day to church, and meanwhile her wounds remained bleeding freely. What was to be done? She thought all night and in the morning tried to rise, but on putting her feet to the ground, so excruciating was the agony she suffered that she thought she would die of it. She got up however, and dragging herself rather than walking she went to the Church for Communion. On coming home, besides her anguish at not being able to hide what had happened, her perplexity was great at not knowing what the wounds on her body meant.

She believed then that all who were espoused to Christ Our Lord by vow bore those marks. Accordingly with modest and ingenuous trepidation, she went from one to another asking them if they had ever had such and such wounds or lacerations, but she got no information. Meanwhile how was she to hide those deep bleeding impressions? When she had thought it over, she resolved to go to her Aunt, and presenting herself with outstretched arms and covered hands, "Aunt," she said, "see what Jesus has done to me." Her Aunt was thunderstruck at the sight, and at Gemma's words. She could not realize what had happened. It was a mystery to her, but later on she came to understand it.

The reader will no doubt wish me to give particulars of the Stigmata of the Servant of God—how they were formed and how they continued to show themselves. Assuredly if this phenomenon were unique I should find great difficulty in undertaking to satisfy inquiries. But, although very rare, it has been made manifest in different Saints, from St. Francis of Assisi in the thirteenth century, to the Belgian Ecstatic, Louise Lateau in the nineteenth. In the case of the last-named Servant of God in particular, this prodigy was witnessed for a long time by thousands of persons. It was studied from a physiological point of view by most learned medical men, both Catholics and rationalists, and from a theological standpoint, by eminent professors distinguished alike for their piety and learning. These and others have written volumes on this subject. Hence it is easy by means of opportune comparisons to arrive at a satisfactory knowledge of what was seen in Gemma of Lucca.

The phenomenon began in the way that we have seen, and as she who was thus favored was, so far, the only witness, there is nothing to be added to her literal account of it. From that day forward periodically it continued to repeat itself on the same day every week, namely on Thursday evening about eight o'clock, and continued until three o'clock on Friday afternoon. No preparation preceded it, no sense of pain or impression in those parts of the body affected by it. Nothing announced its approach except the recollection of Spirit that preceded the ecstasy. Scarcely had this come as a forerunner than red marks showed themselves on the backs and palms of both hands, and under the epidermis a rent in the flesh was seen to open by degrees; this was oblong on the backs of the hands and irregularly round in the palms. After a little the membrane burst and on those innocent hands were seen marks of flesh wounds. The diameter of these in the palms was about half an inch, and on the backs of the hands the wound was about five-eighths of an inch long by one-eighth wide.

Sometimes the laceration appeared to be only on the surface. At other times it was scarcely perceptible with the naked eye; but as a rule it was very deep, and seemed to pass through the hand, the openings on both sides reaching each other. I say seemed to pass, because those cavities were full of blood, partly flowing and partly congealed, and when the blood ceased to flow they closed immediately, so that it was not easy to sound them without a probe. Now this instrument was never used, both because of the reverential delicacy inspired by the Ecstatic in her mysterious state, and because the violence of the pain made her keep her hands convulsively closed. Also, because the wounds in the palms of her hands were covered by a swelling that at first looked like clotted blood, whereas it was found to be fleshy, hard, and like the head of a nail raised and detached, and about an inch in diameter. In her feet, besides the wounds being large and livid around the edges, their size in an inverse sense differed from those of her hands; that is, there was a larger diameter on the instep and a smaller one on the sole. Furthermore, the wound on the instep of the right foot was as large as that on the sole of the left. Thus it must certainly have been with our Savior, supposing that both His Sacred Feet were fixed to the Cross with only one nail.

I have said that the opening of these wounds was effected by degrees, that is, in five or six minutes, beginning underneath the skin and ending with its bursting asunder. At times however this was not the case; their opening was then instantaneous, and came from the exterior like a violent transfixing. Then it was agonizing to see the dear martyr, thus stricken all of a sudden, and trembling in every fiber of her body. Now about the wound in her side. This was seen directly by very few persons and very seldom. For it did not seem right to those good ladies to examine that virginal body too closely, with the sole aim of gratifying their curiosity however devout. I took the same view of it and accordingly deprived myself of the consolation of being thoroughly informed on all the details. Certainly if we are to judge by the excruciating pain that Gemma suffered from this wound, not only near the surface but in the center of her heart, we may reasonably hold that it reached the very heart itself. Besides, if God's end in working such wonderful miracles is to reproduce in some of His chosen servants the reality of what His Own Divine Son, Jesus, suffered for us in His Passion and Death, there is no reason to suppose that He would only do this partially. I read in the Biography of the Servant of God, Johanna of the Cross, that in the examination of her body after death the surgeons wished to follow the course of the mysterious wound in her side, and found that passing through the lung it in reality reached her heart. An examination was also made of Gemma's body thirteen days after her death, and of this I shall have to speak later on. If the miracle of the Stigmata, as seen exteriorly, had not ceased two years before her death, we should now without doubt have, in another palpable example, the clear evidence of what I here state as simply probable.

The opening in Gemma's side was in the form of a half-moon in a horizontal direction with the extremities turned upwards. Its length in a straight line was quite two inches, and its width at the center about a quarter of an inch. This wound also was produced in two different ways; that is, instantaneously from the exterior as if by the stoke of a lance, or else from the interior, gradually by the opening in that part of minute reddish pores that showed themselves beneath the cuticle, and increasing in number ended by bursting the skin, thus forming the fearful wound that we have described. I wondered greatly at the crescent form of this opening, so unusual in other stigmatics of whom we have particulars, until I read the Life of the Venerable Diomira Allegri, a Florentine of the sixteenth century. She had a wound like Gemma's, as is shown by the sworn deposition made in the process of her Beatification by medical men officially appointed, and several eyewitnesses. Now as it does not seem reasonable to think that the shape of a wound so well defined in two different cases, three centuries apart, happened by chance, one would be led to suppose that the lance which pierced our Savior's Side was of such a shape that striking obliquely it would have opened a curved wound.

Blood flowed in abundance from Gemma's side as was evident from her underclothing being saturated by it. The humble, modest Virgin did what she could to hide it, using for this purpose many folds of linen cloths which she applied repeatedly to her side. In less than an hour they became saturated and she hastened to hide them in order to wash them secretly. The flow of blood however was not continuous, but intermittent at irregular intervals, thus allowing the blood to congeal and giving time to cleanse the parts. In this way the raw flesh, after washing, remained as in a wound when healing naturally. But this was not a case of a natural phenomenon, and therefore, on a fresh kindling of the interior mysterious fire the wound suddenly became inflamed and the blood began again to flow in great abundance.

On one of the many occasions on which that happened she wrote thus: "This morning about ten o'clock my heart was seeking seeking…I felt my senses leave me…to the agony in my heart was added an excessive pain through all my members…But before, and above all, was my sorrow for sin. Oh! excruciating this pain! Were it any greater I could not have outlived it, and I may say the same of the stroke I received." She meant the stroke of the lance that opened the wound in her side. "My little heart," she said, "could no longer bear the restraint and has begun to send forth blood in quantities." And in another letter: "Jesus has made His strength felt in my soul and my heart not being able to resist it, the wound in that part has opened and poured out blood."

On this account it was never possible to ascertain how often, apart from the regular days, this wonderful phenomenon manifested itself, nor to calculate the quantity of blood lost by this victim during the twenty hours more or less that it lasted. It can however be stated that the quantity was large, as those who lived with and assisted her are prepared to declare on oath, that from her side alone there came so much blood, that, if not stopped, it flowed down to the ground. The same thing may be said of the other Stigmata of her hands and feet. This blood too was fresh, of rich color, and in all respects the same as flows from a newly opened wound, and so it remained after it had dried on the skin, the clothes, or the floor.

The way in which the Stigmata disappeared was not less wonderful. As soon as the ecstasy of the Friday was over the flow of blood from all the five wounds ceased immediately. The raw flesh healed, the lacerated tissues healed too, and the following day, or at latest on the Sunday, not a vestige remained of those deep cavities, neither at their centers nor around their edges, the skin having grown quite uniformly with that of the uninjured parts. In color however there remained whitish marks showing that there had been the wounds of the day before—which would be opened again as at first, in five days, and closed in the same way. Two years after this marvel of the Stigmata had ceased, that is at the time of Gemma's death, those marks still remained and were then easily observed on her body, particularly on her feet which in her lifetime could only with great difficulty be uncovered during her ecstasies.

Before the prohibition of her directors, the phenomenon of the Stigmata was constant and unvarying on all Thursdays and Fridays. Nor was it ever, except once, manifested on any other days or Feasts however solemn they might be, even though on such Feasts the ecstasies of the seraphic girl were repeated in a more extraordinary way than usual. There was only one exception to the days on which Gemma always received the Stigmata, and I will give the account of it in another chapter. I spoke of the sweat of blood when treating in another place of Gemma's love of God and of her horror at knowing that He was offended, particularly by the accursed sin of blasphemy. Here, as the opportunity is offered me, I will add that this prodigious phenomenon occurred also very often in her meditation on the Passion of our Lord and His agony in the garden. It happened sometimes when she was not in ecstasy, but never occurred during the periodical ecstasies of the Thursdays and Fridays. On these occasions the blood, pressed from the heart by the vehemence of compassionate grief, oozed through the pores of her body, and specially from the left side over the region of the heart, so that she was bathed in blood. The angels no doubt will have received that blood with love, presenting it to God to appease His wrath, through the merits of the victim who, with so much generosity, shed it as our Divine Redeemer did His own.

CHAPTER 8

1900: St. Gemma Participates In All The Sufferings Of The Passion

THERE have been very few Saints who had all the five sacred stigmata. The Spirit, as we read in St. John, "breatheth where He will," and as He will, and whether by much or by little attains His most sublime ends. Gemma was to be among the number of the most privileged, participating not only in the five Wounds of His Crucifixion, but in all the torments of His Passion. After the Sweat of Blood in Gethsemani, the first punishment that Jesus willed to suffer in His Body was the scourging. Gemma was wont to contemplate this painful mystery with tenderest love. She counted one by one those deep gashes with which she beheld the Body of her Divine Savior covered, and kept repeating: "All these are the work of Love." Thus she consumed herself in desire to see them imprinted on her own flesh. Our Divine Lord Himself, being pleased to increase this desire in her, frequently appeared to her, as we have seen, bleeding all over, and invited her to touch and kiss those adorable wounds. She, unable to withstand the torrent of her grief and the love that such a sight enkindled in her heart, fell senseless at His feet.

At last on the first Friday of March 1901, having wept and implored of her Divine Spouse with renewed ardor to grant her some share in the martyrdom of His scourging, her prayer was granted during the usual ecstasy. The torment was horrible. "Friday," thus she told me of it, "about two o'clock Jesus let me feel some slight blows. Father, I am all scars that cause me a little suffering. Jesus be praised for ever!" And now let us hear the description of these scars, that no one could call imaginary, from her adopted mother, who examined them several times minutely. "I noticed," she says, "that on that first Friday evening Gemma was suffering more than usual while in ecstasy. I lifted up her arm and saw great red stripes on it. On applying a handkerchief to them I found it stained with blood. She suffered greatly, and in the ecstasy I heard her say: 'But are they Thy stripes, O Jesus?' Hence I thought that it was the scourging. This was repeated on each Friday in March 1901. The first Friday it was as I have stated. On the second the flesh was torn, and on the third still more bruised, so that the bone was almost visible. On the fourth it was something indescribable—wounds everywhere, that must have been nearly half an inch deep. But after two or three days they disappeared. Once, however, that I bandaged two of them, these only did not heal, they festered; and when I went to undo the bandages it caused her great suffering. When the bandages were removed they healed of themselves by degrees. I speak of these two wounds specially because the others healed at once. This is how they were disposed: two on one arm, from two to three inches long and very deep; two on one leg, round, and about the size of a florin; one near the middle of her breast in the direction of her throat; two very large oblong ones above the knee; one on each knee and elbow, almost laying bare the bone; one nearly round and very deep on each instep, and a long one on each shin. There were others that I could not see so well. At first they were, as I have said, in stripes, then they became deep gashes, and on asking her the reason of this, she answered: 'First they were switchings, now they are scourgings.'" And concluding, this lady added: "If you wish to form some idea of it, recall to mind the large Crucifix that we have in the house before which Gemma was in the habit of praying; she was like that. The same livid marks, the same torn open gashes in the skin and flesh in the same parts of the body, equally long and deep and equally horrifying to behold. Blood came from her wounds in great abundance. When she was standing it flowed to the ground, and when in bed it not only wet the sheets, but saturated the whole mattress. I measured some streams or pools of this blood, and they were from twenty to twenty-five inches long and about two inches wide."

All the others who saw those wounds give the same account of them. Hence it is evident how absurd it would be to think for a moment that Gemma could have punished her body in that way by means of disciplines or other instruments of penance. She was forbidden such austerities, and we know and shall see fully proved that nothing could be more perfect or more scrupulously precise than her obedience.

And then, in any case, how could she have done it, never being left alone in the time of ecstasy, during which the phenomena in question always manifested itself? Moreover it would have to be explained how such deep gashes in the flesh, if the result of natural causes, could have healed in such a short time. It is needless to discuss how the dear victim felt the intense torment of the cruel wounds and heavy blows that tore open her flesh; that was easily seen by her attitude under the torment. "During the scourging," says one of the witnesses, "Gemma is seen to suffer greatly, but does not move. Sometimes she is slightly convulsed and her arms tremble. As to her senses, she hears everything; she becomes slightly exhausted, but soon recovers, and after the ecstasy, as I have proved by experiment, she remembers everything. Poor child, how it rends one's heart to see her undergo so much! When suffering thus, imagine her saying to me, 'recommend me very much to Jesus.' Then I hear her saying: 'My mother! Eternal Divine Father!' On Thursday night about eleven o'clock she said, 'Good-bye till tomorrow.' And, in fact, the blows of the scourging ceased under my hand, and she remained as one dead. Her pulse however beat normally, and the action of her heart was more calm, but after a little while the violent palpitation began again."

We do not know if this mysterious phenomenon of the scourging was repeated oftener than on the four Fridays named. It is however probable that the same thing occurred at other times, but unobserved, because it is well known to how many artifices this humble girl resorted in order to keep God's gifts hidden. Once she asked her benefactress's leave to take a bath in the house, because, she added, "I feel my clothes stuck to the flesh and they are troubling me a good deal." She went to have the bath, and it was found that those sinless members were furrowed all over by deep gashes. The blood in them had dried with that which had saturated her underclothing, so that it was impossible to remove it without reopening the wounds and causing her immense pain. And yet, her way of putting it was that all these torments were only a few little strokes that Jesus let her feel, and in this way gave her "some little thing" to suffer.

The Savior of the world, as we are told by the Evangelists, after He had been cruelly scourged, was surrounded by the soldiers of the praetorium who, having twined a crown of thorns, pressed it on His Divine Head. Adorable Crown! Should not every Christian be enamored of thee, and deem it the greatest honor to wear thee on his brow after having seen thee crown the Man God? Certain it is that such were the sentiments of the Virgin of Lucca, who so thoroughly understood the Mysteries of Christ's greatness, and had already for so long been enamored of the glories of His Passion.

I shall have to mention again the touching vision of the Angel who appearing to her offered her two crowns, one of white lilies, the other of thorns, leaving her to choose which of the two she would have. And Gemma without a moment's hesitation said: "I want that of Jesus," and taking it from the Angel, pressed it closely and lovingly to her heart. On another occasion Jesus Himself appeared to her crowned with thorns and asked her if she too wished to have that Crown. This saintly child having by her mystic purification reached the perfection needed for such extraordinary gifts, passed easily from words to facts, from visions to the reality. Let Gemma herself give us instances of this:

"At last, this evening," (it was the 19th of July 1900) "after six days of suffering from the absence of Jesus, I have been a little recollected. I went to my prayer as I usually do every Thursday, and began to think of the Crucifixion of Jesus. At first I did not feel anything but after some moments I became rapt in thought,

*Jesus was near. My state of recollection was followed as usual
by the loss of my senses, and I found myself with Jesus Who was
suffering terrible pain. How could I bear to see Jesus suffering
and not help Him? Then I felt myself consumed by an
unquenchable desire to suffer, and begged and entreated of Jesus
to grant me this grace. He gratified me at once, and drawing
near to me He took the Crown of Thorns from His own Head,
placed it on mine, and with His Holy Hands fixed it on my
temples. These are painful moments, but happy ones. Thus I
passed an hour with Jesus."*

And in another letter:

*"Yesterday, about three o'clock in the afternoon, to say the truth
I felt greatly upset, weary and weak. I found myself again before
Jesus, but He was not sad as the night before. He soothed me a
little, and then seeming quite contented. He took the Crown from
my head—that also caused me pain, but less than before—and
replaced it on His own. I did not feel any more pain, but at once
regained my strength, and felt better then than before suffering."*

This refers to July 1900, but would seem to have happened earlier.
We have come to this conjecture through some passages in Gemma's
own writings.

Facts were here again at hand to show that all this was not the
effect of imagination. The dear child's head was seen at the time to
be encircled with punctures from which fresh blood flowed. And not
only was this around her head, but all over it. Thus is confirmed what
some contemplative saints have left written, that Our Savior's Crown
of Thorns was so shaped as to envelope the whole head. And Gemma
herself, speaking of the Crown that was shown her the first time by
the Angel, says plainly: "It was not in the shape of a crown but of a
cap." Sometimes the punctures were almost imperceptible to the naked
eye, as was the case with the Stigmatic Louise Lateau, and were only
ascertained by the blood that oozed from them. But at other times

according to the statement of a most worthy priest and eye-witness: "Holes of a triangular shape, from each of which came large drops of blood, were quite visible on her forehead and under her hair." Many others were present at the same time and able at their leisure to observe this wonderful fact. It was repeated regularly for a considerable time from Thursday to Friday in each week—even after the stigmata on her hands, feet, and side had ceased to be visible.

It happened very often, that this bleeding of the head began before the time of the usual Thursday evening ecstasy. Sometimes while Gemma was at supper with the family, drops of blood were seen on her forehead, and as they increased in number they ran down her cheeks on her neck and dress. Another witness says that "drops of blood came from every pore and increased so as to fall to the ground." All witnesses agree that this sight would have softened a heart of stone! And had they but thought of calling a photographer to take a picture of that face, oh! then we should have had an excellent representation of the picture of the *Ecce Homo*. "If you had but seen, father," says another, "blood flowing from her eyes, ears, forehead and temples! They seemed fountains. I soaked two handkerchiefs with it. If you had only heard the sound that we heard within her side!" This was said of her heart that as we have remarked elsewhere beat so strongly during those burnings of love. On one occasion being present I ordered those punctures to be washed and dried and set myself to examine them. In a few moments the blood began to come again from the same points. That angelic face was soon again all covered with it, and I noticed that the flow was very rapid, as if the blood was forced to burst out by some strong inward pressure. It ran down her cheeks but quickly dried on the skin.

Although the Gospel does not mention it, contemplatives, with St. Teresa, are accustomed to dwell on the consideration of a particular Wound of the Divine Man of Sorrows. This was the Wound on His left shoulder caused by the weight of the Cross on His painful way to Calvary. And Gemma had this also, although some may have confused it with the many wounds of the scourging. It was very large and deep, and caused the sufferer so much pain that it obliged her to lean to one side when walking. It bled copiously, and also, like the others closed on the Friday evening, or at latest on Saturday morning. It differed from the others however in that it continued to give her trouble for some time.

Things went on in that way up to February 1901, when I wrote telling her to pray that she might be freed from these outward extraordinary manifestations. This humble servant of God who, of herself, had so desired and besought her Jesus to free her from all publicity, prayed this time with the merit of obedience and was heard. Jesus, as she wrote, assured her that He would remove the marks but increase the pains. The wounds of her hands, feet, and side never opened again except once—in the way and for the reasons yet to be explained. The punctures of the thorns on her head continued for a little time longer and then ceased. The same has to be said of the lacerations from the scourging, and every other lesion of the flesh causing a flow of blood. It was precisely on the 7th and 8th of February 1901, that the scourging began and continued on the four Fridays of March. But on the 6th of April Gemma wrote that the stripes ceased through obedience to her Confessor.

The pain however continued to be felt and indeed, much more than before. The bleeding, as the poor sufferer herself said more than once, gave her some relief. And this conclusion was readily come to by all who saw the increased agony she went through after the bleeding had ceased—how she trembled all over, and tears came to her eyes.

God however willed to give her some relief through her heart, which by its beating would seem to have forced the blood to come in quantities from her mouth. The saintly child rejoiced at this, and while in ecstasy was heard to exclaim: "Jesus, I would give Thee my hands and my feet but I cannot. It has been forbidden me by the confessor. Take my heart, this I can give. My hands also, Jesus, but I cannot." It would seem that Our Lord here let her see His pierced Hands, as if inviting her, almost tempting her, to give Him all hers in exchange for His Most Precious Blood. "But I cannot," she repeated, "I suffer because I cannot, but obedience is worth more than a victim." "Oh, if you had seen her this Good Friday," so her adopted mother wrote to me, "from one to three o'clock! I really thought she would die in my arms. Blood came in quantities from her mouth! and she exclaimed: 'My Jesus, I cannot give Thee blood from all parts of my body, but I give it Thee from my heart." In fact this was the beginning of those ineffable yearnings that almost forced her heart to burst from her breast, violently pressing out her ribs on the left side; and also of those inner fires that, as we shall see, burned the flesh and the skin of the surrounding parts.

To complete my picture, I might here bring forward the dislocation of His bones that Our Divine Savior underwent in His Crucifixion; the dragging asunder of His limbs while hanging on the Cross; the agony caused by the dissolution of all the members of His Most Sacred Body during His last three hours, and His burning thirst which forced Him to call out: *"Sitio*—I thirst." And then I could show how Gemma in reality, after the cessation of the bleeding stigmata, participated also in those other torments of the Passion. She confessed it herself. It was witnessed many times through the external symptoms, and proved by several persons who, struck with wonder, unanimously attest that nothing was wanting in that holy creature to enable her to be looked on as a living image of Jesus in His Passion. But as I have already exceeded the limits of this chapter, I will not detail the statements of those persons or go further into particulars of what I have here stated.

I ought also to make mention of the anguish of Heart which was the most ineffable part of the Mystery of the Cross. Gemma, after having suffered the corporal pains of Jesus Crucified, underwent also with Him His Agony of Spirit on the Cross. But how shall I make the reader understand in what those mystic agonies consisted? I will say only that to judge of them from what appeared externally, in the cadaverous color, heaving bosom, sunken eyes, spent lips, etc., they can and ought to be looked upon as agonies of death, and thus was heard to its fullest extent the fervent prayer that the sight of Jesus Crucified had deeply impressed in the heart and suggested to the lips of the Virgin or Lucca: "Jesus, make me like Thee; make me suffer with Thee; do not spare me; Thou sufferest, make me also suffer; Thou art the Man of Sorrows, and I wish to be the child of sorrow."

Nothing more seems wanting to enable us to assert that Gemma had reached the summit of sanctity. Had she not achieved the end of all the predestined and elect, who according to St. Paul represent in themselves the image of the Son of God?

CHAPTER 9

June–September, 1899: St. Gemma Meets the Passionist Fathers. More About The Stigmata

HAVING considered the marvels of God's Infinite Love in His chosen faithful servant, her full participation in His sacrifice—the excess of His love on Calvary, we are enabled to form an idea of the nature of her Communion on the morning of the 9th of June. It followed the wonderful phenomena of the day before that likened her in body as well as soul to her Crucified Lord. Then for the first time, with her hands and feet pierced through and through, and a deep wound throwing open her heart, she went to the Holy Table. With what ardor will not Gemma have repeated in her thrice happy state: *Dilectus meus mihi et egi illi!*, "My Beloved to me and I to Him!" And with St. Paul: "I am truly crucified with Jesus; I live, but it is not I who now live, but Jesus Who lives in me." On her return home she had no difficulty in explaining things to her Aunt as on other occasions. But she had yet to do what she found most difficult and painful. She had to give a minute account of everything to her Confessor to whom she had previously made known her presentiment of receiving an extraordinary grace.

She had always felt the greatest difficulty in speaking of herself and of her spiritual experiences. Having to make such manifestations caused her intense pain and confusion; rather would she have died. Imagine now what her feelings must be in a matter so far from all expectation and so mysterious. "And what will my Confessor think," she said to herself, "on hearing what I have to say, he who fully knows how unworthy I am of heavenly favors? And won't others also, knowing how sinful I am, be scandalized at all this?" Even repeated admonitions and reproaches of her Angel Guardian were needed in order to overcome her repugnance.

The whole month of June passed in these perplexities and Gemma had not resolved to do her duty. But at last, God in His loving Providence taking pity on her, came to her aid and put her on the way by which He destined her to walk. Here is how it came about: Pope Leo XIII had ordered Missions to be given in all the Dioceses of Italy, and the Passionist Fathers were sent to Lucca where they opened the Mission in the Cathedral Church of St. Martin towards the end of June. Gemma just then was attending sermons on the Sacred Heart of Jesus in another Church, and at the beginning of July, urged by Divine impulse, she hastened to the Mission at St. Martin's. Her joy was great at recognizing in the garb of the Missioners precisely the same habit in which her beloved Protector, Blessed Gabriel of the Dolours, had appeared to her. "The impression was such," these are her words, "as not to be described. The first time I saw those Fathers I felt a special affection for them, and from that day I did not miss a single sermon." On this subject of her first meeting with the Passionists she further adds "It was the last day of the Holy Mission. All the people were assembled in the Church for the general Communion. I also joined with the others, and Jesus Who was pleased at this made Himself strongly felt in my soul, and asked me: 'Gemma, do you like the habit worn by that Priest?' (and He pointed to a Passionist who was at a distance.) It was not necessary for me to answer Jesus in words, my heart spoke by its palpitation. 'Would it please you,' He added, 'if you also was clothed in the same habit?' 'My God!' I exclaimed. He then (without letting His Will be clearly understood) added: 'You shall be a child of My Passion, and a beloved child. One of these shall be thy father. Go and explain everything.'" Gemma taking those words literally, in the sense that she should one day become a Passionist, was overjoyed at it. She also was jubilant at finding that her repugnance to making known the state of her soul had gone. Then wishing to obey the voice of God immediately, she hastened to present herself to one of those fathers who happened to be Fr. Cajetan of the Child Jesus, and at his feet unfolded her whole soul with perfect ease, as in her ordinary confessions, and ended by telling him of the Stigmata and her reluctance to speak of them to her Confessor. The Father, wonderstruck at the recital and at the artless candor of the young girl, gave her prudent advice, and at the same time exhorted her to be very humble and grateful to God. With regard to her more detailed direction, wishing to ponder things well before giving her any final decision, he promised that at his return to Lucca, which was to be very soon, he would see her again. He then granted a few of the requests that she made him, and imposed upon her a formal precept to make known everything to her ordinary Confessor.

The chief among the requests alluded to was, to be allowed to make the three religious vows of poverty, chastity, and obedience; and the father, not wishing to sadden her by a refusal permitted her to make them, as a matter of private devotion, to be renewed at short intervals, with the approval of her Confessor. He was not so ready to give her leave for austerities that she wished to practice, but, on the contrary, he took from her certain instruments of penance that she had made for herself, as he felt sure that her Confessor would not allow her to use them.

Gemma's joy at making those three vows was immense. She herself will tell us of it: "Having always wished," she says, "to make those vows, I quickly seized on the opportunity offered me, and the father let me make them from the 5th of July to the 8th of September. This made me feel very happy and was one of my greatest consolations."

The difficulty experienced by the Servant of God in manifesting the state of her soul to her ordinary Confessor, far from being the result of any caprice, arose in great measure from a combination of circumstances. She was devoted to him and greatly needed and desired his guidance. He had known her and heard her confessions from her infancy, but now, owing to the extraordinary ways by which God was leading her, it became necessary that he should be perfectly informed of all that was happening to her. He, on the other hand, overwhelmed by a multiplicity of official cares, works of zeal, the direction of innumerable souls, etc.—all matters that kept him occupied from morning till night—found it impossible to give much time to Gemma. She could not find him when needed, and his verbal answers to her letters given hurriedly in the Confessional did but increase her perplexities. She therefore had good reason to dread bringing the vast matter of the Stigmata, etc., before him. Father Cajetan having seen how things stood and wishing to facilitate matters, undertook on his return to Lucca, at Gemma's desire, to see her worthy Confessor, Mgr. Volpi, and manifest to him all that had recently happened to her. He did so, and soon after him Gemma also went to see Mgr. Volpi and with her wonted candor told him all. The holy Bishop received them both affectionately, and approved of what the Extraordinary Confessor had done. But with regard to the Stigmata he wished to take time before coming to any decision. He would not allow of the supposition that such a soul as Gemma's could be deluded, hysterical, or possessed; but neither would he too readily recognize in her the work of God until he made certain that God was the author of the phenomena under consideration, or at least that they could only be explained by Divine intervention. As those wonders continued to happen as usual on Thursdays and Fridays, he ordered Gemma to do all in her power and to pray that those singular impressions on her body might not be repeated. Her prayer was granted by our Lord for a short time, but then the phenomena returned as at first. Gemma writing of what had happened at that time said: "I had no longer any fear or hesitation in telling Monsignor everything; and he told me that if Jesus had not made him see things clearly he would not have believed in such representations."

Father Cajetan also resolved to verify the facts of the Stigmata, as appears from the following declaration:

J.X.P.

"I the undersigned hereby testify and declare that in July, 1899, I saw certain extraordinary Wounds on the hands of the young

girl Gemma Galgani. In the inside, that is, in the palms there was seen a raised piece of flesh like the head of a nail about as large as a half-penny. At the back of each hand there was a somewhat deep laceration that seemed to have been caused by a blunt nail forced through the hand from the opposite side.

I, and those who were with me, had no hesitation in saying that those were Stigmata which could not have come from any natural cause. In fact we saw her hands on Thursday free from any marks. On Friday morning we found them as we have described. We examined them again on Saturday and found no mark except a small reddish cicatrix."

—CAJETAN OF THE CHILD JESUS, PASSIONIST.

This verification of the wonderful fact was soon followed by another—that of the Provincial of the Passionists, Fr. Peter Paul of the Immaculate (now Mgr. Moreschini, Archbishop of Camerino) who came to Lucca on the 20th of August, 1899. He received hospitality from the Giannini family, benefactors of our Order, and as Gemma, but a short time before, had come to share their home, he was able then and later on to satisfy himself fully about her Stigmata, etc. I think it well to give here in his words the account of what happened on the 29th of August and his sentiments on that occasion.

"Having heard others," he said, "speaking of this young girl and relating strange things about her, while suspecting that it was a matter of mere feminine delusions, I thought I would make sure of it with my own eyes. I went to her house, it was Tuesday, and saw the child. I felt inspired to ask our Lord to deign to give me a palpable sign if He was truly the Author of those marvelous things. Then mentally, without speaking of it to anyone, I thought of two things: the sweat of blood and the manifestation of the Stigmata. When it was Vespers time she withdrew quite alone to say her usual prayers before the Crucifix. In a few minutes she was in full ecstasy. I entered and with my own eyes beheld her totally transfigured so that she looked like an angel although torn by terrible pain. From her face, head and hands there flowed fresh blood, and I suppose it was the same all over her body. That flow of blood lasted for about half an hour, but did not reach the ground, because it dried quickly while flowing. I withdrew, greatly moved, and Gemma coming out of the ecstasy, being alone with her aunt, said: 'The Father has asked for signs from Jesus, and Jesus has told me that He has already given him one of them and will also give him the other. Oh! what do these signs mean? Does He say it?' In the evening the lady just mentioned asked me quite anxiously: 'But, father, would the other sign you have asked for be that of the Stigmata?' I was astounded, and she continued: 'I ask this because if it was so, Gemma has them already opened, come and see." I went, and found that blessed creature in ecstasy the same as the first time, with her hands pierced (I say pierced) through and through by a large freshly opened wound from which blood flowed in abundance. The affecting spectacle lasted about five minutes," (and he goes into minute description of it all, which coincides in every respect with that already given by me). "With the cessation of the ecstasy the wounds closed, the blood ceased to flow, and the torn skin returned at once to its natural state, so perfectly that nothing more was needed but to wash her hands in order to find that every vestige of what had happened was gone. Jesus had heard me, and thanking Him I laid aside every doubt, established in my belief that *digitus Dei est hic.*"

He also, at the same time, wrote to Mgr. Volpi as follows:

"RT. REV. MONSIGNOR: I make it my duty to inform you of what I witnessed in Gemma Galgani on Tuesday the 29th of August. I saw with my own eyes the wounds on both sides of her hands, and that they were truly torn open. When the ecstasy ended everything healed up, the cicatrices alone remaining. How could such a wound heal thus instantaneously by natural means? My opinion is that it is the work of God, and I still think that you

ought to place her for a time in some convent for the reasons I have given you."

—FR. PETER PAUL OF THE IMMACULATE, PASSIONIST PROVINCIAL

The above attestations served to impress on Mgr. Volpi still more profoundly the delicacy of his own position. Hence he believed it his duty to act with the greatest prudence and reserve. After mature consideration he determined to have recourse to a proof that he thought would be decisive. It was, that a qualified physician, as learned as he was religious, in whom he had confidence, should examine Gemma's Stigmata. The matter was not mentioned to the Servant of God; but Our Lord made known to her what had been resolved upon. In her autobiography she writes thus: "Monsignor thought it well to have me visited by a doctor without my knowing it. But Jesus gave me notice of it and said to me: 'Tell the Confessor that I will not do anything he wants, in presence of the doctor.' I told this to the Confessor as commanded by Jesus." Her words to the Confessor were: "Yesterday evening Jesus gave me a message for your Lordship in these words, 'You shall say to your Confessor that I will give him any sign he wants provided he be alone. He may rest assured that it is not an ailment as they have believed.'"

What then will Monsignor do? Will he go alone? His simple inspection unwitnessed will not lessen his responsibility; and if the suspicion existed that it was an ailment, or, to put it better, a case of auto-suggestion, he alone would not be able to dispel the doubt. He therefore adhered to his decision. And to Signora Cecilia Giannini, Gemma's adopted Mother, who gave him particulars regularly of all that happened to her protégée, he said: "I should like to have Gemma visited by the doctor, and let him examine the Stigmata." It was arranged for him and the doctor to come on the following Friday.

On the 8th of September 1899, Feast of Our Lady's Nativity that fell on the Friday, about ten in the morning Gemma withdrew to her room and went into ecstasy. About an hour later she returned to the use of her senses and wrote a few lines to Monsignor telling him that if he wished to come he was to come alone, and not bring anyone with him, as Jesus was not pleased and would not let them see anything. However, that he was to act as he pleased, and that she was satisfied with whatever he did. She gave the letter open to her adopted mother, who read it and sent it immediately to Mgr. Volpi. About one o'clock Gemma returned to her room again and was rapt in ecstasy. Her adopted mother soon after found her with blood flowing from her forehead, and the open Stigmata in her hands also bleeding. At this ecstasy Signora Cecilia, her brother Signor Matthew Giannini with his wife Justina, and probably others of the family, were present full of devout admiration. About two o'clock Mgr. Volpi came with the doctor and Signora Cecilia ran to meet them, saying: "Come, come, it is just the right time," and she brought them into the room with the above-named members of the family. The doctor took a towel, dipped it in water, and wiped Gemma's hands and forehead. The blood immediately disappeared and the skin showed no sign of cicatrix, scratch or puncture, as if there had never been any laceration. Imagine the effect on those present! The doctor, assisted by Signora Cecilia only, wished to examine her feet and side; but the result was the same. Thus God, Who is admirable in His ways, refused to allow human science to sit in judgment on what He had deigned to operate in the supernatural order, to enliven the faith of His servants. Gemma, in her autobiography, narrates the fact with her usual candid simplicity:

"He" (the Confessor), she said, "acted in his own way, but things went as Jesus said they would." And the same evening she wrote to the Prelate, "If you had been alone Jesus would have thoroughly convinced you. Yesterday He told me that you were coming today."

During the whole of the visit Gemma remained in ecstasy, and knew nothing of what happened. But having come to herself she saw that a certain change had come over the family, who were greatly mortified, upset and puzzled. Her adopted mother, in order to distract her own thoughts and also to revive Gemma, took her as her companion out of doors. As they walked Gemma said to her: "Take me for a while to Jesus, I have need of Jesus." So her companion took her to St. Simon's Church, which was at some distance. After a visit to the Blessed Sacrament of about an hour, when outside the church Gemma said to Signora Cecilia: "I should like to tell you something, but am ashamed to." Being pressed to speak, she showed her open hands, from which blood flowed as on the other Fridays. The good Signora thought of letting Mgr. Volpi see her in that state, and got a confidential friend to take her to him. Thus with his own eyes he saw not only blood but also the small wound in each hand from which it flowed. The prudent Prelate showed no sign of surprise, even not to expose his spiritual child to the danger of vanity. He merely satisfied himself by examining her hands, and then let her go. In this way Our Lord in His Mercy willed to lessen the humiliation of His Servant and relieve in part the minds of her Confessor and of the others who had been present at the fruitless visit of the doctor.

Although God in His Love from time to time afflicts His Servants, yet He never abandons them. No, the ways of His Providence by which He comes to their aid and consolation in desperate conjunctures are most admirable. Gemma, some would say, had fallen to a pitiable state from which she could not hope to rise. Such conclusions are false, for it is written: *facile est in oculis Dei subito honestare pauperem*—It is easy before God to instantly restore the needy. And so it was with Gemma.

In her Autobiography she writes: "From that day of the doctor's visit a new life began for me." She meant a life of prolonged martyrdom. Not only the Giannini family were greatly upset, but even the good Confessor, notwithstanding what he had seen for himself. "I had again," she writes, "the Confessor's prohibition of all the extraordinary things of the Thursday and Friday. And Jesus obeyed for a while, but again returned to the same manifestations and to more than before." The Servant of God who was informed by her

Jesus of all the doubts and uncertainties of her Confessor was greatly afflicted on his account while in her heart she was gladdened by what she called "the most beautiful humiliation that my dear Jesus has given me." She could not help feeling pained at the state of mind of him whom she loved from her infancy and venerated as a father. She also saw that in him she was losing the only comfort she had in her constant sufferings. To no one would she more readily recur. Our Lord however did not long delay to console His Servant and strengthen her weakness of spirit. "My child," He said to her, "you, in your afflictions, weaknesses and adversities, think of them all more than of Me. You have recourse to others for relief and comfort rather than to Me." The Divine Master wished by these words to let her know that however reasonable her attachment, and however holy the confidence she felt in His Minister, she could not lose courage when, through no fault of hers, such helps came to fail her; that having Him she should be satisfied.

Those words so well understood by Gemma were enough to give back peace to her afflicted mind and effect her detachment from every human sentiment together with the total abandonment of herself to God. Regardless of the poor Monsignor's doubts regarding herself, she ceased not to long for his welfare and continued to ask Jesus to enlighten and console him. This is evident from many of her letters to him and to others who enjoyed his confidence. Even in her colloquies during ecstasy, while pouring out her heart to her God in sorrowful patient entreaty, the thoughts of her Confessor would often come before her and then she would suddenly exclaim: "O Jesus, go console Monsignor who is so depressed. Some think one thing and others quite the opposite. But do You wish it to be so? Are You better pleased with me now that all think me crazy, than before when they believed me to be a saint? Is it not the truth now?" And having learned from her Divine Spouse that after the futile effort made through the doctor, another was contemplated, namely to obtain a formal order to have her writings given up to a learned man for examination, she with her usual simplicity, remaining still in ecstasy, thus expressed herself: "O Jesus, and they even wish to have the writings examined by Doctor Boda! May such a thing never happen! O Jesus, they are turning You to ridicule. If they wish to see the writings, let them see only blank paper. Go, Jesus, to Monsignor and tranquilize and console him." Nor was she satisfied with praying. She always showed by facts that she was most devoted to him. She sometimes thought that he had abandoned her because, for various reasons, he sent her now to one, now to another strange Confessor. Yet she continued to use him as her Confessor up to her death, always looking on him as a father.

Ah! How true it is, what Jesus said to Gemma: "In suffering one learns how to love." God so disposed things that in the same month of September 1899, Fr. Cajetan returned to Lucca and remained there for two months owing to sickness. Then hearing all about the doctor's blank visit, and the Confessor's discomforting impressions he too was greatly taken aback and began to have doubts and suspicions. But Our loving Jesus willed to do with him as with St. Thomas: "Put in thy finger, and see My hands, and bring hither thy hand, and be not faithless but believing." He saw again, observed, touched and said: "This is the finger of God." Then in the letter he wrote to the Confessor explaining his convictions, he added that he too had exacted the same proof as the doctor by ordering the wounds, which he says were deep, to be washed three or four times, but they did not disappear. On the contrary, the blood stopped for a moment but soon again began to flow.

In like manner, Fr. Peter Paul returning often to Lucca on his business as Provincial during the last months of 1899 and in 1900 and 1901, was frequently able to satisfy himself fully regarding the Stigmata, and likewise concerning all the other wonderful things that God was operating in His Servant. He thus was able to formulate a definite opinion on all points and give the world a most authoritative testimony of the wonders of God's grace in this chosen soul. Having made his lucid statement giving full particulars of the Stigmata, he proceeded in the following words to speak of the Crowning with Thorns:

"I saw that drops of blood were oozing from the skin around her head, especially from her temples. After the lapse of twenty minutes, when she had come out of the ecstasy and washed, I saw that there no longer existed the death-like pallor and indication of pain which made her resemble Our Savior on the Cross. She had returned to her natural color; nay, after the sweat of blood had ceased her countenance assumed an angelic beauty."

"On another occasion," thus he wrote in 1901, *"it was told me, that not only the stigmata, but the punishment of the scourging, the crowning with thorns, and the three hours' agony on the Cross was frequently renewed in the body of this angelic girl and that she suffered terribly. I therefore proposed to be present at that scene of pain, if God would deign to grant me this favor, as He had done before, and thus see everything with my own eyes. Gemma, as usually happened, rose from the family table after having taken very little or no supper. After a little I went with D. Lorenzo Agrimonti to her room, and beheld her, in ecstasy, already a prey to the cruel martyrdom. I remained in that room for more than two hours and a half being determined not to leave until I had seen at least the flow of blood with my own eyes. She was having such a violent palpitation that it moved the bed-covering in the part near her heart, while her arms remained motionless and extended. The beat was so strong that it made the bed shake, and I confess that I experienced at the same time feelings of terror and devotion. After an hour or a little more the palpitation quieted, and she began to shed blood from her head in such abundance that the pillows and sheets were soaked with it. In certain parts of her head, particularly in*

the upper part of her forehead, blood came in such quantity that, while congealing it became clotted in several places. From the time this flow of blood from her head ceased (it was then half-past eleven), until about three o'clock in the morning, the ecstatic, who previously had made some very slight movements, remained perfectly motionless. Her countenance seemed that of a dead person, and to see her in that state, with such a cadaverous color, her features all drawn and stained with blood, anyone would have thought her dead. All pulsation seemed to have ceased and her breathing was scarcely perceptible. Thus she passed three whole hours and then came out of the ecstasy. I saw her very soon again the same morning. She was then ready to go to Church for Holy Communion, and her natural color had returned as though she had not suffered in the least.

I related that which I had seen with my eyes and touched with my hands to Gemma's Confessor. We spoke at length of these facts and I told him of the good impressions they had made upon me. He begged of me to continue when an occasion offered itself to examine his penitent, and gave me faculties to hear her Confession."

Chevalier Giannini, his wife Justina, his eldest son and in particular his sister Cecilia, of whom we shall have to speak again, all of them worthy of the fullest trust, had for a long time ample and numerous opportunities before, as well as after the Medical Visit, of verifying the Stigmata and other signs of the Passion of Our Lord, which He was pleased to manifest in His faithful Servant. To their authoritative testimony the writer of this life can add his own, having had every facility of testing and all full information regarding the wonders worked by God in this favored soul.

The reader is sure to appreciate my having united, at a slight sacrifice of chronological order, nearly all that refers to the Stigmata and other marks of Our Lord's Passion, as we find them reproduced in the virginal body of His faithful handmaid. Because the concentration of so many marvelous facts, verified beyond all shadow of doubt, strengthens the proofs of their reality and supernatural origin.

We have, it is true, the fruitless visit of the doctor, which counts for nothing, if not to prove the Divine intervention. Gemma, informed by God, had prophetically and repeatedly warned those concerned of what eventually happened. Her stigmata were well attested immediately before and after that visit, and if they had not been withdrawn from the doctor's view, then indeed might the Divine interposition have been questioned. We cannot but admire the most admirable dispositions of Providence in what happened. Gemma was not in a cloister, she was in the world. She was obliged to go out of doors several times a day, but spent the rest of her time hidden at home. Only a few of the members of the Giannini family knew of the extraordinary things happening to her, and they kept them so secret that they were unknown in Lucca. It is easy to imagine what the result would have been had the doctor, or other outsider, verified the Stigmata and the other phenomena. The scientific, the curious, the praters, the scoffers, etc., would all have been set going. No, God would not allow it. By withdrawing the marvelous phenomena from public gaze, He kept His Servant humble and His treasure hidden.

However, the prudence, wisdom, learning and honorable standing of all who have attested the truth of those marvels of Divine Love have amply effected all that was necessary or desirable. Science cannot pretend to explain supernatural things; it can only certify the existence of facts. And surely, in order to verify facts there is no need to call in the aid of scientists. Then in the case before us, as the phenomenon was not constant, but recurred at intervals, all that a scientist could say would be that at the time of his inspection it did or did not appear. And to prove its presence the testimony of a number of most trustworthy witnesses who had seen it several times was even more than was needed.

It would be ridiculous, and a parting with reason, to suppose that by force of imagination anyone, however hysterical or amenable to hypnotic suggestion, could naturally produce deep wounds and lacerations such as were verified in Gemma Galgani. Still more absurd would be the supposition that such wounds and lacerations could be perfectly closed and healed in an instant by any power of nature. All this is fully discussed in the Appendix to this Life. We are forced to conclude that in Gemma Galgani's case what was seen and happened was the work of God. The Devil can and does effect much by his temptations and wiles, but not in souls so rich in virtue and love of God as was Gemma's.

As an appropriate ending to this chapter we give the continuation of Fr. Peter Paul's report of 1901, although he touches on some matters that we must deal with later on. Speaking of his first intercourse with the Servant of God, he writes:

"According to the opportunities offered me I often conferred with Gemma. I heard her General Confession which she wished to finish at three intervals, and I had then the opportunity of knowing that she had preserved her baptismal innocence. I have seen her several times in ecstasy. When she set herself to pray or was spoken to of spiritual things, specially of Our Lord's Passion, she went into ecstasy. Then she seemed to be transfigured, with her eyes open and fixed on one point, remaining immovable in her person although her limbs were quite flexible. She was during ecstasy insensible to any noise that was made near her, or to the puncture of a pin, or to the burning with a taper. But although so dead to sense during the ecstasy she was all alive to heavenly things, and was heard to give vent in fervent expressions to her love of God: 'Yes, I love You, my Jesus; I will be all Yours. I will suffer all I can for You.' Her bearing during those moments was truly angelic, and her

countenance was resplendent with beauty joined with a marvelous majesty."

He said that what moved him most in Gemma were her virtues, and that they enabled him to assert without fear that the extraordinary things that happened to her were from God. He ended his report by giving an account of those virtues, as follows:

"I have been able to notice in her an angelic purity. Not only did she preserve her baptismal innocence but, as far as I could ascertain, she never committed a deliberate defect during her whole life. Her humility was most profound. She was devoid of self-esteem, desiring to be humbled and corrected; and having been despised and mortified without measure, she gave no sign of the least displeasure or resentment. On the contrary, in her countenance she showed that she was more pleased than otherwise. Her obedience was singular and admirable. She never gave any opposition, even to the least hint or desire of others. She obeyed with promptitude, simplicity and joy, no matter what the nature of the command might be. She gave clear proof of this perfect obedience with regard to her prayers. Our Lord had raised her to the highest degrees of contemplation, and when her ordinary Confessor bade her keep to the method of prayer for beginners, she obeyed at once, and did herself violence in order to carry his wishes into effect. She underwent this sort of martyrdom for nearly two years.

Her mortification of her senses was continuous and most severe. She took very little food, so that it seemed a miracle how she lived. And if she had not been restrained by obedience she would have deprived herself of that little; for, as she said, she felt satisfied by the bread of Angels which she received every morning. With her everything was good, everything was equal. In her attire she never had any ambition and never asked for any special garment. Nor did she ever seek any amusement or recreation, nor complain of cold or heat, as though she were insensible to everything. A love of suffering was with her almost characteristic. No one ever heard her utter a complaint even in the midst of the terrible pains she underwent during her long sickness, or from the violent assaults of the devil. Her constant remembrance of Jesus Crucified stimulated her to suffer always, so that she desired nothing more than suffering and whatever she suffered seemed little. This perfect creature had offered herself a victim to the Sacred Heart of Jesus for the conversion of poor sinners and for this end she willingly offered every suffering. For the same end, and still more through love, she desired continually to suffer with Jesus on the Cross, to live always on the Cross, and to die with Him on the Cross. And in this it would appear that her Divine Spouse satisfied her because in life and in death she suffered always a cruel martyrdom of body and soul.

What shall I say of her union with God? I can certify that this was unceasing. Even in the midst of the most distracting occupations she was always recollected and in mind and heart united to God. On account of this habitual and profound recollection her voice was never heard. She answered briefly the questions that were asked her and then resumed her silence. Indeed, so intimate was her union with God that she seemed more a celestial being than a creature of earth. Behold these are, put briefly, the virtues which Gemma practiced always, and which go to show that she was full of the love of God. Hence I hold that the wonderful phenomena which we have admired in her, are the work of that God Whom she loved so much and served so well."

—Fr. Peter Paul of the Immaculate, Passionist

The above statement of the distinguished Passionist in praise of the Virgin of Lucca is most important, and adds great value to her Biography, precisely because of the man who has written it. Better recognized as Mgr. Camillo Moreschini, Archbishop of Camerino, he is widely known and esteemed for his learning, zeal and prudence in the guidance of souls and in the Apostolic ministry. The Holy Father Pius X, owing to his rare good qualities and after he had been Superior General of the Passionists, employed him in the Apostolic Visitation of some twelve important Dioceses and then raised him to the Archbishopric of Camerino. Who does not see the importance of such a man's testimony in such a story as Gemma's? When she had been discredited by a few because of her Stigmata, God in His pity and love sent first, Father Cajetan, and after him Father Peter Paul, to vindicate her reputation and make known her virtues. *Jacta super Dominum curam tuam et Ipse te enutriet*—Cast thy care upon the Lord and He shall sustain thee."

CHAPTER 10

July-September, 1899: St. Gemma is Received Into the Giannini Family as an Adopted Child.

THERE is in Lucca a truly patriarchal family, that of Chevalier Matthew Giannini, in which virtues are held as the greatest riches. It consists of father, mother, the father's sister Cecilia and twelve children. They are greatly esteemed, and dear to all the citizens. This family have gladly given the hospitality of their home as benefactors to the poor Sons of St. Paul of the Cross, who often pass that way in the exercise of their apostolic ministry.

Signora Cecilia Giannini is a lady wholly given to doing good. She only knew Gemma by sight; that was when they met daily at Holy Communion. To see the child was to be drawn to her. She seemed to her future friend like an angel in human flesh. About this time Father Cajetan of the child Jesus, on his return to Lucca from the Mission of S. Martino of which we have spoken, asked Signora Cecilia to fetch him the Servant of God as he had promised to see her. She readily embraced an opportunity of becoming acquainted with Gemma, and having sought and brought her to the father, realized at the same time that she had found a treasure never to be relinquished. Gemma in her turn was struck by the lady's charming ways and by the solid and vigorous virtue of her whom she felt she was to have in the place of a mother. The family was away for the bathing season, and this gave the signora a good motive for asking her to come often and spend a few hours of the day with her. Gemma's people, knowing the high reputation of the other family, made no difficulty. From having the angelic girl's company by day followed the wish to keep her overnight, and on the pretext of needing a companion because feeling so lonely she obtained this favor also, at least now and then. Gemma rejoiced greatly at this leave as she seemed thus to find herself as it were in her proper place. She breathed a purer atmosphere and felt her soul uplifted whenever she was able to be with such a valued companion. In her own home difficulties increased every day, and she was obliged to treat with all sorts of persons. She tried hard to stand aloof attending to her work and to prayer but she could not always succeed. It happened once that in a quarrel she heard the Divine Majesty spoken of irreverently, and so great was her grief at it, that she began to sweat blood from her whole body to such an excess that it ran down to the ground. Her consternation was great. What was to be done? For some time back her family had noticed a change in her bearing. Doubts were raised about her, and they asked one another what it meant. A few gossipers, even outside the family, caused uneasiness particularly to her Aunt to whom the candid child had a short time before shown her hands bleeding from the stigmata. Gemma herself giving an account to her Confessor of what happened, after the phenomenon of her sweating blood wrote thus:

"Monsignor, one of my aunts, yesterday when I went to my room, followed me in a great rage, and said: 'This evening thou hast not thy sister Julia to defend thee, let me see at once whence all that blood has come or I will beat thee into obedience.' I remained silent, while she with one hand held my throat and with the other tried to undress me. She did not succeed. Just then the bell rang and she left me. But that was not all. When I was going to bed she returned saying that it was time to put an end to these fooleries and that I had done enough to deceive others. 'If thou dost not tell me,' she said, 'whence that blood has come, I will not allow thee to leave the house alone, or send thee anywhere.' You can imagine at those words I began to cry, and knew not what to do. At last I determined to tell her, and answered thus: 'Blasphemies are the cause. I see how much they make Jesus suffer, and I suffer with Him, and my heart suffers, and that blood comes from it!' She then cooled a little and left me alone."

This was not the only time that the Servant of God suffered in her family through her relatives' ignorance of God's dealings with her. Her kind Aunt Helen, through illness, could not accompany her to church. The other would not allow her to go alone. The curiosity of some, even of the servants, beset her. They watched her everywhere and even espied her actions through the chinks in her room door. Coming on her unawares while in ecstasy, in the same way, they judged wrongly of what they beheld and invited others to come and see her in that state. She deplored all this to her Confessor, and also to Our Lord Who likewise had commanded her to keep everything hidden from profane eyes.

One can easily imagine Gemma's gladness at the prospect of being away from such surroundings and able to commune freely with God without any fear of disturbance.

Meanwhile Signora Cecilia had better opportunities of admiring her charming young friend's virtues, her ingenuous simplicity and striking modesty, and thus came to love her more and more. She, at first, was somewhat perplexed by the phenomena she so often witnessed, and set herself to carefully and continually examine them. Gemma, on the other hand, through her innate bashfulness and modesty did all in her power to keep hidden. Being convinced of her own unworthiness she feared she would scandalize her benefactress were the latter to become aware of the heavenly favors she was receiving. But her delicate reserve was of no avail, as God willed the gifts of His grace to become known. Here is how she wrote to her Confessor of one of her misfortunes as she called them:

> *"Yesterday Jesus made me suffer greatly. I sweat blood all day, but not at home. It was with Signora Cecilia Giannini. Jesus continually warns me not to let my personal happenings get known, otherwise He punishes me. He always tells me that I ought to be ashamed to let myself be seen by anyone being so full of defects."*

The pious hostess, without displaying any surprise in order not to disconcert her guest, blessed Our Lord in her heart and more and more venerated and loved her charming protégée. *"Viva Gesù!"* she used to say, "we have an angel in the house. How shall I act? How can I prove my gratitude to Our Lord for such a grace?"

Two of the Passionist Fathers, Cajetan and Peter Paul, passing through Lucca at this time had an opportunity of seeing Gemma and of witnessing the phenomenon of the stigmata which was repeated every Thursday and Friday as has been said. Signora Cecilia, who saw these things regularly, asked explanation and advice of the fathers. They approved of her prudent reserve, exhorting her to observe the favored child and inform them at intervals of what happened.

When the family returned to the City, Miss Giannini, who was greatly troubled at the thought of having to part with her dear Gemma, took courage, and presenting herself to her brother and his wife said to them: "God has sent me this Angel whom you see here. Could she not remain with us? We have eleven children in the house, what signifies one more?" They gave their consent. No sooner said than done. She proposed it to Gemma's aunts, and they seeing too truly that it had become impossible for her to live at home, owing to the want of means, gave their consent, although it cost them much to be separated from their only comfort in the midst of so many privations. At first they allowed her to go during the day only, but finally, in September 1900, agreed to her living permanently with this good family.

Does not all this appear to be a miracle of Divine Providence? Pious single women, widows or otherwise, living in their own homes are sometimes found willing through a spirit of penance, or for their own convenience, or for company's sake, to adopt poor little destitute or orphan girls. But in a numerous family composed of father, mother, aunt and eleven children (all under twenty) with not a few servants, and already insufficient house-room, this does not happen. Surely the thought of that good lady might seem not only precipitate and rash, but impossible to be carried out. And this more so when it is considered that the young girl whom it was proposed to adopt lost her mother through consumption, and was the sister of five consumptives either dead or dying. By what strange caprice then could they have been led to introduce so much that was dangerous into their home, and to bring one with such antecedents to live with healthy children?

But God willed it thus, and when God wills, "there is no wisdom, there is no prudence, there is no counsel against the Lord." The pious lady spoke to her brother and his wife, the mother of the children, and both were favorable. She spoke also to the elder children, to others in the house, and to a priest, D. Laurence Agrimonti, who for some time had been living with the family as a second father. All were fully satisfied.

"Gemma is most welcome," said these pious parents, "she shall be the twelfth child that heaven has given us. Let everyone honor this new daughter. Let the servants respect her, and let her want nothing."

But nothing more was needed than to look at this girl of twenty, in order to be rapt in admiration. The reader already knows something of this. Humble, docile, courteous, free from all levity or caprice; and, moreover, so devout and so good to all. During the four years she was with the family of her adopted parents she never gave occasion for the least misunderstanding or dispute, either with the young people or with the servants. And yet who will not acknowledge it to be an extraordinary thing that from children of different ages, sex and temperament, there was never heard a disparaging word against one who had come to live with them, not as a servant, but as an equal taking part in everything as one of themselves? The facts that are related in this Biography of Gemma Galgani are all recent and can be verified by anyone. "I am able to declare on oath," says the mother of this family, "that during the three years and eight months that Gemma was with us, I never knew of the least trouble arising in our family on her account. And I never noticed in her the least defect. I repeat, not the smallest trouble, not the smallest defect." All other witnesses bear the same testimony as we shall see by degrees.

CHAPTER 11

1899-1903: St. Gemma's Mode of Life
in Her New Home.

LET us look at Gemma more closely in her new home. On account of want of space in the house she had sometimes to sleep in the room of one of the girls, or in that of her adopted mother, whom to avoid confusion we shall call "Aunt." Gemma, with ineffable tenderness, used to call her "Mamma Mia." All the belongings she brought with her were a little linen, two dresses and a hat. Nor would she ever accept anything more, as we shall be better able to show when we come to speak of her detachment. Jesus was enough for her, and Jesus engaged the greater and better part of her day. In the morning she rose without delay. She slept very little, if at all, and when she noticed that her Aunt was awake she got up at once. In less than five minutes she managed to dress, wash, do her hair, and with her hat on was ready to go out to church. At that hour she attended to nothing else, no matter what other important matters might be going on about her. She did not even speak a word to anyone. She wished the first fruits of the day to be for Jesus, and accordingly by agreement with Aunt, who was of the same mind, she rose before day when all the others, being asleep, had no need of her.

She went to one of the nearest churches and generally heard two masses, one in preparation for her Daily Communion (which she never omitted) and the other in thanksgiving. An hour's prayer was indeed little for this fervent soul, who would gladly have remained in church in communion with her God all day. On no occasion however did she show the least objection to being called away too soon. And at the very first sign to leave, even when in ecstasy, as was generally the case, she returned to herself and silently followed her Aunt towards home. On entering the house she immediately set to work to help the grown girls and the servants with the younger children, dressing them, and joining in their prayers. Then to gain time she usually took in hand something she could do while moving about and thus engaged she was to be seen here and there, wherever her presence was needed.

While at school she had learned to embroider and do other kinds of fashionable work to perfection. Yet she always avoided occupying herself in this way as she thought it was little less than vanity and loss of time. She preferred mending, darning, knitting and other less showy work, that needed more patience and was much more useful in such a large family. She never hesitated to take part in the most servile works of the house, although accustomed from her infancy to be served by others. She would draw water from the well, help the maids to clean the rooms, wash up the kitchen things and assist the cook to prepare the meals.

She gladly took on herself the entire care of anyone who was sick in the house, and she saw to whatever was needed during the whole time of the sickness. One of the servants fell ill with pustules of a repulsive nature on her legs. Gemma at once was to the fore, and without making any distinction between servants and others, set about attending to her as if she herself was the last and least among the servants. She did all the cleansing about the sick room, and washed, and on her knees bandaged those purulent sores. And although the sick woman, who was of odd and irritable temperament, instead of gratitude, heaped reproaches and abuse on her little nurse, even so far as to say that she disgusted her and must leave her bedside, still the Angelic servant of God did not detest but redoubled her care, seeking always new ways of contenting the sufferer.

If left to herself she would have found occupations all day long in various employments of this kind without ever resting. But her adopted mother would not allow it. Gemma had come into their home, not as a servant, but to be a consolation and a bright example to the whole family. Hence having allowed her to do quite as much as any of the others she wished her to desist, and used to say: "Now let me enjoy my Gemma," and with these words she would take her away to her work-room or into the open air, allowing her to continue her knitting or needlework.

Their conversation generally turned on the affairs of the soul and on Jesus. They talked of the Communion of the morning, of the mystery or feast of the day, of the longing for heaven. On such occasions this observant friend used to lay innocent snares, in order to draw out Gemma's spiritual secrets. Having first set her soul on fire by fervent words, she followed up with numerous questions dexterously put so as to extract from her the lights received and resolutions made at Holy Communion, as well as what had happened during her ecstasy and so on.

I had instructed her to act thus. And in this way it pleased Our Lord to make known to us many extraordinary things that, without this device, would never have been revealed. The conversation was always new, although from early morning till late at night it occupied all the intervals of their free time, and never caused them the least tedium or weariness.

When however it happened that the good lady had to absent herself for some time, or that others came to take her place, Gemma seized the first opportunity and quietly withdrew. She then betook herself to the solitude of her room, or to the domestic chapel, there to continue her work and at the same time more easily to commune with God in prayer. Thus these two souls passed their days, and this seems to me almost a miracle when I consider the vast amount of work that her household cares entailed on this lady. She was kept on foot and occupied nearly all day without time to rest. Yet while omitting none of her duties she was able to spend long intervals with her beloved adopted child. "With Gemma at my side," she used to say, "I rest, I find myself refreshed, and no longer feel the weight of my work, nor the bitterness of disagreeables." And then she was wont to add: "What account shall not I have to give to God, if I don't value the treasure

He has given me, in this Angelic creature, and profit thereby for my soul's good!"

And as this lady thought, so likewise thought all the other members of the family, as well on the first day they came to possess Gemma as on the last when heaven took her from them. The mother of that family bears testimony by letter as follows:

"Of our Gemma I have only to say, that the most extraordinary and wonderful things continue more and more to happen to her. And when I look at her I seem to behold in her something that is not of this world. What a happiness to have lived thus with such an angel! A world of things would not be enough to give you an idea of what goes on in her. She is an angel in human form, and that expresses all."

That venerable Priest, D. Laurence Agrimonti, spoke in his turn thus: "To know and to admire this dear child, so adorned with virtue and rich in the gifts of God, was one and the same thing. I was charmed by her extraordinary ingenuousness, which seemed almost to challenge her more than ordinary intelligence. Full of admiration I observed her continually, and during the whole time that she was in our house I had constant opportunities of remarking not only her scrupulous exactness in every duty, but also her denial of her own will and her exercise of every virtue. Her virtues were practiced with such promptness, diligence and calmness, that they seemed to have become part of her nature. I admired in particular her spirit of recollection and union with God. Even in the midst of domestic occupations of the most distracting kind she was always seen as if absorbed in God, and in continual meditation. This did not hinder her from attending with great care to whatever she was doing. The fervor of her piety seemed to radiate from her person, especially from her eyes which she was wont to keep modestly downcast. Indeed I must confess that on her glancing at me I felt so impressed that I could not look her in the face." Those were his words, and after having added many other things in his long deposition he concluded as follows: "Oh! what a great grace it has been for me to have known this privileged soul. God only knows the comfort it brought to my heart! I feel now and must ever continue to feel the influence of those angelic ways, that more than ever became evident during the time of my sickness. I was astonished at her vigilance, her promptitude, and her precautions. They had in them a something truly maternal."

Another most worthy Priest made similar declarations. He was a friend of the family and often visited them. The reader will be pleased to see part of his evidence also: "The modesty, the luminous simplicity, that one reads in her countenance," so he goes on, "made a most grateful impression on me. And although I often came in contact with her, yet I could not find in her the smallest imperfection. If she had to treat with others she did not seem in the least put out, but full of a natural affability that revealed the beauty of her innocent soul. Her words were few and in answer only to the questions that were asked her. I never heard her speak of herself or of her doings. And while knowing well that she had a most delicate conscience and a beautiful soul, all intent on loving God, I should never have thought that she was so far advanced in sanctity."

Gemma came to the family table, morning and evening. But you would have said that she did so rather for form's sake than for any other reason. Her food was scarcely a few ounces in weight. When she had taken a spoonful or two of broth, she rose on some good pretext and went into the kitchen, but returned in a short time to taste in the same way of some other food. Thus she left the table almost fasting. She then withdrew to her room, leaving the others to chat among themselves as was their custom. She never sought or accepted restoratives of any kind in the course of the day, although they were frequently offered her. Nothing ever induced her to go for a walk, and the others, knowing how she disliked it, never pressed her to join them. But she used to go in the evening to the church for Benediction of the Blessed Sacrament, a devotion largely practiced in the devout city of Lucca.

At home it seemed as if Gemma was not in the house. Her voice or her laugh was never heard. She never was seen to run or fuss about, although by reason of her ardent temperament it would be natural for her to move with vivacity. When strangers made their appearance she disappeared, as much to leave the family free, as to avoid distractions in listening to conversations that were of no interest to her. In this particular, she was so exact and scrupulous that at the end of four years, it may be said, that she hardly knew one of the many visitors who frequented the house, nor even anything of what was going on. When she heard people talking, she paid no attention to what they said.

This angelic girl also found great satisfaction in exercising charity to the poor, of which we have seen her give proof in her father's prosperous days. She was continually asking Aunt for leave to put by whatever was left in the kitchen, in order to give it to the poor. Whenever she heard the door-bell ring, she thought it might be some poor person, and if the door was not quickly opened, she would ask to be allowed to answer the call. She would hasten to the door, and almost invariably on such occasions some poor needy one was there. Then as if she had found some treasure, she made the poor soul come in and sit down, while she, all contentment, went to select the best from her little store. This she brought and presented with great grace, and sitting down beside this member of Christ Our Lord, she began at once to catechize and talk of holy things: "Have you heard Mass this morning? How long is it since you went to the Sacraments? Do you always say your prayers morning and night? Do you ever think of all that Jesus has suffered for us?" By such questions as these, she sought with great tact to insinuate salutary thoughts of faith, devotion and resignation into the hearts of the sufferers, who thus restored in body and spirit went away contented. Her Aunt, who was well aware of those pious tactics, often watched her secretly, and, to her great satisfaction, beheld her saintly child full of animation and her countenance all aglow. It happened that coming on Gemma unawares she heard her say: "And am not I also poor? Jesus has taken everything from me and yet He lets me want for nothing. Indeed I am too well provided for; then why should the other poor ones want what is necessary?" Returning to the same idea she once said to her Aunt: "What you do for me, remember that you ought to do it as for a beggar that you would meet in the street, otherwise there would be no merit in it."

Here I ought to call attention to Gemma's great gratitude towards her benefactors. It was simple, uniform, and devoid of compliment; nevertheless what was in her heart was clearly read in her countenance. "My God," she used to exclaim when alone, "how shall I be able to correspond to all they do for me? I don't even know how to thank them. I am so uncultivated and ignorant. See to it Thou, O my God. Make them prosper, and repay them a hundredfold for all they do for me. If any misfortune is about to befall them, let it fall on me instead." At other times turning to this or that one of the family, with a voice full of affection she used to say: "Don't regret having to exercise your patience with me a little longer. I won't forget you with Jesus. When I am with Him I will always pray for you." From these words it is easy to see that this favored child, although she knew how much she was loved, and realized the exquisite care with which she was treated, yet felt keenly the humiliation of her position, and in a manner was ashamed of it. So resigned was she that she calmly awaited His dispositions regarding herself and all that concerned her. She knew so well how to hide her feelings, that no one ever became aware of the pain she felt at her family reverses. "I turn to my heart," she wrote to her director, "Jesus is owner of my heart, and, being in possession of Jesus, I find that I can smile, even in the midst of so many tears. I feel, yes, I feel that I am happy even in the midst of so many discomforts."

The prayers of this faultless child for her benefactors deeply touched the Heart of God, and moved Him to be most bounteous in rewarding them. Hence she was able to exclaim when writing to me: "O Jesus! If you only knew how He helps them. He blesses them every moment. He withdraws them from danger." Once the mother of the family fell seriously ill with internal spasmodic pains that made the doctors speak unfavorably of her chances of recovery. Gemma was deeply grieved, and asked her Jesus that she instead might suffer those pains. Here are the words she used in telling me of it: "I have taken on myself those pains you know of, that the Mother of these children was suffering. They are indeed fierce pains, and I really don't know what is going to happen to me." The lady in fact got well in an instant, and poor Gemma, for many months, suffered a long martyrdom that brought her to death's door. Meanwhile God was bringing about His own divine ends in this chosen soul. He willed to make her pass by most wonderful ways, and to be singularly glorified in her, not only in secret, but by manifest signs and wonders. In fact, during the course of the four years that she dwelt in the house of her loving benefactors, all the marvelous phenomena that we shall have to relate came to light. Now, if she had been in her own home, how difficult it would have been to deal with such phenomena! There was no one there able to attend to her, guide her, and hide her from the curiosity of the profane. Gemma herself was so persuaded of this that she trembled at the bare idea of returning to her own home, even for a day. On the other hand, she found herself better off in the house in which God willed her to be received than if she were in a convent. All members of the family from the first to the last were most religious Catholics. The lady who adopted Gemma, herself far advanced in the ways of the soul, could easily understand the secrets of her child's inner life, and be of the greatest help to her. Prudent likewise beyond measure, she knew well how to ward off every inconvenience and those occasions of gossip that are never wanting when there is question of extraordinary events, more especially if of the supernatural order.

And, as a matter of fact, she succeeded. In the midst of a numerous family, largely engaged in commerce, Gemma lived comparatively unnoticed, and the special gifts with which heaven enriched her remained known only to her confessors and spiritual directors. How good Our Lord is in the exercise of His providence!

And here I turn to you most well-deserving family, refuge of this Gem of Heaven, and with an overflowing heart thank you on the part of that same God Whom you intended to honor by benefiting His faithful servant.

CHAPTER 12

1900-1903: St. Gemma and Her
New Spiritual Director.

GOD, wishing to console His Servant and help her in her many needs, particularly in those that followed the appearance of the Stigmata, brought her into contact with the sons of His Passion—Fr. Cajetan, Fr. Peter Paul, and several others. On her first coming to know them He manifested to her by distinct locution that one of them should be her future director. But although those Fathers helped her greatly in her spiritual necessities, none of them was to be the director whom God assigned her. Hence each one, having accomplished his mission, withdrew rejoicing at having beheld the wonders of God in that favored girl. Gemma had never seen her future director nor heard of him, yet she knew him, his age, disposition and appearance. He was living in Rome, and as soon as it was made known to her that he was the one destined to be her father, taking courage from the boundless confidence that she already felt in him, she wrote him the following letter on the 24th January 1900:

"VERY REV. FATHER: For a considerable time I have felt a great desire to see you and to write to you. I asked leave to do so from my Confessor, but he always said no. Last Saturday I renewed my request and he said yes, thus giving me great consolation. But now as I begin to write a great fear has come over me; this is because I have to write such strange things that even you will wonder at them. I tell you frankly that my head is a bit strange, and I sometimes imagine that I see, sometimes that I hear, impossible things. I say impossible, because Jesus has never spoken, never appeared to those among His servants whose souls are as sinful as mine."

Then, having related how Our Lord in vision showed her her new Director, she goes on to give him a minute account of what had happened to her during the previous two years—of her serious illness and miraculous recovery, of Blessed Gabriel, of her vocation to the Religious State and of her first acquaintance with the Passionists. She speaks to him of the foundation of the Convent of Passionist Nuns that would be made later on in Lucca, and describes minute details with as much exactness as if they were present. I will point out later how exactly her predictions were verified. This first letter to her Director was quite ten pages long and ended in the usual way: "I beg of you to bless and help, and pray for poor Gemma."

A little later she wrote another letter of six pages:

> *"Yesterday evening, when praying before Jesus in the Blessed Sacrament, I was called—I think it was Jesus. (My father, before you go on reading I beg you in charity not to believe what I say. I act only through obedience or else I would not write another word.) He said to me: 'My child thou mayest write to thy father that the Confessor would willingly correspond with him. Do this. It is My will.' 'I see my Jesus Thou willest that the father know everything about me.' I was continuing to speak, but it seemed to me that Jesus (or perhaps my imagination) would not let me finish, and He said to me, 'This is My will, that the Confessor should henceforward make known everything to thy father."*

And it was precisely so. Mgr. Volpi, Auxiliary Bishop of Lucca and Gemma's ordinary confessor, feeling so inspired, wished to share his responsibility, but with whom he knew not. The direction of his beloved spiritual child weighed on him greatly although he, better than any other, could appreciate Gemma's soul. In his humility, and because of his many occupations, he thought the whole burden of this important spiritual direction too much for him. He accordingly sent her now to one and again to another Confessor, and asked the advice of a great many persons. The more frequent repetition of the phenomena of the Stigmata, of the Sweat of blood and of the ecstasies increased his fears, and notwithstanding Fr. Cajetan's and Fr. Peter Paul's assurances, his doubts and fears continued to return. On coming to Rome he sought an interview with me, but we were not able to meet. We then tried to come to an understanding by letter and in August 1900, through our Provincial, he invited me to Lucca in order to examine his penitent in person. I, who on principle have always been slow to believe in such extraordinary things, replied advising him not to attribute too much importance to what was happening, but rather to put his penitent on the ordinary path pursued by the majority of the faithful. He wrote again giving me some particulars of those extraordinary things, and I, still persisting in my way of thinking, was so far wanting as to suggest to his Lordship to have recourse to exorcism. His perplexities increased and still wishing that I should judge of things in person he prevailed on the Provincial to oblige me to go to Lucca. I went there on the 1st of September 1900, and stayed with the Giannini family with whom Gemma was living. On seeing me the dear child recognized me at once, and coming forward to welcome me showed great gladness, blessing Our Lord in her soul. I confess that on meeting her, my first sentiments were those of devotion and veneration. We went together and knelt before the Crucifix in the family Oratory. Gemma wept and I likewise.

My feelings on that occasion, still vivid in my memory, baffle explanation. Our Lord was then assuredly preparing me to see great things by which every shadow of doubt remaining in my mind should be dispelled. It happened to be Thursday, and about the middle of supper Gemma, feeling signs of the coming ecstasy, rose from the table and left the room. After a little time her adopted mother came to call me. I followed her and found the child in ecstasy. The subject of the ecstasy was the conversion of a sinner and the form was a wrestling between the blessed maiden and the Divine Justice to obtain this conversion. I confess that I never beheld anything more affecting.

The dear child was sitting on her bed with her eyes, face and all her person turned towards a part of the room where Our Lord appeared to her. She was not agitated, but earnest and resolute, like one in a struggle who is determined to win at any cost. She began by saying "As Thou hast come, Jesus, I renew my supplications for my sinner. He is Thy child and my brother; save him, Jesus;" and she named him. He was a stranger whom she had met in Lucca, and moved by spiritual impulse she had already warned him very often by word of mouth and by letter to listen to the dictates of his conscience and not be contented with the mere public reputation of being a good Christian. Jesus seeming disposed to deal as a just Judge with this man, remained unmoved by the entreaties of His servant. But she nowise deterred rejoined: "Why today, O Jesus, dost Thou not heed me? For one soul only Thou hast done so much! Why then wilt Thou not save this other one? Save him, Jesus, save him. Be good, Jesus. Do not say that to me. In Thy mouth, Who art Mercy itself, that word 'abandon' sounds badly. Thou must not say it. Thou hast not measured the Blood Thou has shed for sinners, and now dost Thou wish to measure the enormity of our sins? Dost Thou not heed me? And I, to whom must I turn? Thou hast shed Thy Blood for him as well as for me. Wilt Thou save me and not him? I will not rise from here. Save him. Promise me that Thou wilt save him. I offer myself victim for all, but particularly for him. I promise not to refuse Thee anything. Dost Thou grant it me? It is a soul. Remember, O Jesus, it is a soul that has cost Thee so much. He will become good, and not relapse."

In answer to all her entreaties Our Lord put forward the Divine Justice. But she growing still more fervent replied: "I am not seeking Thy Justice. I am imploring Thy Mercy. Then Jesus, go in search of that poor sinner. Press him to Thy Heart and Thou wilt see that he will be converted. At least try it. Listen, Jesus, Thou sayest that Thou hast made many forcible attempts to convince him, but Thou hast not called him son. Try that now, and tell him that Thou art his Father and that he is Thy child. Thou will find that on hearing this sweet name of Father, his hardened heart will soften." And here Our Lord, to prove to His servant what reason He had for remaining firm, began to show her one by one, with the most minute circumstances of time and place, the evil deeds of that sinner, adding that he had filled up their measure. The poor child showed her dismay. She let her hands fall, and heaved a deep sigh, as if she had almost lost the hope of succeeding. But quickly recovering from the shock she returned to the attack. "I know, Jesus," she said, "I know it, that he has offended Thee thus grievously. But I have done worse and, for all that, Thou hast shown me Mercy. I know, I know, O Jesus, that he has made Thee weep. But now Jesus—Thou must not think of his sins. Thou must think of the Blood Thou hast shed, what immense Charity, O Jesus, hast Thou not lavished on me! Use with my sinner, I implore of Thee, all those delicacies of Infinite Love that Thou hast used towards me. Remember Jesus, that I want his salvation. Triumph, triumph, I ask him of Thee in Charity."

In spite of all these efforts, Our Lord remained inflexible, and Gemma again relapsed into anguish and discouragement, remaining silent, as if she had abandoned the strife. Then, of a sudden, another motive flashed to her mind that seemed invincible against all resistance. She became all animated, and spoke thus: "Well, I am a sinner. Thou Thyself has told me so, that worse than me Thou couldst not find. Yes, I confess it, I am unworthy that Thou shouldst listen to me. But look, I present Thee another advocate for my sinner, it is Thine own Mother who asks Thee to forgive him. Oh! imagine saying no to Thy Mother! Surely Thou canst not say no to her. And now answer me, Jesus, say that Thou hast saved my sinner." The victory was gained, the whole scene changed aspect, the tenderhearted Savior had granted the grace, and Gemma with a look of indescribable joy exclaimed: "He is saved, he is saved! Thou hast conquered Jesus, triumph always thus." And then she came out of the ecstasy.

This most affecting scene lasted quite half an hour. The words in which I have described it were in part taken down in writing, and in part preserved in my memory from which I have faithfully drawn them. When it was over, having withdrawn to my room, with my mind engrossed by a thousand thoughts, I suddenly heard a tap at my door. "A strange gentleman, father, has called and wishes to see you." I bade him come in. He threw himself at my feet sobbing and said: "Father, hear my confession." Good God! I thought my heart would burst. It was Gemma's sinner, converted that same hour. He accused himself of all that I had heard repeated by her in the ecstasy. He had forgotten one thing only and I was able to remind him of it. I consoled him, told him what had just happened, got his leave to narrate these wonders of the Lord, and after a mutual embrace we parted. Some years have passed since that event and I still seem to find myself present at it. In my copious notes I have particulars of other conversions similar in many ways to that just described and equally well authenticated. For the sake of brevity and to avoid uncalled-for repetition I have not given them here.

The fact narrated speaks for itself. There is no place for imagination or hysteria here. The devil is able to drag sinners to perdition, but not to convert them, much less in such a way as we have seen.

Notwithstanding my admiration at what I had witnessed I did not stop there. I began my studies with great earnestness in order to make certain of Gemma's spirit. These studies lasted nearly three years without interruption. Guided by Ascetic and Mystic Theology and by modern physiological science, I put her through lengthened trials so as to be able to say at last that I had not neglected any such steps, and it is worth observing that not one of them failed. The pious Bishop, her Confessor, in his turn was satisfied. He approved of all that I had done, and expressed his desire that I should take up the direction of Gemma. She, who more than anyone else feared being the victim of delusion, seemed to rise from death to life on learning my final assurance that what was happening to her was from God, and that she could freely allow herself to be guided by the Holy Spirit in that way. To humble her I treated her rudely rather than otherwise, and mortified her continually, yet she remained undisturbed, addressed me with child-like expansiveness as Babbo. Sometimes with the same amiable ingenuousness modifying this name she would add the word wicked: "Oh what a wicked Babbo Jesus has given me!"

Her gratitude to God from whom she acknowledged having received such help, and to His poor Minister whose services and labors in her behalf she exaggerated, was without measure. "What patience," she would say, "you need with me! O Father, infinite thanks for all the care you take, and, I think, wish to take of my poor soul. If I succeed in saving this soul you shall see what I will do for you. When I shall have reached Paradise I will drag you with me at any cost. If you only knew what good your letters and your little sermons do me! I hope that by this time you know me well. Pray to Jesus for light to guide me and then convert me. Will you succeed, Father, in converting me? It is so hard to move me, and when your last letter brought this fact before me I cried, as always when I think of it. May Jesus lead us to life!" From those words one can gather that Gemma's direction was effected principally by letter. Still, as it was God's Will that she should have better help, He so disposed things that very often, even without thinking of it, I had, when travelling, to pass through Lucca. While staying there, at Signor Giannini's, I had every facility of helping the little saint, and of continuing my studies and trials of her virtues. Grateful indeed was the task of guiding this favored soul, so detached was she in mind and heart from everything earthly, and specially from herself. She was humble, docile, lovable, ready for every sacrifice, full of faith and love of God, and at the same time so natural that you would scarcely have distinguished her from any ordinary young girl. I must not stop here to describe all the rare qualities of my spiritual child. I will say only that to treat with her, to labor in helping her to advance in perfection and correspond to the impulses of Divine grace, caused no weariness but rather intense satisfaction. One could speak to her for many hours on heavenly things without feeling the time pass. She spoke little even to her director, and seemed to find a difficulty in answering the questions put to her. Still what she said was so much to the point, so wise and so full of unction that it was enchanting to listen to her.

She was much more free when writing. It seemed as though being alone removed the difficulty she always felt when speaking of herself. She consequently wrote long letters without any art, just as her heart or rather the Spirit of God dictated. And the arrangement of the subject matter left nothing to be desired. At first her letters regarding herself were addressed to her Confessor, then to her Director, and much more frequently and without restraint to her new Director. I kept her letters and frequently thought over them. I compared the earlier with more recent ones and always had to conclude that the Spirit of God was working in her and enabling her to speed by giant strides along the way of perfection. In the year 1900 I published in one volume several of her letters to me with others to different persons. I am sure that whoever reads them will agree with what I have said.

I should not perhaps have styled myself Gemma's Director. Her Confessor and Director from her earliest years was Monsignor John Volpi. I did nothing more than help him in this work. It remains however to be said that her true Director was the Holy Spirit, Who delights in reserving to Himself the immediate guidance of certain chosen souls. Jesus her Divine Spouse was her Director. So was her heavenly Mother and her Angel Guardian. What I hold as a certainty is, that from my contact with this Servant of God my poor soul has derived the greatest advantage. I have felt reanimated in my faith, in my desire for Heavenly things, and in my love of virtue. All praise be to Thee, O Jesus, Who in most admirable ways dost provide for the welfare of those souls who desire to please Thee alone.

CHAPTER 13
St. Gemma's Characteristic Virtue.

BESIDES the essential spirit of sanctity common to all the just, there is also an individual spirit, more or less clearly manifested by each one in particular. The first consists in the possession of all the virtues taught us by Christ our Lord, model of all His Saints. The second becomes evident in a characteristic prevalence of some particular grace or virtue that gives, as it were, a special form to the others, and distinguishes the individual. We have seen that Gemma from her earliest years labored with unwearied energy in the acquisition of every virtue. She possessed and practiced them all in such an eminent degree, that it would be impossible to know which was her greatest perfection. She had, for all that, a characteristic virtue, and gave continued proof of it through a peculiar trend of mind that was entirely her own. This virtue was transparent in her whole person. It shone in all she did, and made her the beloved of all. It was her extraordinary, her evangelical simplicity.

It will accordingly be well, before giving a general description of her virtues, to make her rare simplicity thoroughly known and valued. In worldly estimation this virtue is thought little of or wholly undervalued. But the true valuer of things is God, and He says in the Gospel, "If you do not become simple like children, you shall not have part in the Kingdom of Heaven." These words of Our Lord clearly show the importance in the Divine Mind of evangelical simplicity, and surely mean that a Christian for Virtue's sake has to become what children are naturally, by keeping the soul free from malice and deceit, and all the faculties disposed to rectitude. According to St. Thomas, holy simplicity is the fruit of truth and modesty.

It is quite evident that Gemma possessed this precious virtue to perfection, and in a way that was surpassingly rare. She was simple in thought, thinking no evil, and therefore incapable of forming a rash judgment. In her soul there reigned an unalterable serenity. With her mind ever fixed on God, in Him she saw all else, whether good or bad, agreeable or the reverse. She was like a spotless mirror, that receives all images and upon which none leave an impression. This perfect quality of soul was apparent in her exterior. Hence it happened that not only her presence dispelled restraint, but it inspired at the same time feelings of veneration and sweetest confidence. Once a venerable Prelate, who had spoken to her for a while, was heard to say: "I should have no difficulty in making my general Confession to that girl, or in confiding to her the most intimate secrets of my soul, so great is the confidence with which the candor of her mind inspires me."

Indeed, many, attracted by this candor, used to consult her on most delicate matters. The saintly child listened to them modestly, gave her answer in a few words, adding if needed even an admonition, and then, re-entering into herself, thought no more about the matter. She feared lest, if other ideas came to mix themselves with those heavenly ones which always occupied her thoughts, they might lessen the simplicity of her soul. I myself, on more than one occasion, determined to prove her angelic mood by introducing irrelevant matter into our conversation. But she always turned the subject. "I prayed to Jesus, Father, as you know, for that unfortunate. I have thanked Him for the happy termination. Don't let me think more about it."

Because of this rectitude and candor of soul she seemed incapable of conceiving thoughts of vainglory. As a matter of fact she never had any, and no matter how insidiously Satan tried to put her merits and good qualities before her eyes, he never was able to take her unawares. That "Yes, yes; no, no" of the Gospel, on which she had established her rule of life, was as a compass that kept her on a steadfast course. Praise was certainly painful to her, but reproach and abuse failed to ruffle her. Everything came alike to her just as happens with infants. Because of their simplicity, they know not how to give a thought to things that, for certain, would upset their elders.

And as the mind, so was the heart of this innocent dove. Here to perfect order, calm lucidness, and shining candor. Her most pure heart belonged to all, was all in all, but ever in God. She was grateful to those who loved her, and, as we have already shown, knew not how to wish harm to those who were against her. She desired nothing, sought nothing, and nothing made her sad, because she was devoid of all earthly affection. During the horrible sufferings with which the evil spirits continually tormented her, her only affliction was her fear of offending God. Otherwise she would not have spoken of such trials, even to her Director. The same may be said of all her other pains, even as the Prophets foretold of the Divine Lamb, Who, led to the slaughter, opened not His mouth, and offered His face to those who insulted and struck Him. How often when she went to the Church to ask for her Confessor, was she not publicly insulted and all but turned out by insolent boys dressed up as Clerics? And she always remained silent, not wishing to speak of it even to those of her home. But more of this hereafter.

As Gemma's simplicity of mind and heart was so great, and as from the abundance of the mind and heart the mouth speaketh, great indeed was the simplicity of her speech. She never thought ill of others, and so knew not how to speak disparagingly of anyone. "You would need a wrench," said a witness, "to draw a word from her regarding others, even when the information was necessary or useful, if that word had to be one unfavorable to them." Such was her way of acting, not only with those of the family around her, but also with her Director. When interrogated by him, her answer reduced itself to an allusion to facts, out of which one could make nothing. And when she answered by letter, she interposed dots in blank, as if to say "You know the rest," and passed on quite naturally to other subjects. This extreme caution on her part was all the more marked when of her own accord she made up her mind to speak of such things to her Director. "Father, pray. That person is not going on as Jesus wills. Write to him (or her), on the subject, admonish him to amend." Then dots, and there it ended.

When beginning to speak or write, she avoided the preambles that are ordinarily used, and in many cases called for. It appeared to her that such were a loss of time and little less than an artifice to ensnare the reader or listener. Hence she entered at once on her subject, and she did so without any special regard to the dignity of the person addressed, unless indeed we regard as introductions certain expressions full of ineffable simplicity, and peculiarly her own, with which she often began her letters. Here are a few of them:

Monsignor, stay and listen, today so and so has happened to me.

Countess, Jesus has said that you are the one who will have to carry out that holy work.

My Father, Viva Gesù! *Listen to the curious thing I am going to tell you.*

These, and other similar words should please sensible people infinitely more than all the affected phraseology that as a rule one meets everywhere.

In her conversation, as we have said, Gemma was of few words, and reserved. When writing, being free from the restraint of another person's presence, she was less reserved, unless she had to write about herself and her own affairs. But as a general rule she was only perfectly free and open when treating with her Director. She was not in the least concerned about the style of her speech or writing—if well put or not —if it would bring her praise or blame—if it might be taken in good or bad part. And, when her letter was finished, she closed it without waiting to read it over, and thought no more of what she had written. When she had not a whole sheet of paper by her, she wrote on half a sheet. And when there was not even so much, she used any bit of paper at hand. On one occasion only I knew her to apologize, because, having need to write, and not being able to find a postage stamp, she posted her letter unstamped. "Who knows what Father will say at having to pay double postage? But forgive me. I am poor, poor, and have no money." Who could be displeased by negligences like these, accompanied as they were by such lovable ingenuousness.

It happened sometimes however that this dear child, yielding too freely to the instincts of her large heart, was the cause of some slight inconvenience. And then it was most difficult to persuade her that she was not to trust everyone so readily, or to make her see that she deserved to be scolded for what had happened. She believed that everyone acted with candor like herself, so that all could be trusted alike. Likewise, as she could not think that those who scolded her excessively were moved by anger or other inordinate passion, she sought to persuade herself that their action was of diabolical suggestion permitted by God to humble her. Yet, as we have seen, Gemma was far from being deficient in talents and intelligence. But she felt and acted in this way because she had virtually become a little child through her love of God. As then the rare simplicity of this admirable girl was the fruit of the virtuous habits she had acquired, it is not to be wondered at that this virtue should accompany her in everything and everywhere. Simple in her bearing and ways, simple in her dress, simple in whatever belonged to her (if indeed she could be said to possess anything), nothing in her was superfluous. She interpreted the word simplicity in its strictest sense, and contented herself with bare necessities. It was enough to look at her to become rapt in wonder. And yet there was nothing singular about her except a certain dignified gravity, the result of her continual union with God. In the church, where every day she passed long hours at the foot of the Tabernacle, she remained immovable as a statue. If her fervor of soul forced her to tears, she no sooner became aware of them, than gently bending her head, she covered her face with both hands. In a word this all-pervading simplicity was evident in Gemma's whole person, and in her virtues of which it was the form and as it were the savor. Therefore we have every right to say that simplicity of soul was truly the distinctive characteristic of the holiness of this virgin spouse of Christ.

She entered this mystic life a baby in spirit as well as a baby in age. In spirit she always remained a baby, and as such treated with the Majesty of the Lord, listened to His ineffable secrets, and tasted their sweetness. This was always what I found most to be wondered at and to admire in Gemma, and this likewise was the most convincing of the arguments which from the beginning made me pronounce the spirit of her sanctity to be true—so unconcerned, so natural, so spontaneous, was she, in the midst of all that is most sublime in the supernatural order.

Moreover, who does not know that the transcendent things of the faith are of such a nature that in their presence mortal man is overwhelmed, and that even those who are most versed in them never on that account become accustomed to them, but in fear and trembling, hoping and loving, receive the communications with which Our Lord favors them? Yet it was not so with this Angel. With her, faith seemed no longer to be faith but evidence. With its most hidden mysteries she seemed to find herself at ease, as if in her natural sphere. She had no need to make the least effort in order to nourish her mind and heart on the great truths of religion. God, the sacred Humanity of the Divine Word, the Blessed Eucharist, the Angels and Saints of Heaven—she sees them all, she speaks with them, heart to heart, she humbles herself before them, adores, prays, weeps; but always as if she beheld them without veil. Nor was this only during her ecstasies and raptures, and in the more hidden depths of contemplation, but, so to say, in an ordinary and habitual way even during the time of profound spiritual dryness. These are wonderful but undeniable facts.

I must confess that because of such clearness of evidence, appearing to be almost excessive, a suspicion or doubt once came over my mind. It was but for a moment. Gemma, as if aware of it, began to give me an account of some of the sublime communications she had from God, and then added the following words, which, to my mind, are worth a treatise of theology. "Without doubt this is a Paradise on earth, and yet I wish to go to Paradise all the same, because, see, Father, here I behold my God, I behold Jesus, but not entirely. He does not let me see His whole Self, although what He does let me see is so much that it surpasses all human understanding. I want instead to see Him wholly and entirely." Behold then the merit of faith that remains undiminished in the desire of future glory, even in spite of so much evidence and such great intimacy.

Gemma thus passed her life in God's presence, singularly privileged, and so far as it is allowed, seeing God even in this life. Yet that Infinite Majesty did not dazzle her. She talked to her Lord with the same ease and confidence as a little child speaks to her father while sitting on his knee, as in her right place. Nay, without being wanting in reverence, she addressed Him with the same simplicity of words and ways that we use with our fellow creatures. In order to give an adequate idea of this, it would be almost necessary to produce all that has been preserved of her long colloquies with our Lord during her ecstasies and contemplations. For the present let one suffice, which she herself related to her Director. Others will be seen as we go along. "On Friday Jesus appeared to me, and this time He was serious, serious. He seemed to weep, and I said to Him: 'O Jesus, what is it that makes you weep so? Oh! would it not be better to leave the weeping to me, who feel I want so much to cry?' But Jesus did not answer me. And then, moving aside quietly, I got near my Heavenly Mother, and said to her, 'Tell me, Mother, what is it that makes Jesus weep so? What can I do to content Him?'" Nevertheless, while this child as it were plays around her God, He lifts her up by means of the highest contemplation to a clear understanding of the mysteries of His justice and mercy in the government of the world, and of His infinite love of souls.

The visible presence of her Angel Guardian, with which Gemma was singularly favored by God, was for her one of the most natural experiences. Her Angel used to talk to her as ordinary mortals talk to their friends. She gave him commissions of every kind for the inhabitants of heaven and earth, and that with the most humble reverence, but full of affectionate confidence. If, while engaged talking with him, she was called away, or some duty intervened, she arose at once, and without excuse or compliment went quickly away to her duty, leaving the Angel to wait for her. At night, when lying down to rest, she begged of him to sign her on the forehead, and watch by her pillow; and being assured that he would, she immediately turned on the other side to sleep. What a blessed virginal repose, at which the Angels are visibly present! In the morning on awakening, when she saw her faithful Guardian still at his post, she paid little or no attention to him. Her anxiety was to fly to the Church and Holy Communion, of which she had been thinking all the night, for she slept very little. "I have what is so much better in my thoughts," she used to say to him. "I am going to Jesus," and left immediately. But if the Angel was taking leave of her she would reply charmingly: "Good-bye, dear Angel. Offer my salutations to Jesus."

Every week for a long time those wounds of the stigmata were renewed, and the punctures of the Crown of Thorns around her head, the shedding of tears of blood, and other extraordinary graces were added. From Thursday to Friday evenings in particular she was made to participate in Our Lord's Passion, and suffered excruciating pain, such that she then believed she would die of it. But no sooner was she out of the ecstasy, than she rose as if nothing had happened, washed her hands and head, to remove the stains of blood that had flowed in profusion, drew down the sleeves of her dress to hide the large marks on both hands, and, believing that no one had noticed her, with her wonted serenity and gentleness, returned to join the family gathering.

Does it not seem a wonder that a woman, a girl, to whom such strange things happened, should not even stop to think of them, or to ask herself what it all meant; if they were a good or bad sign; the work of God or a wile of the Devil? Gemma did not put to herself any such questions. She, without waiting, simply told all to her Director, in order to have his advice and guidance, whilst she herself remained perfectly tranquil about it all, and did not further inquire into what was taking place in her. After having seen face to face her crucified God, after having suffered with Him, and after having contemplated the hidden mysteries of Redemption, she no sooner returned to the use of her senses than she was quite ready to join in amusing the little children of the house.

One more instance of this Angel's holy simplicity must suffice for the present. She often, when in ecstasy, received light from God regarding things that had to be done or avoided either by her or by others. She then hastened in person or by letter to inform her Director of what had happened. "Jesus," she would say, "has said so and so. He has commanded me to tell it all to you. If I have not understood Him rightly, make Him explain it better to you Himself." So said, she thought no more about it. But if the same locution was repeated three, five, ten times, she each time returned to manifest it to her Director with the same calm and candor, as in the Sacred Scripture the child Samuel is related to have done with the Priest Eli. "Jesus has said so and so. Kind Father, listen to what He says and please Him." Surely we have in this favored child the essence of holy simplicity.

CHAPTER 14

The Means by Which St. Gemma Attained to Perfection. First, Her Detachment.

CHRIST Our Lord has said: "If any man will come after Me, let him renounce all that he possesses, let him deny himself, and take up his cross and follow Me." He wished all to know, that in order to put on the perfect man, that is Himself, God and man, it is necessary to put off the old man, earthly and vicious, renouncing all inordinate appetites, and doing continual violence to self. Without this one cannot be His disciple and follow Him in the way of sanctity. Hence the need of constant mortification, of profound humility, of absolute detachment from every created thing, more particularly from oneself, of generosity of soul and great patience in the endurance of trials and sufferings. These are in fact the means that all the Elect have used in order to become perfect, and those who have signalized themselves most in their practice have become the greatest saints.

Gemma from her earliest years ardently desired to follow Jesus, to be like Him, to become a Saint. She had then to put in practice Our Lord's own teaching, such as has just been specified. And indeed she practiced it so well that from the very first she gave proof of being one of the most humble, mortified, patient, generous and strong among the Servants of God that are venerated by the Church. In this chapter we shall treat of her detachment. Of her other means of attaining sanctity we shall speak separately in the chapters that follow.

Everyone knows what a difficult thing it is for a girl in good position to renounce the vanity of dress both in heart and deed, while remaining in society. Nature itself inclines the weaker sex to wish to appear to advantage, and does so with such impulse that without a special grace it is not possible to repress it entirely. Now God gave this grace to Gemma from her very infancy, as I have already pointed out, and confirmed her in it definitely. Her dress was most simple, and consisted of a costume of black woolen stuff, with a cape of the same color and material, and a black straw hat. No cuffs, no collar nor clasps, no ornaments of any kind, nor flowers nor extra trimming to her hat. In vain her friends remonstrated. This was the only way she dressed, winter and summer, on festivals and ordinary days, nor would she hear of any other.

And what we say of her dress applies to everything she used, such as books, purse, pictures and similar articles that even the poorest possess. A rough wooden box holding a little underclothing, a crucifix, rosary, and two or three little books of devotion made up the belongings of this chosen spouse of Christ. "I have nothing," she used to say so sweetly, "I am poor, poor, for the love of Jesus." When little pictures or the like were given her she quickly got rid of them, feeling much more free when she had given away what she did not absolutely need. "Jesus has said to me," she used to repeat, "remember that I have created thee for Heaven. Thou hast nothing to do with the earth. Oh what then would you have me do with these things of which I have no need." Even when ill she was never known to manifest the least desire for anything. Nay, in order that the servants should not have extra work on her account, she used to say she was well and had no need of anything. And she strove to appear well to them so that they might not become aware of her great sufferings, and try to procure her remedies and restoratives. Without doubt she was quite dead to herself.

Gemma loved her parents tenderly, particularly her mother. And yet we have seen how calmly she received the announcement of her mother's death, and how bravely she assisted her father in his last moments, as she had previously assisted her beloved brother Gino. Later on in one year she lost an aunt, another brother, and her younger sister Julia, eighteen years of age, the dear confidante of her spiritual secrets. Announcing these losses to her director, she wrote: "Father, my aunt, whom you knew to be ill, is dead. She was so good!

Recommend her to Jesus, in case she may have need of prayers. Tonino (Antony) also is dead. My poor brother! He suffered so much! Ask Jesus to be merciful to him." Somewhat more expressive is the letter in which she tells him of Julia's death, her grief is more transparent, yet resigned and calm. "You, Father, knew how good this sister was, but Jesus has wished to take her to Himself. The day before yesterday Julia died. Don't scold me, Father, for not having cried, for I knew that Jesus did not wish it. *Viva Gesù!*" We are assured that these were the true sentiments of her heart, by her benefactress and adopted mother, who wrote to me thus: "Father, you know how much these two sisters loved each other, and yet poor Gemma is not upset. She immediately made an offering to God of her sister's soul, and then thanked Jesus. See what heroic virtue! I instead have shed many tears and it was Gemma who consoled me saying: 'You must not cry.'"

It is certain that this holy child, although she seemed to be more of heaven than of earth, and indifferent, indeed almost rude, to strangers, was nevertheless of most tender and affectionate heart. Not knowing, because of her perfect detachment, what share the senses might have in her affections, she never had any doubts or scruples on that point. Hence, she loved with fullest liberty of spirit all those with whom she came in contact. It was not always easy to discern this, but whoever watched her closely became well- aware that she knew how to love, and that with the most exquisite delicacy. Her great heart at the same time remained perfectly free, and the receiving or not receiving correspondence to her love was one and the same thing. For even though she might feel pain at the loss or absence of persons that were dear to her, this was only an impression of the moment. She turned at once to Jesus, and said to Him, "O Jesus, for Thee I willingly make this other sacrifice. Alone with Jesus only!" And then her soul remained in peace. Even from her spiritual father, whom with child-like simplicity she used to call "My Papa," she was most detached. Nor did she ever complain to him either of the rarity of his visits, or delays in answering her letters. "Don't scold me," she wrote to him, "when I tell you that I really need to see you. But if you don't come, I shall be content all the same. At any rate ask Jesus about it, and if He says yes, come at once. I have written you three letters, and you have not given me any answer. It seems to me that Jesus really wishes you to tell me how I should act in that matter. I will be good, mind and obey. But if you have no time nor wish to write, do as you think best. I have abandoned myself entirely to God." And when she was near death, being asked if she wished the father to be called from Rome by telegram, she answered "Yes," but immediately corrected herself, saying, "Even of him I have made the sacrifice," and did not wish him to be sent for. And, as I shall relate in its place, she died alone with Jesus only, drowned in an ocean of pain.

Our Divine Savior Himself acted as her good Master in order to perfect her every day more in this most important virtue of detachment. To give one example out of many: I had made her a present of a precious relic, a tooth of Blessed Gabriel. She valued it as a great treasure, and carried it always about her. It happened then that, treating with Our Lord in familiar colloquy, as often happened, she said to Him with her usual ingenuous candor, "Jesus, the Father is always talking to me of detachment, but I understand very little or nothing of what he says, because I have nothing and don't know from what to detach myself." Then said Jesus to her, "And art thou not too much attached to that tooth?" I remained thunderstruck—these are her words to me—"and was about to remonstrate, saying: but my Jesus, it is a precious relic. And I was almost crying, but Jesus, somewhat seriously: 'My child, Jesus has said it, that is enough.' Ah Jesus, Jesus," she afterwards exclaimed, "what have You not seen and weighed? Nothing is small or to be disregarded that gives Thee glory, or that would prevent our giving all to Thee."

I should not end soon were I to relate the many edifying particulars that I have in my hands on this subject, and to repeat the sublime outbursts in her conversation, letters and ecstasies, to which this dear child so often gave expression. She did so in order that all in heaven and earth might know that her only wish was to love God. "I wish to be all and only of Jesus," she used to say, "and what is there to love on this earth now that I possess Jesus? World, creatures, all you are no longer for me, nor am I for you, and so I cannot love you and will not love you more." Once, when giving me the account of her progress, she wrote thus:

> *"Yesterday morning, in a meeting that I had with my loving God, I besought him to detach me from everything, to free me from my body, and let me, having broken every bond, go straight to Him, to Him only and for ever. But Jesus answered me, 'Where wouldst thou fly to?' To Thee, my dear and sweet Lord. And Jesus again, 'Let me come yet a little longer to thee, and then, when I set thee free, thou shalt come to Me.'"*

Thus life had become a weight and pain to this dove. As she kept her heart turned towards heaven, she felt like a stranger who knows no one and takes no interest in earthly things. Let her again speak for herself: "I live on this earth, but I seem to dwell here like a soul that has lost its way" (see what an expressive figure: "like a soul that has lost its way"), "because never for a moment do I cease to look back to Jesus, apart from whom I despise all things." Thus wearied, unsatisfied, she counted the days like a pilgrim, who, longing to reach the desired land, from time to time, standing still, looks back to see the distance done and count the remaining way. The simile is Gemma's, who so gracefully applies it to herself. "I greatly rejoice that time flies so quickly, because that means so much less to spend in this world, where there is nothing to attract me. My heart goes incessantly in search of a treasure, an immense treasure that I do not find in creatures, a treasure that will satisfy me, and console me, and give me rest." We shall return elsewhere to consider Gemma's desire to fly and be at rest with her Jesus in heaven.

If temporal life was of such small concern with this young girl, it was not a wonder that she was always so ready to give it away, as happens with valueless things. Did anyone fall dangerously ill, then you would see Gemma running to her director for leave to give that one, two, three, four years of her life, saying to him: "Jesus, you know, will accept the exchange, provided you, father, approve of it." And in order to get my consent, she used to bring forward certain arguments of her own, putting them with such dexterity, that if I was not on my guard, I was in great danger of giving way. "Look, father," she would say, "it concerns the mother of a family with many children. Oh! what would these little ones do without their mother? Let me tell Jesus about it. What difference can a few years less make to me?" The same thing used to happen when she had the conversion of any sinner at heart, and she was sure to have some such in hand. "Jesus, I give you three years of my life. Convert him for me." That was a way she had of putting it. At last I allowed myself to be persuaded by her amiable and forcible eloquence. I gave the leave asked. God accepted the exchange and Gemma died exactly at the time agreed upon, in the richest bloom of her youth, and contrary to all human expectation.

It is well known how attached women are to their own judgment in matters of piety, and how difficult it is to get them to alter their minds, even when a wise director judges them at fault. From material and external things perhaps they will keep their hearts more or less detached, but it is not so with spiritual matters. They do not know and do not wish to believe in any but themselves. How much more strikingly is this the case when it is a question of supernatural things, as of supposed visions, locutions, and the like! The Confessor must give in to these deluded creatures on all points, thinking as they think, praising their highly favored state, etc. Otherwise, complaints, grumbling, and often declared hostility. So great is the pride of the poor daughter of Eve! The contrary however was manifest in our Gemma. She had good reasons for believing that the wonderful things continually wrought in her were, without doubt, the work of God. God Himself, by evident and palpable truths, assured her of it, and said to her: "Don't fear, it is I who am operating in thee." And yet that was not enough. She wished that her spiritual father should give judgment, and to his decision she bowed unreservedly. "Let you, my father, decide it for me. Am I to believe it is Jesus, or the devil, or my own imagination? I am ignorant, and may be deceived. What would become of me if I were deluded? You know that I don't wish these things. I only desire that Jesus be pleased with me. What must I do to please Him? Tell me. I wish to do His Will at any cost."

It happened that one of her first directors, either to try her, or because he really was in doubt, opposed her. He went so far as to mortify her bitterly, saying that she was a victim of delusions. Another director also, full of perplexity in the presence of facts that were so new to him, in order to get himself out of all difficulty commanded her to ask Our Lord to remove or prevent these extraordinary manifestations, and put her on the common beaten path. Gemma thanked the former with all humility. To the second she brought the following answer: "Yesterday you told me to ask Jesus to take all these things away or to make them quite clear to you or to whom you desired. I prayed so much! because I want this favor granted. Oh yes, I want it at any cost. I feel persuaded that He will do all that the Confessor wants. I said to Jesus that if it is He who really manifests Himself to me, well and good. But if it is the devil, to drive him away, because I won't have him. And if it was a delusion of my brain, I could not bear it any longer, my head would split. If you think these words were not sincere, tell me so, for I would not willingly tell lies, and I am resolved not to commit any more sins."

One day Our Lord reproached her sweetly because, after so many proofs, she still seemed to doubt. She answered modestly, "I doubt because others doubt. But if Thou art Jesus, make Thyself known for a certainty. Believe me, neither the Confessor nor I can bear the strain."

When Our Lord drew her to Himself, so that she could not resist, she had to yield to His power. No sooner however had she returned from those Divine communications, than she hastened to her Confessor to repeat the old story with humble simplicity. "Tell me, Father, what must I do?" And how touching and tender the contest that she was often obliged to have with Jesus Himself, when He made Himself felt. "But the Confessor," she would say, "has told me that you are not Jesus. Or can the Confessor be mistaken?"

The life of the just on earth is a network of consolation and pain. Of this mystery I have already said something, and intend to say more later on, when treating of the mystic trials to which Gemma was subjected by Our Lord. Here I will only observe that this virgin soul made no account of her consolations, which were many and frequent. She was perfectly detached from them. When God sent them, she received them with gratitude, and knew well how to use them as a stimulus to greater perfection. But when He withdrew them, leaving her to languish in darkness and abandonment—imagine what agony this must have been to a soul on fire with the love of God!—even then she declared herself content. "Let Jesus do as He wills! Provided He is pleased let all be satisfied. Do I forsooth deserve His consolation? It is enough for me to be able to enjoy Him in the other life. I don't mind suffering here."

And now, find supposed illusions if you can in such a soul. Those only who are ignorant of the things of God, and those with idle minds could think it. We, on the other hand, are aware that whoever denies himself for the love of Christ, divests himself of the old man, and is reclothed in Christ, and in His virtues. And whosoever is reclothed in Christ cannot be subject to illusions.

CHAPTER 15

St. Gemma's Perfect Obedience.

SOMETHING has now to be said of the obedience of which this blessed child gave proof, denying her own will in order to give it entirely into the hands of her spiritual guides. This subject is of the greatest importance, as it is in this denial of the will that the virtue of obedience principally consists. We have already shown how necessary this self-denial is for the attainment of perfection. Of this Our Lord speaks when He says, "If any man will follow Me, let him deny himself."

When Gemma, having been left an orphan, entered the house of strangers as a guest, she obeyed her loving benefactress in all external things. Aunt had only to say, "Gemma get up and let us go out; go back to your room; go to bed," and Gemma, always ready, hastened at once to obey without making the least demur. This even when she was suffering from fever, which must have rendered certain acts of obedience very difficult.

When in Church, and intent on heavenly delights with her Jesus, after Holy Communion, on receiving a sign from her companion to come home, she immediately stood up and followed her. One would think that she was only waiting to be called. The force of this virtue of obedience, as we have likewise seen, was felt by her even when in ecstasy. Let us hear the same Lady describe it: "After Holy Communion, and the blessing of the Priest, I called Gemma to come back to her place; but she was already in ecstasy. Fearing that anyone might notice her, without uttering a word, I said within myself, 'O Jesus, if it is Thy will, make her return at once to her place through obedience.' Would you believe it? She immediately raised her head. I told her to go to her place, and she did so. Seeing how well this plan succeeded, I continued to act afterwards in the same way, and God, Who so loved His faithful servant, was always present and made her obey."

When she was in bed at night, although surrounded by many persons talking among themselves, if the aforesaid Lady said to her, "Gemma, you need rest, sleep!" she then and there closed her eyes, and fell into a profound sleep. I myself wished to prove this, and being in the house when Gemma was ill, standing by her bedside with other persons, I said to her, "Take my blessing, sleep, and we will go away." Gemma turned on the other side and fell fast asleep. Then I knelt down much moved, and lifting my eyes to Heaven, I gave her a mental precept to awake. And behold! as if aroused by a voice she awoke, and as usual smiled. I reproached her, "Is it thus you obey? I told you to sleep." And she in all humility said, "Don't be vexed, Father, I felt someone touch my shoulder, and a loud voice called out, 'Rise, the Father is calling you.'" It was her Angel Guardian who was watching by her side.

Let no one think that this holy child's great readiness to obey was the effect of natural timidity or indecision. We have already observed the trend of her natural disposition. It would have impelled her to command and domineer, rather than to obey and submit. Hence it was entirely the fruit of solid virtue when, with such astonishing simplicity, she submitted herself to the will of others. Nature had no part in those acts. Nay, she had to repress nature, and constantly do violence to herself, in order to yield so unreservedly to others.

And as she was so docile in conforming to the will of others in external things, it is easy to understand how much more perfect was her obedience in spiritual matters, to which she devoted all her attention. In her humility she felt that she was totally incapable of taking a single step unassisted. Hence in her desire to walk, nay fly, in the way of perfection, she was thoroughly convinced that her only course was to place herself in the hands of a spiritual guide assigned her by Heaven. "The time has now come," she said, "for me to do the will of my Confessor, and never again my own. Even Jesus has said this to me, indeed He often repeats it, telling me that I must no longer have a will or opinion of my own and that my wish must be that of the Confessor." For this reason she constantly had recourse to him, at one time to ask him if she had done rightly on such an occasion, at another to know how she was to act in some undertaking. From every one of her letters it will be seen that she wished to be guided in everything by her Confessor. It is certain too that, had she not felt such need of direction, we should have known hardly anything of the interior work of grace in this privileged soul.

And into what details was she not ready to enter, although so gifted with infused knowledge of heavenly things! "Provided you, Father, approve of it, I should like to ask Jesus to calm my head a little." (She was alluding to the excruciating pains, that were causing her a martyrdom.) "Shall I ask him? Do you approve of my making a general confession to Father Provincial? If you do, I will make it; but if you don't wish it, I am satisfied all the same. Will you allow me to ask Jesus to make the hour of agony every night?" Again, writing to her ordinary Confessor, "I should like to ask you to put me in a convent, but I think the Father" (her director) "does not wish me to speak of such a thing. If it is so, I will say nothing. You are satisfied, are you not, that tomorrow I go to spend the day at the convent? You may be sure I shall enjoy it." All will I think be gratified by my many quotations of Gemma's words, and that the beautiful soul of this perfect child may be made known to us in her own language. "On Saturday," she says, "you gave me leave to rise early in the morning. I rise and pray, but I should like to do what the nuns do in choir. Do you approve of my asking a Passionist Father to teach me what they do, and allow me to do it? Were I to ask Jesus to make me die of consumption," (of course in His own time, not now), "would you be satisfied? This would be my desire, but in any case I am willing to do what Jesus wants of me." And taking fresh courage from her filial confidence, she writes in another letter, "Give me leave, Father, to ask Jesus again to take me quickly out of this life to be with Him in glory. I live always trembling at the danger of offending Him."

To all these and similar proposals the Confessor and Director replied as they felt inspired by God. And Gemma, showing by deed the sincerity of what she had said, remained perfectly satisfied with the answer given her, whether it was yes, or no, and thought no more about it. When the no was preceptive, this saintly child kept it carefully in her mind, and set her whole being into conformity with it. Here I have to mention things so strange that if they were not true they would seem incredible.

I have said already that Gemma, in order to obey her spiritual Father, was obliged to struggle with Jesus Himself, because she was given to understand that it was not Jesus she saw, but the devil. Here I go further and add that she even resisted her Divine Spouse, although recognized as such by her director, solely because the obedience had forbidden her to stay to listen to Him. Such a struggle surely was superior to all human strength! Yet Gemma sustained it courageously and triumphed. "Oh! how my good Jesus tempts me!" she said, "but I hold steadfastly to the obedience though it entails great strife. O beloved sacrifice! O beloved and beautiful obedience!" Once when Our Savior appeared to her all covered with wounds, He invited her to approach and kiss Him. At such a sight, and at the thought of the prohibition laid on her, she burst into tears, but would not approach her Jesus. Meanwhile, as her affections grew more excited, she began to feel the usual indication of the sacred stigmas in her hands and feet and side. "My God," she said, "what is to be done? The moment I felt it, I rose and quickly fled. I left Jesus and thus obeyed and was content." "Poor Jesus!" she said again, "how many times have I not been rude to Him, and resolutely turned Him away in obedience to the Confessor. And He stood there, so good, so good!" At another time she had leave to remain with her Lord, when He came to visit her, for a limited time, in order, (as her Confessor wisely thought), that she might have time to sleep. What happened? Jesus appeared to her. It was one of the usual evenings from Thursday to Friday. Gemma took part as usual in the pains of the Passion, and was being consumed with love in company with her suffering Redeemer, when, lo and behold, the clock struck the allotted time. "What was I to do?" these are her words, "Jesus remained, but He witnessed my embarrassment. In obedience I was obliged to send Him away because the fixed time was passed. He then said, 'Give me a sign that henceforward thou wilt obey Me.' Then I exclaimed: 'Jesus, go away, I don't want you any longer.'" The same thing happened frequently with her Guardian Angel, but of that in another chapter.

I learned once that, while at Our Lord's feet, it was made known to her when my letters would reach Lucca. And she, with her usual simplicity, made it known at home. "This morning—tomorrow—by such a train a letter will come from Father. He posted it yesterday—or today—at such an hour." And as she said, so always without fail it happened. I wished to mortify her in this, saying that thus she gave evidence of levity and subtle pride. This is how she took the correction, "Father, on my knees I ask your pardon for all. No, no! I will never again attempt to do what I have done, or say what I have said. I will obey you. Do you know, Father, all day on Sunday I felt your reproof. I will take care not to make any more prophecies about the arrival of your letters. I always feel sorry for what I said and did, and I hate it and will not do it again. Write when you will, I won't dare to disobey your command." Then knowing well that she had gotten that knowledge from Our Lord, with humble bashfulness she added: "I feel inclined to excuse myself, but no, no! I wish to obey and hold my tongue. *Viva Gesù!*" And, as she never forgot what she had been told by her director, after some months she was able to write as follows: "Father, as you know, I have conquered! This morning early, before Holy Communion, I knew by inspiration that today for certain a letter would come from you. I have suffered somewhat from my longing to come out with it, but I have repressed it. According to the warning I had from you, I have not said a word. That is right, is it not?"

I have already mentioned the extraordinary phenomenon of bursts of blood from her mouth, that Gemma very often had, when, while in ecstasy, her heart throbbed violently, so as even to bend her ribs considerably. Her ordinary Confessor forbade this, though well knowing that it did not depend on her will. No matter, this saintly girl made every effort to please her spiritual father, even when in ecstasy, and when she knew that her efforts were in vain, she felt remorse at her failure, and accused herself of it, as of a disobedience. "I have disobeyed the Confessor," she writes to me, "as he had forbidden me to bleed from my mouth. I obeyed up to now, but this morning, in a movement of my heart, a little came away. How shall I have courage to meet the Confessor?" In these words I don't know which is more to be admired, the simplicity of the dove, or her heroic obedience.

I have also stated how her prudent Confessor, fearing that the excruciating pains to which this precious victim was subject every week from Thursday to Friday, might ruin her health, ended in forbidding her cooperation in any of these extraordinary things. And this under precept of obedience. Behold the wonderful result! The Divine Author of this extraordinary phenomenon willed the precept of His minister to be respected, until he withdrew it. The phenomenon ceased, at least as to its outward manifestation, and Gemma rejoiced at this, although the precept cost her so much. Here is how she writes to me: "The Confessor put me under obedience not to do anything extraordinary, and all is going well. But oh! what violence I have to do myself in order to keep good." And in ecstasy she was heard to exclaim, "Oh dear obedience, that deprives me of all the sweetness of my love, I long to embrace thee!"

In a suffering that troubled her shortly before her last illness, her stomach became so upset that she was unable to take any food, liquid or solid. Here again recourse was had to obedience, with the same success. "I am ready," she said to me, "to do all that you tell me. I hope that Jesus will enable me to obey. Nay I am certain that from the first of the month I shall never again reject any food." And indeed from the beginning of the next month she was able to take and retain her food without any difficulty. After such an easy experience precepts were multiplied one after the other. In every need recourse was had to the Confessor or director, and he sent word to Gemma that through obedience she was to recover, through obedience she was to get up, through obedience she was to come to her senses. Then in an instant the fever left her, she rose, the ecstasy ended, then was Gemma up and free and well. Great God of infinite love, how wonderfully dost Thou deal with Thine elect!

That this holy obedience was pleasing to Our Lord was made manifest by the earnestness with which He deigned to inculcate it to His servant either directly or through her Guardian Angel. "Obedience! Obedience!" This was the dominant note and aim of every one of those celestial interviews, with which she was so often favored. "Blind obedience, perfect obedience! this is the first thing to be remembered," said the Divine Master to her, "be as a dead body and do henceforth everything that is required of thee promptly." Nor did she escape severe scoldings when in the least bit wanting in the perfection of this virtue. "If thou dost not obey," said Jesus to her, "at the cost of every sacrifice, I will leave thee alone in the hands of thine enemy." "If thou dost not overcome thyself," said her Angel Guardian, "by promptly doing whatever is commanded thee, thou shalt not see me more." Everything was turned to profit by this watchful virgin; severe threats and sweet exhortations alike; the words of her spiritual director just as those of Our Savior and of the Angel. Her consequent advancement in this virtue as well as in all others was seen by everyone.

So perfectly had she accustomed herself to obey that in obedience alone she found tranquillity and repose. "What consolation," she exclaimed, "does not my heart find in obedience. It generates in me a calm that I cannot explain. Obedience for ever! Source of all my peace. I thank you, my Father, who have taught me the value of this precious virtue, and given me so much good advice and instruction, by means of which I have escaped so many great dangers. I will always, with the Divine assistance, put in practice whatever is commanded me, in order to please Jesus." And in another letter, "Don't be afraid, Father, recommend me to Jesus, and I will always and everywhere obey. Nay, with regard to certain things, by force of habit I no longer feel any difficulty in obedience. It was Jesus who a few days ago gave me this grace, for which I will ever thank Him." Again, "Jesus has promised me to make known to you His Will in my regard, provided I ask it of Him with humility, and I have already done so. Thus I am in peace, awaiting that the most holy Will of God be perfectly fulfilled in and by me in all things." Now this is the highest degree of perfect obedience—joy in the denial of self. Gemma had reached it. She has therefore a right to the Divine Promise: *Vir obediens loquetur victorias*—the truly obedient will recount victories.

CHAPTER 16

St. Gemma's Profound Humility.

PRIDE separated man from God. Humility brings him back to God. Pride is the fatal principle of every vice. Humility is the fruitful mother of every virtue and the foundation of all perfection. Gemma, when on her death-bed, being asked by one of the Sisters in attendance what virtue was most important and dearest to God, answered with great vivacity of spirit, "Humility, humility, the foundation of all the others."

In accordance with this doctrine I made humility the test of her spirit from the moment I was called on to examine it. Many persons, including even her ordinary Confessor, manifested hesitation, and all but doubt, on witnessing such extraordinary things in a simple child from the first moment that she entered on the way of perfection. "It may be so," they said, "but can all this, so rarely to be found even among the greatest saints of the Church, be from God?" My answer was: "This certainly is from God, if accompanied by humility." I set myself to examine, and from the very start it became evident that for a long time this holy child had understood the importance of humility. Nay, she had aimed at acquiring it before all the other virtues, and with her whole being studied how to practice it. In a word I found her to be most humble. There was accordingly no room for doubt, and, deeply touched by what I witnessed, I remained rapt in admiration of the blessed child, who thus enlightened by God, had learned so soon and so perfectly how to correspond with grace. To me her sanctity seemed more than proved.

When thirteen years of age she made a course of spiritual exercises at the Convent of St. Zita in Lucca. In a little notebook she wrote of this retreat: "Exercises made in 1891, in which Gemma has to change and give herself entirely to Jesus." Among the many and holy maxims inculcated by the preacher was this: "Let us remember, sisters, that we are nothing, and that God is all." These words from that day forward made a profound impression on the mind of this child, and she never forgot them. There is not a letter of hers, especially those written to her director, in which this sentiment of her own nothingness is not expressed with ever increasing emphasis and renewed eloquence. Thus she kept growing more and more in the knowledge of God and of herself until at last it seemed impossible to her for anyone to be proud. The truth is that during her whole life she never entertained a thought of self-esteem. "And how," she used to say, "could I become vain? Was there ever greater madness than that?"

On one occasion I reproved and mortified her, and at the same time admonished her to be on her guard, lest she be taken unawares by pride. I also let her imagine that I had noticed some secret germ of this vice in her heart. Observe the terms in which she answered me:

"I have read your letter. O my God, have mercy on me! It is true, too true, that pride is in me. Listen, Father, I no sooner read that word pride than the devil seized on it in order to drive me almost to despair. I had already passed a very bad hour, and at last, driven to extremes, I ran to the Crucifix and, prostrate on my face, asked pardon many times, and implored of Him to let me die there and then at His feet. But this was not granted me. A few moments later tranquillity and peace suddenly returned. Poor Jesus! Oh how often do I not cause Thee pain! Where am I going to end if I continue in this way? But no! I won't be wanting any more, and I ask your pardon, Father. Don't be angry with me, you shall see. I won't do the same thing again. Your letter said what was true, and I thank you for it on my knees. But why let me trouble you so? Don't you know that I have a thick head and little intelligence? Then forgive me, and I will never again displease you. What pain I must have given Jesus by these proud thoughts!"

Not even she could tell what those thoughts were, but simply she believed what her director had said. Then she continued:

"Father, ask Jesus to forgive me in pity for my poor soul. Instead of being always good, I have managed to get filled with malice and iniquity and pride. Yet Jesus has given me the grace to acknowledge this wicked sin, and now He enables me to correct it." Then she further adds, *"I tremble, I fear that Jesus will punish me because I have offended Him and displeased you. Do you know the punishment I fear?—and I shall deserve it—to be condemned not to love my Jesus any more. No, no! Let Jesus punish me in any other way that He chooses, but not this. Father, if you still find pride in me, don't delay, kill me, do all that is possible, but take the pride quickly from me."*

Her actions corresponded to her words. No one ever saw her ruffled. She neither boasted of, or made any display of her talents and gifts. Quite the reverse, no one could equal her in modesty and in her efforts to hide herself from the eyes of others. "For charity's sake, Father," thus she wrote, "don't speak of me to others, if not to tell them what I am in reality. I will humble myself and change my ways, and ask forgiveness of all for having deceived them. Jesus Who is infinitely good will pardon me."

I must now speak of her natural qualities. I have already said that they were many and exceptional—quickness and clearness of intellect, strength of mind and fixity of purpose. Yet to see and deal with her, one would almost think she had no mind of her own, as she asked for advice and direction about everything. At school she acquired a great proficiency in French, drawing, and painting, but once done with school and study, she never was heard to utter a word of French, or seen to take her brush and colors in her hand. It was only after her death that it became known from her teachers that she was proficient in those things.

She moreover wrote verses with great facility. But of this talent she was not known to make much use. Once at the request of a Religious, with whom she was very intimate, in less than half an hour she wrote a poem of fifteen stanzas in form of devout aspiration to God, directed to sanctify the principal actions of the day. It would be difficult I think to say what was most to be admired in these stanzas, the smoothness of the verse, the variety and naturalness of the ideas, or the piety of the poetess. A very charming sonnet of hers on the happiness of life in the cloisters also came into my hands. I do not know of her having indulged in any other poetic compositions. On the contrary, it is known that having been requested to write one for a festivity, she stoutly refused to do so, notwithstanding many entreaties, saying that it was mere vanity or at least a loss of time. This favored child was also gifted with a charming voice and a marked taste for music. Anyone who had known her ardent longing to praise her beloved Jesus and her Heavenly Mother, would certainly have expected that at least while alone at work she would have opened her innocent lips in devout song of praise. But no; no one ever heard her sing, even in an undertone. Do not these constant uniform practices in a young girl of natural vivacity and ease of manner constitute a strong proof in themselves of profound virtue?

Gemma's spiritual endowments were without measure. She had such extraordinary gifts that one marvels at their very description. All saw them and were struck with admiration. She alone seemed unaware of them, or at least gave them no consideration, except in order to humble herself the more before God and men. How often did she not implore of Our Lord to withdraw from her those marked favors for which she did not believe she could possibly be fitted, and give them instead to others who would know better how to correspond to them. "O Jesus," she would say, "don't let me do these things that are above me. I am not good in anything. And then I know not how to correspond to so many great graces that Thou hast given me. Seek, oh seek someone else who will know how to do better than I." One of the many times when she was thus bewailing her own shortcomings, Our Lord, Who deigned to act as her loving Master in the school of humility, in order to confirm her the more in this virtue, made her hear in her heart these words: "Do what thou art able. I will to make use of thee precisely because thou art the poorest, and so great a sinner among all My creatures." To these words she replied with ingenuous familiarity, "Then Jesus, do as Thou pleasest and I am satisfied."

On another occasion He let her see her soul through rays of His infinite light, in order that she might humble herself at the sight, and said to her in spirit that she ought to be ashamed to let herself be seen by others. Gemma not only humbled herself and was filled with shame, but she remained stupefied. "If you only saw," she confided to me one day, "how horrible my soul is! Jesus has made me see it." Sometimes our Gracious Lord, in order that she might love Him with greater earnestness, appeared to disregard her, assuming an aspect of severity. "Jesus," she said, "scarcely looks at me any more, and if He does glance at me, He is so very, very serious that sometimes I am even obliged not to look at Him. It seems as though He drives me from Him. This is a real torment. Now, Father, I am almost abandoned by Jesus on account of my sins. And what shall I do? To whom shall I go? You, Father, ask Jesus, and hear what He says."

Not only in the time of trial did Gemma feel unworthy to look at Our Lord, but also during the frequent apparitions with which He favored her when her soul was full of sweetness, so great was the shame that covered her in the presence of His Divine Majesty. Such being the disposition of this pure soul, grace was able to descend in torrents upon her without fear, so to say, of lessening her humility. The more she was favored, the more deeply did she descend into the depths of her own nothingness. I, on my part, can affirm that this holy child never spoke to me either in person or by letter of any special communication she had from God, that she did not end with some act of the most profound humility. In proof of this let one example suffice, in addition to all that has been said. Our Lord had on a certain occasion filled her with such great consolations that she seemed to come from them born again to a new life. In giving me a short account of what had happened this is how she expressed herself, "Oh how much ought not I to marvel at the infinite mercy of God! Yes, Jesus is indeed my Jesus, all full of goodness to me, miserable and most ungrateful sinning creature. He has again wrought the miracle of my conversion. Hence through the light that He has deigned to grant me, I have come to know my baseness."

From these and like words that on every opportunity came to her lips and were expressed in her writings it is easy to understand that Gemma was not only dismayed at realizing her own nothingness before God, but also that she believed herself unfaithful to the immense favors she had received from Him. She was fully aware of the value and beauty of the gifts bestowed on her, and used to say that their price was the Blood of Jesus Christ. Hence her great confusion and contempt of self. Here are some of her words in this connection:

> "*I ought to think, dear Father, of all that is wanting in me in order to be a worthy child of Jesus; and instead....?*" (These points that are often met with in her writings are meant to signify so much more that she sees and feels, but is unable to express.) "*I ought to fight bravely, doing violence to myself; and instead...! There is nothing left me but to humble myself beneath the powerful hand of God, and pray, without seeking my own satisfaction. Behold the month of May!*"

She wrote again:

> "*I am thinking of the great benefits I have received from my Heavenly Mother during these first years of my life, and I am ashamed, because I have never repaid the hand and heart that so lovingly bestowed them on me. Nay, what is worse, I have repaid with ingratitude all that she has done for me.*"

On one occasion, well knowing with whom I had to deal, I took the liberty to humble her by saying: "I cannot understand how Jesus can bring Himself to soil His hands in such a cesspit." The angelic maiden smiled and was filled with joy, as though she had found in those words what she had been seeking for a long time, namely the best epithet that she could apply to herself. She stored it in her heart, and every now and then brought it out when speaking or writing, and even when ravished in ecstasy she exclaimed, "Oh Jesus, how is it that you wish to soil Your hands in this cesspit Gemma?" And when her Angel Guardian appeared to her, she exclaimed, "Don't soil your hands, I beg of you, in this cesspit." To this epithet she used to add another that she herself invented, that of "worthless being." "What is to be done, Father, with this worthless being?" And she meant to say "with this discarded contemptible creature, become vile and repulsive in the eyes of God and man." And in prayer, "Dear Mother," she would say in tears, "my dear God, this miserable being has to be lifted up, and when?" With this same sentiment in her mind, having learnt that I was going from Rome to Isola to visit the tomb of her Confrère Blessed Gabriel, she wrote me a long letter charging me with several messages to him. The principal one was the following, "Say to Venerable Gabriel these precise words: 'What am I to do with Gemma?' Mind, say this, Father, and let me know his answer."

Not only was the confusion of this humble virgin great indeed at finding herself so lovingly treated by God, it was the same when she saw herself benefited by those around her. In her exterior, as already observed, she knew not how to be complimentary. Besides that, so great was her pain at noticing that she was the object of attention from others, that, had they known it, they would, in order to save her suffering, have been watchful not to let her notice their solicitude.

"I am asking Jesus," she wrote me, *"for patience, not for myself but for my Aunt here, because she needs it with me. I would rather have nothing of all that is done for me. If you only saw,*

Father! In some things she prefers me to the others. She goes so far as to have my bed warmed for me. Now ought these things to be done for me? Will you speak to her? Heaps of things are done for me, who ought to be treated as worthless, and yet not even a thank you escapes my lips. Oh! if at least with my cold prayers I could benefit those who are kind to me! My wish would be that they should all treat me as a slave."

It is well known how inclined devout souls, especially those who have made vows, are to call Our Lord their Spouse, and themselves His Spouses. Not so Gemma. Although she loved with all the ardor of her soul this Divine Eternal Word, true Spouse of our poor humanity, and found herself treated by Him with exceptional tenderness, yet she would not dare to call Him Spouse. "Child, useless servant, foolish virgin, wretched creature"—these are the titles she gave herself, never "spouse," at least when not in ecstasy. Two or three times only, when ravishcd in the highest contemplation, she was heard to call her dear Lord "Spouse of Blood."

In her letters, when she had finished what she had to say, she always wound up with these words, "Pray for me, who am poor Gemma." One day I said to her that she had better add a surname; that if she did not wish for any other she might take "Gemma of Jesus." At such a proposal the humble maiden was wholly confused and mortified, as it seemed to her to be too great a pretension, and she made difficulties. I insisted that such a name did not mean that she was worthy of Jesus, but that she did not wish to glory unless in Jesus alone. She seemed convinced, and from that day began to sign herself "Poor Gemma of Jesus." But it was not for long. The sentiment of her own vileness drove my suggestion from her mind, and she ended by forgetting it altogether. Returning to her old custom she henceforth signed herself, "Poor Gemma."

This deep sentiment of her own nothingness made her recommend herself to the prayers of everyone to whom she spoke. In this, to her eloquence, always found new forms of expression: "Recommend me to Jesus and also to the others. Whoever prays for me will do a great act of charity. I ask your blessing, and then tell our confrère Venerable Gabriel to think also of poor Gemma." And in another letter:

"If you only knew, Father, the means Jesus uses to confound my pride. Oh, if you were to know how wicked I am! Who will give me the virtue I need to attract Jesus? Pray and get the others to pray that He may quickly help me to heal my great wretchedness, clearing my mind and letting me see through the horrible darkness in which I am enveloped, so that although I remain confused, Jesus may be glorified in my poor soul."

Great was her embarrassment when others turned to her for help in their needs, and this was of frequent occurrence because of the high opinion in which she was held by many. To a confidential friend she wrote thus:

"Listen, I was greatly astonished that you in your letter should have obliged me to pray for that Lady. If you did not know me you could be excused, but now that you know me well enough…! I say no more. What can you expect to obtain through a sinful soul, full of defects, that is so little, if at all, concerned for Jesus? Nevertheless I will obey, but don't trust me, because I am good for nothing."

Her words to a priest were: "I will pray, be assured of that. But you know well that my poor prayers are weak and without force, and Jesus, Who is gone to hide, will not hear them."

Thus she was accustomed to speak of Our Lord, when withdrawing His sensible Presence, He allowed her to languish in aridness, "Jesus gone to hide."

Elsewhere I shall say more of this interior martyrdom with which, from time to time, Our Lord was pleased to try the fidelity of His servant. Here I need only observe that however great His severity, she never made the smallest complaint, being convinced of her unworthiness of all consolation. She thought instead that she deserved to be abandoned by God in punishment for her sins. This made her write with trembling hand to her director as follows: "Let me tell you Father, Jesus at last is tired of me because of my great want of fervor. But He has reason to be so, therefore I thank Him always and adore Him."

The very inflictions with which the spirit of darkness tormented her so often, of which I must speak later, gave her a motive for self-humiliation in the thought that she herself through some hidden fault had provoked the Divine Justice to chastise her in that way. She accordingly was not grieved thereat, but bore all as a just punishment, saying, "I know, Father, I know why Jesus lets the devil torment me thus, and I will tell it you in confession. But it has grieved me exceedingly. Even my Angel Guardian seems ashamed to stand by me." And it seemed to her that all in the family must have noticed her Angel's displeasure. For this reason she once said to me with indescribable simplicity: "Perhaps you, Father, would think of it, and tell the Angel to keep hidden you know, and not let the others see him." In a word, everything offered this child of benediction an opportunity of humbling herself. When the tormenting pains of her stigmata oppressed her, she reproached herself in her heart, saying: "Look there, Father, how I am always behind-hand, how suffering deters me. Oh! what weakness of spirit! I would almost dare to choose from the hands of Jesus the kind of suffering that would please me! Pray for my soul." If there was any upset in the family, she attributed all that went wrong to herself, and even in the event of any public disaster she believed unhesitatingly that she was its cause.

We have already seen how assiduous this favored child was in revealing the state of her conscience to her spiritual father. Anyone who did not know her well might perhaps have believed her to be one of those lightheaded creatures who take the greatest pleasure in talking of themselves and their affairs. It was the reverse with our humble Gemma. The manifestation of her inmost thoughts cost her pains of death, and she would have preferred to be sunk in the abyss, rather than say or write a single word about the extraordinary things that Grace was operating in her. Let her tell us this herself: "I have been making these manifestations to you," she says, "for such a long time that the shame it causes me ought now to have passed away. On the contrary every time I have to write or confess such things, my confusion increases. I don't know how to express myself, but it is not shame, it is a sort of fear."

In reality she was influenced by both these sentiments; shame, because she would rather not have told any human being of things that could in the least redound to her praise; and fear, because she dreaded not being able to express herself clearly, and that others on her account might thus be led into error. "I fear," she said, "that in the midst of the extraordinary things that happen to me daily, I may be duped, and also lead others astray. This I should regret beyond everything. Beg of Jesus earnestly to help me, and not let me deceive others. My fear is so great that on certain days I would fain be hidden from the eyes of all." But where was there room for deceit in this candid soul, who did not even know how it was possible to impose on others? She once said to me: "Father, I wish you to explain to me the meaning of the word 'deceit,' for I wish not to deceive anyone."

If then, Gemma felt such great difficulty in manifesting the "things of Jesus," as she used to call them, to her Confessor, we can imagine what repugnance she would have felt to reveal them to others. That great maxim of the Prophet Isaiah, "*Secretum meum mihi,* My secret to myself," was with her a rule of conduct. And none did know them except her spiritual director, and, by his express command, the pious lady who acted as her mother. But, notwithstanding all the precautions she took, her anxiety was ceaseless for fear that something might get known. "I do myself all the violence I can, but I fear that, on the occasion of some sudden impulse, others may come to know what Jesus wishes to be kept secret. In the street, in church, I try to distract my thoughts, but I do not always succeed. Hence I may excite an estimation in others that I do not deserve."

It was this great fear that made her so long to be enclosed in a convent. "In the cloisters," she thought, "I shall be hidden, at least from the eyes of seculars." All the time that I have had to do with this child of Heaven, as already stated, I have invariably noticed her indifference to all her surroundings. Without desires, without inclinations, without will, she seemed completely dead to self. Only in this one desire to be enclosed in a convent have I found her somewhat tenacious, and I often scolded and mortified her for it. There is scarcely one of her letters in which she does not return with earnestness to the subject. "Father, don't leave me in the world. The world is not made for me, it keeps me in fear. Come soon to Lucca, and shut me in. Oh why do you leave me exposed to the gaze of all? And what would happen to me if they came to know certain things?" Thus she continued for a long while, until God made known His Will to dispose of her in another way. It is certain that she carried this excessive fear and reserve so far as to keep herself hidden even from her directors, except when she felt an urgent need to consult them. A holy reserve, this indeed, but how many holy things, and what a mine of important information regarding this child of grace has it not hidden from us!

What has been mentioned will go far to explain how Gemma felt wounded to the core whenever she noticed that anyone held her in esteem. She often had letters from very distinguished persons. Many who desired to meet her made arrangements with members of the family so as to succeed without her suspecting that she was the object of their visit. On such occasions she did all in her power to get out of the way and hide herself. But when obedience forced her to remain, it could be seen that in spirit she suffered violence, unless perchance she succeeded by some studied industry to pass as a simpleton. As an instance of this I remember that, while I was at the house, an eminent Prelate was announced as wishing to see Gemma. She, not being able to escape, immediately on being called ran and seized a large cat that was near, and appearing to be greatly delighted with the animal, fondling it around her neck quite childishly (a thing, be it noted, she never before had done), she presented herself to the Prelate. Her artifice succeeded, and he, shrugging his shoulders, showed that he despised her. Then Gemma, full of joy at having attained her object, sped away with the cat in her arms without making her homages to the visitor.

Blessed folly, that in the eyes of God is wisdom and virtue! Blessed humility, that keeping man in his place, moves God to come down to him and load him with graces! *"Humilibus dat gratiam!"* The second motive that urged this servant of God so to humble herself, was the great number of sins that she believed she committed continually, and the numerous defects with which she beheld herself as with a leprosy defiled.

Some think that the Saints, because Saints, cease in a certain sense to be human, and become, so to speak, celestial beings. Even the writers of their lives are frequently so mistaken. They would represent them as ideal beings, who have little in common with our human miseries. But they are wrong. The Saints are ideals, if you will, but truly human, children of the same father Adam, from whom they inherit a fallen vitiated nature. Grace lifts this fallen nature, and restores it to perfection. But this work is not effected at once, and therefore side by side with supernatural gifts, there remains the human with all its miseries. This human side is undeniable and by its contrast with the supernatural, the virtue of Divine Grace in the Saints is admirably manifested. According to St. Paul, *"Virtus in infirmitate perficitur"*—virtue in infirmity is made perfect. The Saints are subject to our weaknesses, to our repugnances, to our wearinesses and distastes in the practice of virtue. They feel the weight of the flesh, and the impulse of passions. They, too, have great reason to fear and tremble for their souls, and need to do violence to themselves in order to remain faithful. It is because they so love God and are so deeply impressed by His infinite beauty, that every shade of fault seems to them a monstrosity, and every least failing a serious sin. Hence their tears, their penances, and the contemptuous titles they continually give themselves, as though they were great sinners and criminals unworthy to be allowed to live.

Gemma's defects and those she called great sins were certainly not willful. Nay she would have passed through any torment rather than deliberately consent to even the merest shadow of venial sin. "I would not willingly commit them," she used to say, "but I am so wicked. I am on the watch not to sin, but no matter how much I strive, I always relapse. The misfortune is that I am not aware of it when I fall, and I only come to see it afterwards. Otherwise Jesus knows that I would not offend Him." Nevertheless in the tribunal of penance she knew not how to make any distinction between voluntary and involuntary faults, and with an eloquence that would have led the most expert confessors astray, she declared herself culpable in everything. There was an absence of the timidity, affectation, and sighs that weak souls but too often give way too. She told her faults with order, openness and precision of terms, distinguishing their number, species, and gravity. I let her speak, and then, reconsidering those faults, I had always to conclude that they were either virtuous acts or mere frailties. After my experience with her for many years, and after having several times heard the general confession of her whole life, I am able to declare that this saintly girl never committed even one formal sin, that is, with full deliberation. Also, that having lived twenty-five years in this corrupt and corrupting world, she took to Heaven unstained the robe of her baptismal innocence. The same thing has been attested by other confessors, whose authentic depositions I have before me as I write.

It is evident that Gemma judged herself differently from others, and in truth it needed time and labor to persuade her to the contrary, and to prevent her, terrified as she was at her own state, from falling almost into despair. "But can it be true," she said to me in great anxiety, "that Jesus is content with my soul? Oh, how often I blush and tremble at seeing myself so unclean in His presence! I have turned away when

He called me. Oh Father, do ask Jesus often to have mercy on my soul! Implore Him to pardon my sins. Tell Him that a thousand pains of body and soul will seem to me nothing if only I can make atonement for my faults. O my God, the chastisement will never be as terrible as I deserve. Punish me as Thou wilt, but take off the weight of so many sins, for this weight oppresses and crushes me. Woe to me if for one instant I were to lose sight of my faults and my iniquities! Oh, what disgust I feel for myself! Jesus dishonored by me! The goodwill that I seem to have is my only comfort in the midst of so many miseries." These and similar words, repeated in a thousand ways, each one more expressive and touching than the other, came from the pen of this humble servant of God in almost every letter she wrote. This was specially the case when she wrote while in ecstasy.

Once Our Lord appeared to her in tears, and she as I stated when speaking of her unbounded simplicity, asked Him why He was weeping. Later on one day, when thinking of this appearance, she said to me, "I know myself to be guilty of a thousand iniquities, and yet I had the courage to say, 'Why does Jesus weep?'" On another occasion, after some little family disturbance, having as usual attributed all the fault to herself, she conceived such horror of it that it required every effort and every art to restore her courage. "But see what I have done, Father!" she exclaimed. "I shall end by forcing all to abandon me. Despair would fain lay hold of me, but no, my Mother, *Mater orphanorum.* I do not wish to offend God, nor you, Father, nor the others. I don't wish it. I don't understand myself. There is something mysterious about me." She meant to say that she could not understand how a prompt and resolute will to do right could co-exist with the human frailties that seemed to her so enormous.

God Himself, Who willed to keep His servant in these humble sentiments, allowed the enemy to disturb her mind to such an extent, that he sometimes led her to believe that she was all but lost. Then it was that the poor child could give herself no rest, and used with trembling hand to write to her director, "If ever you see, Father, that my soul is in danger, or that I am in the clutches of the enemy, oh, be quick and help me. I wish at any cost to save my soul. How shall I succeed in this?" Now, as it pleased God to give some efficacy to my words, Gemma was constantly seeking to profit by them, and find comfort in her fears. "Oh, Father," she wrote, "you do not yet know the great need I have of your advice. Oh, if you knew the relief I find when I receive a line from you! For your words give me courage to suffer and shed tears. Help me! Help me! If you don't you will see me soon reduced to the ashes of sin." See what sentiments her profound humility excites in the heart of this innocent girl, and with what delicacy of thought she expressed herself.

The horror that Gemma had of sin was not inspired merely by its deformity and the eternal loss it entailed. It was much more the result of her great love of God, whom sin offended. And inasmuch as this love had immensely increased in her, so her contrition for the great offences of which she believed herself guilty against the Divine Majesty became immeasurable. "How is it?" she was often heard to exclaim, when she thought no one was near, "that a God so great and so worthy of being loved, should be outraged by me! And who am I, to dare so much? My poor Jesus!" This thought caused her to grow pale, and torrents of tears to fall from her eyes, as an eye-witness tells us. Even in her ecstasies, when Our Lord ordinarily gave her to taste of the sweets of Paradise, she reproached herself and fervently exclaimed: "Pardon me, Jesus! Oh Father, Father, forgive me my many sins."

Although this sentiment of vivid compunction was a habit of her life, there were nevertheless certain days on which Our Lord made her feel it in a way that was altogether extraordinary. She herself besought the Divine Spouse with fervent supplications to hasten the return of those days, valuing more than any heavenly consolation, and as the greatest grace, that of being able to deplore her faults with unusual intensity. She kept this in mind, and counted the hours that passed between one and another of these ineffable grievings. And when she had gone through them she hastened to tell her spiritual Father of it. "So many days had passed that I had not felt that sorrow for my sins. But Jesus willed anew to give me this grace. Yesterday evening I wept much at His feet. Oh how bitter were those tears, Father, and at the same time how sweet! And how great the throbbings of my heart, as if it would burst with compunction!"

It used to happen in this way: Whilst the holy maiden was absorbed in prayer a sudden bright light flashed in her mind, and laid bare the most hidden depths of her soul. She then beheld herself all covered with the blackest stains of sin, and sometimes it seemed as if God was greatly incensed against her, at others He appeared sad and afflicted by the affronts she had offered Him. Such a sight made this tender-hearted girl tremble, and often losing her senses through the shock of excessive grief, she fainted away. This inner heart-anguish sometimes lasted for hours, sometimes even for a whole day. We have heard her call it bitter and at the same time sweet. This was because in her grief she knew she was able to offer her Lord some compensation for her offences against Him. Here are her words, "This evening, Father, as usual all my sins came to my mind, and so vividly in their enormity that I had to do myself violence in order not to cry aloud. I felt greater sorrow for them than ever before. Their number surpassed a thousandfold my age and capacity. But what consoles me is that I felt such great grief for them, and I would not wish this sorrow ever to be cancelled from my mind or ever to grow less. My God, how immeasurable my iniquity!" The words "as usual" in the foregoing passage clearly show that this grace of extraordinary contrition had become habitual with her whenever she entered into deep recollection and union with God. But it was so more particularly from Thursday to Friday every week, when it was given her to participate in the Passion of Our Lord, as she herself made clearly known to me. "During the whole of Thursday evening, in particular, such great grief lays hold of me at the thought of having committed so many sins, all of which come back to my mind, that I feel ashamed of myself, and become greatly, oh so greatly, afflicted. I only find some solace in the little suffering that Jesus sends me, by offering it first for sinners, more particularly for myself, and then for the Souls in Purgatory." In this way, purifying her soul in sorrow and tears, this holy virgin prepared herself for the Divine communications that she received every week in those wonderful ecstasies.

When in September 1900, I was invited to Lucca for the first time to examine Gemma's Spirit, I found her engaged in writing by order of her Confessor a diary of all that happened to her in the practice of perfection. Being on principle opposed to such a method, as it appeared to me useless and dangerous to keep penitents occupied about themselves I advised that it should cease. Thereupon Gemma's holy Confessor acting on my advice forbade the journal. Very soon however I had to acknowledge that I had been precipitate and that my maxim, though good in itself, should not be applied to Gemma's case. Having taken all that she had written and read it carefully, I found it full of celestial wisdom and of important particulars that would of themselves have formed a most edifying biography. While thinking how to remedy the harm done, all of a sudden an idea presented itself, as if an inspiration, and I seized it immediately. Aware as I was of Gemma's child-like simplicity, I said to her: "You, according to your own saying, have committed an infinity of sins beginning from your earliest years. I know well those that you commit at present. Now, would it not be well, that you should make me in writing a general Confession of the sins of your whole life with all their minute and special circumstances? Knowing then with what class of sinner I have to deal, I shall be better able to direct you in the path of virtue." The innocent child, whose most ardent desire was to have a sure guide, fell into the snare, although showing some repugnance at first to what I asked of her. "O Father," she said, "what need have you of explanations? Of what sins am I to inform you? Think of all that the greatest sinners have committed, I have committed as many. And then, when you have read this paper and known the sins, you will be horrified and won't wish to be my Father any longer; then indeed!" But I insisted, and this docile creature through pure obedience, after having earnestly prayed and besought her Angel Guardian to assist her by recalling to her mind all that seemed to her so wicked, set to work. She began thus:

"MY FATHER, be prepared to hear all sorts, sins of every kind. By my writing all, good and bad, you will be better able to know how guilty I am and how good others have been with me. How ungrateful I have shown myself to Jesus, and how I have given a deaf ear to the advice of my parents and mistresses. Now I begin, Father. Viva Gesù!"

While writing she had to battle continually with her reluctance to speak of herself. This repugnance and struggle increased as she drew nigh the end of her task. The more so because in order to tell the tale of her sins she was forced to relate this story of her whole life, and because she could not emphasize her ingratitude to God without manifesting the great graces she had received. The manifestation was precisely what I had in view when setting her to write. Let us hear from herself how great her pain was at having to act thus:

"My Jesus, may Thy Holy Will be done! How I suffer at having to write certain things! The repugnance I first felt at having to do so, far from growing less, has kept on increasing and makes me feel a pain that kills. And then, wouldst Thou, O my God, wish me to write even those secret things that Thy Goodness makes known to me in order to humble me and keep me in my nothingness? If Thou willest it, O Jesus, I am ready to do even this for Thee. Make me know Thy Will."

To the fear she felt at making known what was so repugnant to her humility she added a doubt which she expressed as follows:

"But these writings, what use are they? For Thy greater glory, O Jesus, or to make me commit more sins? Thou hast willed that I should do this and I have done it, so Thou must see to it.

In the Wound of Thy Side I hide every word of mine, O lovable Dear Jesus!"

The devil, no doubt, had a great part in Gemma's anguish, for the good that her writing would surely produce was most hateful to him. Once he appeared to her visibly, and said with a bitter sneer: "Well done, write everything, dost thou not know that all those things are my doing, and if thou art found out imagine thy shame! What will then become of thee?" Obedience, however, triumphed and in a very short time Gemma had written a good-sized volume in excess of a hundred pages. But in it, with what exquisite art, did not the humble maiden strive to hide herself. Placing the splendor of her virtues and God's best gifts, as it were, beneath the shadow of the sins by which she declared she had profaned them! To form an idea of this Volume one should read it. But Gemma's efforts were in vain. Her simplicity betrayed her, and where she believed she would disgust others by relating sins and disorders, she composed on the contrary a most charming biography. I had gained my end, but Satan was enraged at it and used all the arts of his cunning to overthrow it. I have here to relate what seems incredible but it is a real and historical fact in which there was no room for the play of imagination. I will say without comment simply what happened to myself. Then let my readers judge of it.

Gemma's manuscript, when finished, was by my orders given in charge to her adopted mother Signora Cecilia Giannini who kept it hidden in a drawer awaiting the first opportunity of handing it to me. Some days elapsed and Gemma thought she saw the demon pass through the window of the room, where the drawer was, chuckling, and then disappearing in the air. Accustomed as she was to such apparitions, she thought nothing of it. But he, having returned shortly after to molest her, as often happened, with a repulsive temptation, and having failed, left gnashing his teeth and declaring exultingly: "War, war, thy book is in my hands." So she wrote to tell me. Then, owing to the obedience she was under, to disclose to her vigilant benefactress everything extraordinary that happened to her, she thought she was obliged to tell her what had occurred. They went, opened the drawer and found that the book was no longer there. I was written to at once and it is easy to imagine my consternation at having lost such a treasure. What was to be done? I thought a great deal about it, and just then while at the Tomb of Blessed Gabriel of the Dolours a fresh idea came to my mind. I resolved to exorcise the Devil and thus force him to return the manuscript if he had really taken it. With my ritual stole and holy water I went to the Tomb of the Blessed Servant of God and there, although nearly four hundred miles from Lucca, I pronounced the exorcisms in regular form. God seconded my ministry and at that same hour the writing was restored to the place from which it had been taken several days before. But, in what a state! The pages from top to bottom were all smoked and in parts burned as if each one had been separately exposed over a strong fire, yet they were not so badly burned as to destroy the writing. This document, having thus passed through a hell fire, is in my hands. It is truly a treasure, as I have already said, of most important information which, had it been destroyed, could never have become known.

CHAPTER 17

St. Gemma's Heroic Mortification.

WHOEVER wishes to follow Jesus and be perfect, must deny self, that is to renounce all things and take up the Cross—*Tollat crucem Suam*. Because without the Cross it is impossible to become like Jesus Christ, Who is God Crucified—the Author and Finisher of Faith, Who having joy set before Him, endured the Cross. For this finishing of the Faith centered in the Cross, this mystery of suffering is, so to say, the climax of all that is sublime and perfect in God; it is God's own free choice and must surpass in infinite wisdom, splendor and Love all that it came to complete. Therefore it is impossible to become one with Jesus without embracing the Cross. Furthermore in order to become like Jesus and be transformed into a lover of the Cross, man vitiated by sin must subjugate all his wicked appetites of heart and sense. This cannot be effected without doing great violence to self by means of assiduous mortification. Hence the Divine Master Himself has said: "The Kingdom of Heaven," that is the sanctification of the soul, "suffereth violence," *Regnum coelorum vim patitur*. These words became the rule of Gemma's whole spiritual life. She realized the force of the above doctrine. It moved her to the heroic practice of all virtues, by the constant thought of Jesus Crucified, and hence her determination to overcome every obstacle to her self-mortification and likeness to Him. Let us treat first of her mortification.

Gemma wished to become like Jesus at any cost, having drunk in this ardent desire so to say, while in her mother's arms. It went on increasing until it absorbed all others and she no longer wished to know of anything else. Hence it was enough to look at her face, or movements, or hear her speak, in order to know that she lived in this one desire: to become like Jesus, to please Him alone. It was then to be expected that this child of grace would set herself to employ every means to the desired end, particularly that of self-mortification.

The first thing she gave evidence of in this undertaking was her uninterrupted diligence in bridling her senses. She never made a bad use of them, yet she seemed to wish to punish them as if she had been a most abandoned sinner recently converted. From her infancy she had become mistress of her eyes, and kept them habitually lowered, but without affectation. As she advanced in years and in virtue she became more firmly established in this practice, owing to a resolution she made, when one day in church she happened to look with curiosity, for a moment, at the dress of a little girl who sat next her. She was so angry with herself for this, which seemed to her a crime, that she resolved never more to turn her eyes to look willfully at anyone in this world. From that day forward those innocent eyes remained closed to exterior things and subject to her will. In order to make her use them a formal command was needed. She then obeyed but only for a few seconds and again modestly blushing lowered them. On this account whoever desired to observe the beauty of her soul that shone in her eyes, was obliged to do so while she was in ecstasy, as then she generally kept them raised to heaven.

As to her sense of taste, nothing could induce her to gratify it. No one was ever able to ascertain what meat or drink pleased her most, and in order to induce her to partake of what was on the family table it was necessary to press her, otherwise she would deprive herself of what was absolutely necessary. To hide her mortification she used a thousand artifices, feigning to take food while her hands moved but nothing entered her mouth. She went so far as to carry into effect the thought of making a small hole in her spoon, so that the broth might leak through before she brought it to her lips. We have seen that she found pretexts to rise frequently from table, now for one thing, now for another. When in the kitchen helping the servant she would never taste any of the viands, nor would she ever partake of sweets or fruits that were offered her out of meal time. And in order not to be wanting in courtesy by refusal, she managed gracefully and dexterously to get away.

Being a healthy girl she had a natural taste for food and a good appetite. This seemed to her a sort of derangement, and little short of sensuality. With a view to overcome it she would willingly on her part have abstained from taking any nourishment, but this was not allowed her. She thought and rethought, and at last, all gladness at having found a means of remedying her difficulty she came to propose it to me. Note with what delicate skillfulness she did so.

> *"Father, for a long time Jesus seems to have inspired me to ask you a favor. Don't be vexed with me, for in any case I will do as you wish. There will certainly be no harm in granting my request, but you will have a thousand reasons to bring forward against it—that I am thin, that it is not necessary, etc. But these are valueless reasons—don't wonder at my way of putting it, it is Gemma who writes. Listen, will you be content with my asking Jesus the grace not to let me feel any satisfaction in taking food, as long as I live? Oh this favor is necessary, and I hope Jesus will tell you to grant it me. At all events I am content."*

As I did not answer this letter she repeated her request several times. And at last, more to see how such an extraordinary thing would end, than from any other motive, I gave my consent. Then the simple child went at once to speak to her Jesus, and at once her prayer was granted. From that day forward she lost all sensibility of palate, and never again felt any impression of taste in eating and drinking; neither more nor less than if she had eaten straw or drunk only water. Thus did this young girl mortify a sense that may be considered one of the most difficult to subdue.

The same may be said of the mortification of her other senses. She was never known to gratify herself with the perfume of a flower or other scents. As to her sense of speech, she seemed almost to have no tongue, so rigidly did she bridle it; and yet she continually reproached herself with having failed in words, and renewed with earnestness her resolution to curb the erring member. On one occasion she wept an entire day at Our Lord's feet, because, not having been able to put off some friends who came to see her, she spent a short time talking with them on innocent matters that seemed to her excessively worldly. "O God," she exclaimed, "and I have allowed myself to speak of such things! Oh! tongue, wicked tongue, from this day forward I shall know how to keep thee in bounds!" At another time humbling herself as she was accustomed to do, after her victories in the spiritual combat, she wrote thus:

> *"Yesterday I gained a good victory over my worldly tongue, but I had a hard struggle to keep from speaking! And then I more resolutely renewed my determination never to answer unless questioned. If you only knew what a storm there was between Aunt and me! But silence has overcome all. I have begun, I may tell you, to keep these my resolutions, but with such difficulty!"*

The fact was, she began to observe them when she was almost a baby, with only this difference, that then in order not to transgress with her tongue in any dispute, she got out of the way, and hid herself; but when more advanced in years and in virtue, she remained in modest silence allowing her adversary to cool down.

Of curiosity in Gemma it is needless to speak, inasmuch as, dead to herself, she cared for nothing in this world. It all wearied and weighed on her. Games, amusements, recreations she would not hear of; and not even in the days of her infancy did she care for them. One year in carnival time an attempt was made to take her with other children to some private theatricals. She was dismayed at it, and so influenced her spiritual father, convincing him with such strong arguments that, through compassion, he caused her to be left at home alone.

What was most admirable in this charming creature was the continual war she waged against her inner impulses. I have already called attention to her great vivacity and sensibility. She would in consequence be naturally inclined to impatience. But she never allowed herself to give way to it. On the contrary, the more violent her impulses, so much the more earnestly did she apply herself to curb them and bring them under control. "I will not give them peace," were her words, "until I find them dead within me." This contest was in her mind, and she was most watchful lest anyone might notice it; nevertheless those who lived with her knew quite well that she had to strive without ceasing in combating her impulses.

In order to succeed better she very early began to crucify her flesh by means of severe austerities. How many times has she not importuned her confessor to allow her to discipline herself, to wear a hair shirt, chains, and other instruments of penance! And she knew so well how to insinuate her wishes, that she often succeeded in obtaining his leave, which she looked on as a singular favor. More frequently however it happened that her instruments of penance were taken from her; and she made an offering to Our Lord of at least her will to use them. I was the last one who confiscated them. They consisted of a band armed with sixty very sharp iron points, a discipline likewise of iron, having five strikers, and a long knotted cord, with points and nails in the knots, to be used as a girdle. She did not on this account desist from her austerities, but in a hundred other ways sought means of compensating her losses. "This nature of mine," she used to say, "within and without, is always seeking its satisfactions, and always on the look out for a respite. Give me leave to do all I can to overcome self. The flesh would like to command, and instead I wish to make it serve as it ought, now and for ever." And again: "I want, father, to have a certain leave from you, and I am certain that if Jesus inspires you a wee bit, you will grant it me at once. It would be to promise Jesus not to seek solace henceforward in anything; and rest assured, father, that if this request be granted me, I shall know how to regulate myself so as not to fall into excesses. Think it over." Once, when speaking heart to heart with her God she was heard to say with filial simplicity: "Look Jesus, it is my body that rebels, but I shall know well how to manage it. It often cries out, and would fain not obey me, but I'll see to that. Yesterday it seemed as if it would revolt, and I made it keep quiet by dint of hard blows." As I knew too well to what extent she would have gone, I took care not to yield to her repeated pressing requests. Besides, I was well-aware of the immense internal and external sufferings to which God Himself subjected her. These alone were enough to make her a real martyr and we shall consider them in the next chapter.

Let us pause a little to consider the striking effects that such assiduous mortification produced in Gemma's soul. The first was a complete dominion over all her affections and all her senses. She commanded them as their mistress, and they all were obliged to obey. Hence that most sweet peace that she enjoyed, which according to the Holy Spirit, is the fruit of victory—*In Victoria pax.* Hence also that spontaneousness, with which her innocent body lent itself to all the movements of her soul, and to its sublimest flights. One would have said that those members were only there in order to serve her soul; for they were as ready to leave her free to pray when in church as to go in ecstasy when she sat at table or when walking in the public streets, or when having a bath. In all places as well as at all times she was able to dispose of every one of her senses. If she wished to commune with heaven, in an instant her imagination was silenced and ceased its wanderings; her memory became powerless to remember any created thing as food for thought or expression; the importunate movements of her heart stopped still; and even her physical pains were no longer a trouble or distraction. But no sooner did she return from those celestial interviews than all her senses, as if they had been dutifully waiting outside, returned, each one to its proper office, as fresh and active as before.

This was of almost daily occurrence, except during periods of trial and spiritual dryness; for then, God, in order to refine more and more the virtue of His servant, permitted that the full dominion of her soul over its lower powers should remain at least in part suspended in order that she might feel the struggle. At no other time did her senses offer Gemma, now an adult in virtue, any opposition, any repugnance, any weariness.

As the result of such an enviable serenity there reigned in the heart of this happy child a joy of paradise that could only be ruffled by the fear of offending her Lord and the thought of His inscrutable judgments. Outside these limits nothing caused her disquietude. And this was quite evident in her exterior, always so bright and affable, and in her perpetual smile, that so strangely contrasted with the dignity of her countenance and the gravity of her bearing.

Another fruit of Gemma's untiring self-denial not less precious than the preceding, was her purity of heart, than which nothing more perfect could be desired. The reason of this is clear. Sin, which contaminates the soul, is the effect of the three great concupiscences that reign in man, pride, sensuality, and love of earthly goods. Now Gemma from her very infancy had not only checked in her heart, but absolutely destroyed these incentives of evil. We must then conclude that sin, not having the means of approaching her, left her soul free from every stain of fault. Even after she had reached the heights of perfection she did not stop there. She knew too well how full of contagion the air is that we breathe, and how corrupt the world in which we live. Hence she was always afraid of herself, and not content with what she had already done in bridling the disorderly appetites of nature, she wished to continue without ceasing the work of her perfection, as though those appetites were still rebellious within her.

In this meritorious exercise she gave the first place to the avoidance of dangerous occasions. Clear-sighted though she was and of accurate judgment, notwithstanding her child-like simplicity, she could always discern the danger of such occasions at any distance. "Here," she used to say, "Jesus is not to be found; then Gemma, let us fly." Without thinking evil of anyone she feared all company; and knowing that she had nothing to share with others, she kept aloof. For the same reason she desired to remain alone, and if it had not been necessary to go out to church, and sometimes to the city on business, she would never have left the house. The same may be said of talking, mixing in the affairs of others, making friends, writing letters, and such-like. She used to say: "Gemma, don't trust yourself; remember that every occasion may be dangerous to you; outside Jesus all is deceit; keep with Him alone and go on without attending to anything else."

Yet the most beautiful fruit that our heroic maiden gathered from the tree of the Cross and from the mortification of Jesus, was chastity. Adorable virtue, how rare thou art in this depraved world! And yet thou shouldst be the dowry of every Christian soul, whose vocation according to the words of the Apostle is to be holy and immaculate. Jesus loves this virtue infinitely and declares the souls that possess it to be His chosen spouses, reserving for them also the sweetest tenderness of His Sacred Heart. Our Angelic Gemma learned all this while yet a child from her saintly Mother, and as from those first moments she began to love her Jesus, so also thenceforth she became smitten by the lustre of this priceless jewel and strove with all her energy to keep it untarnished in her soul. Among the practices to this end suggested by her solicitous mother, one was to recite devoutly every evening, with her hands under her knees, three Hail Marys to the Queen of Heaven in honor of her Immaculate Conception. The innocent child though knowing so little at that early age, took keenly to this devotion, and never omitted it. Rising from this prayer and joining her little hands she added these words: "Mother, never allow me to lose holy purity. Place me under your mantle, guard this treasure for me, and I shall become more pleasing to Jesus." A few days before her death, finding herself alone, although she had lost all strength and could not stand, she rose, and taken by surprise, was found with her hands beneath her knees, in the fulfillment of this devout practice.

As she advanced in years, her love of this angelic virtue and her desire to preserve it without spot grew with her. This was a special object of her mortifications, penances, and the custody of her senses.

It seemed to her that every liberty however innocent and insignificant, might discolor this beautiful flower, and to avoid this she took every precaution. She never went near a mirror, not even to do her hair or wipe away the stains of blood that flowed from her forehead, when crowned with mystic thorns, or from her eyes during her dolorous contemplation. And when during impulses of divine love, her heart took fire and burned the corresponding exterior part, and when by a dart of fire from the side of Jesus Crucified she felt a large wound open in her side; and when her heart itself by its mysterious throbbings greatly distorted three of her ribs, although ignoring at first what such phenomena meant she refrained from looking at or touching herself, and never did so on the frequent renewal of these wonders.

We have seen already that from her earliest childhood she shrank from being touched by others, and from the most innocent caresses. Not even was her father to kiss her. When she lay on her death-bed and of her own accord asked for Extreme Unction, great was her consternation at the thought of having to get her feet washed by other hands. What was to be done? Her love of holy modesty gave her strength, and seizing on the first moment that she found herself alone, she put out her hand, took the basin, water and towel, and did all for herself; then full of joy, to those who came to do her the needful service she was able to say: "Thanks; I don't need help; I have done all by myself."

She was quite as scrupulous with regard to her words. Not only was she never heard to use words of double meaning, but not even less delicate though harmless expressions that are used without scruple by good people, specially in Tuscany, where everything is called by its proper name. If obliged to make herself understood on delicate subjects, she resorted to paraphrase, but with such good taste, that no one could have taken it for affectation, but rather as her own peculiar style. All this exquisite delicacy in Gemma's ways must appear the more singular as she never mixed with the world, and knew little or nothing of its hateful looseness. She however feared exceedingly, and moved with the greatest caution. "I know nothing whatever," thus she confessed to me, "about many things. But what, if perchance I have been wanting? It appears to me that I have not." And then she concluded: "No I would not willfully commit sin; and now, once for all, I would rather die than be guilty of the least sin, I would rather become blind for ever than offend Jesus in the least against holy modesty; so I would rather be deprived of all my senses than that, in the least way, they should be to me an occasion of sin."

I don't know how far I am to trust a pious soul of my acquaintance to whom Our Lord, in a distinct locution, is said to have made the following splendid eulogy of Gemma: "This child, whom I love so much, and by whom I am so much loved, is always asking Me for love and purity, and I Who am Love itself and Purity itself, have lavished on her as much of these treasures as a human creature is capable of possessing. I have always guarded the purity of this child's heart as the heart of one chosen by the Divine Spouse Himself, and I have preserved her as a spotless lily of paradise in My pure love."

The angelic purity of Gemma's soul was reflected in her body, which in many ways presented quite unusual qualities. You would have said it was formed of some crystalline material. Although neglected by her, it was resplendent in its exquisite regularity. And not even during the trying maladies that confined her to bed for such a long time did her body ever emit the least unpleasant exhalation. Some marvelled at hearing of this, and to satisfy themselves proved it by remaining near her night and day. More than that, on several occasions those near her remarked how her person and what she touched exhaled a delicious fragrance, that certainly was not of the earth, for as we have already said, Gemma never used unguents or perfumes, or even soap for washing except when necessary. Moreover that grateful fragrance seemed to be supernatural, because it came quite unexpectedly, and moved all to devotion. "Don't you perceive a fragrance?" said the bystanders one to another. "Our dear Gemma!

Assuredly Jesus, or the heavenly Mother, or her Angel Guardian is here with her." At all events such a fact is not new in Christian Hagiology; nay, it is told of many saints, and in particular of Our Founder, St. Paul of the Cross, and of St. Mary Magdalene of Pazzi whose body even now, three hundred years since her death, diffuses a delicious perfume.

A gift of such rare purity could not fail to be an object of hatred to the evil spirit, who certainly must have raged with fury against this Angelic Virgin so favored by God. An assault on so much virtue was a difficult undertaking even for hell. How was this simple dove to be assailed? She so to speak did not even know the name of vice. How then could this foul spirit insinuate his gross suggestions into a heart so pure and full of delicate sentiment? The wicked enemy himself foresaw from the start that he would have striven in vain, knowing for certain that God would not have given him power over her. Hence he employed all his guilty machinations in tormenting her externally. He represented lurid objects to her imagination, and appeared to her himself, uttering vile words, and sometimes even coming to open violence.

Although the saintly child knew not what he meant by his wicked expressions, nevertheless through an instinctive sense of delicacy that penetrated her whole being, she felt that it was wrong. Accordingly from the very outset she armed herself against her enemy and gave him determined resistance. And he, although he found on trial the uselessness of his attempts, renewed his attacks merely to frighten and torment his innocent victim. Indeed it is impossible to express what a cruel torture it was for this angelic girl to see and hear such abominable things. Let her give us an idea of it herself in words spoken in tears at the feet of her spiritual father: "O father, what terrible temptations these are! all temptations are painful, but these against the holy virtue, how they torment me! What I undergo is known only to Jesus, Who secretly guards me, and (note the sense of this expression) is pleased with me." In order to avoid seeing those representations, the poor child, not knowing what else to do, used to shut her eyes and keep them so until the angel of impurity had gone. She also seized her crucifix, called for aid to her dear angel guardian, to her patron saints, and above all to her Heavenly Mother. By these means, after long hours of fighting, being left free, she returned immediately to her soul's peace, and full of joy exclaimed: "Let us thank Jesus, that today also things have passed in the way most pleasing to Him."

But Gemma was not satisfied with this. Having learned that the saints in order to repress similar temptations, had resort to scourges, hair shirts, plunging into frozen water, etc., and not knowing the distinction between internal temptation—the result of sense—and objective temptations as with her, and believing that she ought to imitate those servants of God, she made up her mind to do so. And so earnestly did she set about it, that if obedience had not interposed, she would have cut her innocent body into bits. But, for all that, so great at times was her fear of being led in those horrible moments to offend against the Angelic virtue, that she lost sight of all else, even of the necessity to ask her confessor's leave to do extra penance. Then without let or hindrance she had recourse to the lash and the hair shirt, and the knotted cord and sharp points, with which she tightly girt herself; and very often the pain of those sharp points penetrating her flesh caused her to faint!

But she went even further. One day on rising from the table the demon appeared to her in his wonted attitude of livid insolence, and snorting with rage threatened to overcome her at any cost. Gemma turned pale, raised her eyes and hands to heaven, and without hesitation ran straight to a deep tank in the garden. It was winter and the water was frozen. There and then, making the sign of the cross she threw herself in, and for a certainty would have been drowned had not some invisible hand come to her assistance and drawn her shivering from the water. So in this particular also she emulated the heroism of the athletes of Christian Hagiology in the arena of penance.

Now in the face of such examples ought not we all to blush; we who, professing to follow Jesus Christ in the ways of sanctity, show ourselves so tender towards our bodies, and so adverse to curbing their unruly appetites? Has not our Divine Savior said: *Regnum coelorum vim patitur et violenti rapiunt illud:* "The Kingdom of Heaven suffereth violence, and the violent bear it away?"

CHAPTER 18

Of The Great Trials To Which God Subjected His Servant And Of Her Heroic Patience.

EVERY follower of Christ has, so to say, to impose on himself, during the whole of his life, the cross of mortification and self-restraint. God also assigns another Cross to His elect—that of direct suffering. It is of this Our Divine Master more particularly spoke when He said: "If any man will come after Me, let him deny himself, and take up his cross." The saints by voluntary suffering, self-denial and penance do their part in the work of their sanctification. God, through the suffering which His grace enables them cheerfully to accept, accomplishes this work. And the more perfect He wills the work to be, the more abundantly does He supply opportunities of suffering. This is the philosophy of the Gospel: *Per multas tribulationes oportet nos intrare in regnum Dei:* Whoever wishes to see the Kingdom of God established in his soul must be prepared to pass through many tribulations, for there cannot be true sanctity without this test. Nay, every new degree of sanctity must have its corresponding trial, called by mystic doctors the *Passive Purification*, until at length the great work is finished, and the soul, arrived at the last degree, that of union with Jesus Christ, is able to say: "With Christ I am nailed to the Cross, and I live, now not I, but Christ liveth in me." Hence as Gemma had been destined by God to great sanctity, and to pass through all the degrees indicated in mystical theology, it was to be expected that the bitters of the Cross would be given her not in draughts, but in torrents.

From what has been written so far, it is easy to understand why Gemma was tried by the fiercest and most exceptional pains from her very infancy. I do not intend to return to what has already been said, but only to describe accurately the martyrdom of the latter part of her life, when her virtue had reached the climax of perfection. Those first sufferings were but trials in which grace advanced step by step preparing her for the grand immolation that was to be accomplished on the Calvary of Jesus—her death bed.

Since the immolation could not be meritorious, nor in conformity with the scope of Divine Providence unless it was voluntary, our Lord began kindling in Gemma's heart an ardent desire of suffering. For this purpose He used many persuasions, each one more tender and efficacious than the others. Once He appeared to her with the Cross on His shoulders and said: "Gemma, wilt thou have it, My Cross? See, this is the present I have prepared for thee." And she, "My Jesus, yes, give it me, but give me also strength, because my shoulders are weak; at least that I may not fall under it." And Jesus again: "Would it sadden thee were I to give thee to drink of My chalice even to the last drop?" And Gemma: "Jesus, may Thy most Holy Will be done." At another time He appeared to her nailed to the Cross all covered with wounds and bleeding. "At that sight," she said to me, "I felt such great grief, that thinking of the infinite love of Jesus for us, and of the sufferings He had endured for our salvation, I fainted and fell. After the lapse of an hour or so I came to myself, and then there arose in my heart an immense desire to suffer something for Him Who had suffered so much for me."

As time advanced this desire increased, till it became a real passion, and, unable to contain it within her heart, she used to exclaim: "I wish to suffer with Jesus. Don't let me hear of anything else, I want to be like Him, suffering always as long as I live, and living in order to suffer always." When in ecstasy these ardent expressions came repeatedly to her lips. I could quote innumerable instances. Hers were the feelings of all the saints when contemplating the Divine Man of Sorrows. "No," they cried out with St. Bernard, "it is not just that, under a Head crowned with thorns, His members should give themselves up to delicate living. If He suffers, let them also suffer. It must not be otherwise. It must be so, aught else would be a monstrous ingratitude."

On one occasion, in order to set ablaze the fire that always kept alight in this holy virgin's heart, her angel guardian appeared to her with two crowns in his hands—one of thorns, the other of purest lilies, and told her to choose which of the two she pleased. "I will have that of Jesus," she said immediately, "give me that of Jesus, the only one I care for." The Angel handed her the crown of thorns and kept the other. She then seizing it with ardent desires covered it with kisses, and clasping it lovingly to her heart, exclaimed: "Thanks be to Thee O God for ever! Thanks be to Jesus for His gifts, for His Cross!" Such was the fruit gathered from the Divine teaching by this child.

Greater depths had yet to be sounded. The Divine Spouse had yet to give the last masterly touch to bring His work to perfection. This He did by revealing to His servant the true secret of the mystery of suffering. And this secret is, that the mission of our Savior in this world, having been a mission of expiation, whoever is with Him must by expiation continue and, as it were, complete it, according to the words of St. Paul: *Adimpleo ea quae desunt passionum Christi.* The majority of mankind, instead of appeasing the anger of God by works of penance, provoke it still more by fresh sins, thus rendering His Redemption useless to themselves. It therefore falls to the lot of the just to offer satisfaction for those poor sinners, and thus console the Heart of God according to what is written: "In His servants the Lord will be consoled." Now as He willed to instill this great truth into Gemma's heart, He thus one day spoke to her in intimate distinct locution: "My child, I have need of victims, and strong victims. In order to appease the just wrath of My Divine Father, I need souls who, by their sufferings, tribulations and difficulties, make amends for sinners and for their ingratitude. Oh! that I could make all understand how incensed My Heavenly Father is by the impious world! There is nothing to stay His Hand, and He is now preparing a great chastisement for all the world." Aided by the Divine light that accompanied these words, God's holy servant understood their full meaning, nor was there need of more to set a furnace of zealous love ablaze in her soul. Beside herself with joy she went about exclaiming and repeating: "I am the victim, and Jesus the sacrificing Priest. Act quickly O Jesus! All that Jesus wills, I desire. Everything that Jesus sends me is a gift." Then prostrate on her face she made the following prayer, and afterwards put it in writing for my approval:

> *"Behold me at Thy most Sacred Feet, dear Jesus, to pour forth my acknowledgment and gratitude for the repeated favors Thou has granted me. I thank Thee; but I want yet another grace, O my God, if pleasing to Thee. Wait, Jesus wait. I am Thy victim, but wait. My life is in Thy hands, but wait. Thou canst use me as Thou wilt, but wait if it please Thee. May Thy Holy Will be done in all things!"*

What did she mean here by the delay she asked of Our Lord with such earnestness? I have alluded to it already when speaking of the fear this humble maiden had for everything extraordinary being noticed in her by others. Now the words that Our Lord spoke to her seemed to specially include the external sufferings that could not be concealed. Therefore it was that trembling she besought Him to defer to another time when it might please Him to enclose her in a convent, all that concerned the exterior aspect of the expiation announced to her.

From that day forward Gemma did not seem herself. The thought of the mission entrusted to her by God had as it were transformed her into another creature. The thirst to suffer torments of every kind seemed to consume and rend her whole being. To satisfy her, torrents of fire would be needed. Listen to her exclamation: "To suffer, but without any consolation, without any comfort; to suffer for love alone." And, in truth, for her to love and to suffer was one and the same thing, as it was one and the same thing to be loved and to be pained. Hence she added: "I am quite happy. Jesus does not cease to love me. I mean that He does not cease to afflict me more than usual." It was indeed Our Lord Himself Who had taught her this sublime doctrine. For when she asked Him for the grace to love Him more ardently, His answer was: "If truly thou dost wish to love Me, behold here is My Chalice. Canst thou drain to the last drop this Cup to which I have already put My lips?" And Gemma: "Dear Lord, my lips are ready as my heart is ready. Satiate me with Thy Chalice, and inebriate me with Thy bitter draught."

What more? Even the ineffable consolations with which she often found herself favored in prayer had become in a certain sense distasteful as compared with the longed-for bitternesses and Chalice of Jesus. Hence she was able to say to me: "Believe me, Father, I willingly renounce all the consolations of Jesus, I don't want them. Jesus is the Man of Sorrows, and I wish to be the Child of Dolours." Let not the reader imagine that these and like expressions were the effect of momentary passing fervor, such as may happen to any devout soul in the glow of meditation, which soon growing cold, finds what at first seemed easy and desirable to have become on experience hard and insupportable. This is but a proof that to man created by God in happiness, pain is not natural.

The more Gemma's trials and pains were multiplied the more she longed for their increase. If she prayed or meditated, if things went well with her or the reverse, she always and in everything found motives inciting her to suffer. And what she went through not being enough, she earnestly besought our Lord to redouble her pains and multiply their forms. In a word, as she put it, to satiate her. "On Saturday evening," she writes to me, "I went to make a visit to the Most Holy Crucifix. There came upon me an ardent longing for suffering, and with all my heart I implored of Jesus to satisfy me. And, since that evening, He has granted me a ceaseless pain in my head, but such a violent pain! And I am almost always crying through fear of not being able to bear it." You see, reader, she feels that she may not be able to hold out, and yet she does not desist, but continues to pray that her great longing to suffer more and more may be gratified. Nay, she declares that in suffering she finds all her delight. "Yes," she says, "I am happy in every way that Jesus wills, and if Jesus wants the sacrifice of my life, I give it to Him at once. If He wants anything else I am ready. One thing alone is enough for me, to be His victim, in order to atone for my own innumerable sins, and, if possible, for those of the whole world."

It seemed to her once that she beheld Blessed Gabriel of the Dolours, who drew near to comfort her, while she was suffering excruciating pains that had lasted some time. He offered to assuage them, but she said to him: "No, I beg of you, do not take them from me. O! leave them to me at least a little longer, for if you do not I shall have nothing to offer Jesus when evening comes." It seemed to her a positive loss to have passed even one day without particular sufferings. "Some days I have passed," she complained to me, "and at night I had nothing to give Jesus. Oh! how it grieved me!" From Thursday evening to that of Friday each week, as we know, this heroic child went over all Calvary in body and soul, suffering unspeakable agony in company with Jesus Crucified. Whoever could have passed but once through such torments would shudder at the thought of them. Gemma, who again and again passed over that way of sorrow and pain, longed for the day, counted the hours she had to wait until it came, and, in the words of those who were around her, "prepared to suffer as if she were preparing for a banquet."

Our Lord took infinite delight in such great generosity and heroism, and by open proofs of tenderness, showed His complacency at having chosen a spouse so entirely according to His Heart. Thus, on one of many occasions, making His presence felt in her soul, He asked her if she had suffered much in a long trial that she was still undergoing. Gemma's answer: "With Thee, O Jesus, one suffers so well! What is it to suffer thus for many days, if then Thou comest quickly and consolest?" And Jesus: "Know that when thou wast suffering, I was always at thy side. I beheld thy distress and was gratified by it." Then to reward her for the courage she had displayed in the conflict, He told her she might draw nigh and kiss His Sacred Wounds. And she, all humility: "But O Jesus, why for so little, a reward so great?" Then emboldened by her filial confidence she approached her Savior, and kneeling, with her heart all on fire, she kissed one by one those precious Wounds. But when she came to the Wound in His Side she could hold out no longer, and fell in a swoon at the Feet of her Jesus.

Beyond all doubt this victim, after such lengthened and heroic proofs, was more than fit for the sacrifice. Jesus had so disposed her that she was capable of taking into her soul an ocean of bitterness and sorrow. Now the time had come to complete the work. Among the means leading to the consummation of this sacrifice—the martyrdom of the heart—are those of so-called aridities. This trial is one of the most frequent in the ways of mystical perfection. After having for a time drawn the soul by spiritual sweetness God begins to wean and detach her by degrees, hiding His face and withdrawing all sense of His presence. He then leaves her alone, abandoned as it were in an abyss of darkness and uncertainty of fears and heart-rendings, so that she comes to feel all but lost. In order to understand how terrible this ordeal becomes to the saints, it would be necessary to appreciate as they did the goodness of this God Whom they seem to have lost, and to love Him as they did. But who will give us to rightly understand these two things? Who will tell us how sweet to our Gemma was that Jesus for Whom alone she lived? And how ravishing that flood of consolations that she drank in so often at His feet from her earliest years? And how dear that hope of being happy with Him for eternity? Ordinary souls feel certain privations very little, or not at all, because distracted by many cares and not finding consolation in heavenly things, they turn to seek it in those of the earth—they try to find it in sense. But Gemma, who was dead to all created things, who wished for nothing, loved nothing, held all as nothing, except Jesus, how could she possibly live without Him?

Listen to her longings: "I seek Jesus and cannot find Him. It seems as if He is tired of me, and does not want to know anything more of me; and I, where shall I go? And what is to become of me? Poor Jesus, what have I done to Thee! But Thou wilt let me find Thee again, wilt Thou not? Be pleased, oh be pleased and come back to me, because I cannot endure it; to be away from Thee, no, no!" During these periods of agonizing desolation her Angel Guardian often came to console her, and even her Heavenly Mother sometimes appeared to her. But Gemma seemed not to attend to them. She wanted Jesus Who was more precious—Who was her all. Hence like Magdalene at the Sepulcher, without wishing for comfort from anyone, she asked the Angel: "Where is Jesus?" And to the Holy Mother: "Tell me, Mother, Jesus, where is He gone?" And writing to her director: "Would not you at least be able to tell me what I can do to find Jesus? Tell Him that I cannot bear it longer." Exteriorly she strove to hide her feelings so that no one might become aware of her profound martyrdom. Yet she could not prevent those most familiar with her from noticing how pale and wane she had become. Occasionally also, coming unawares, they found her alone in her room kneeling with outstretched arms, her tearful eyes raised to Heaven, and heaving deep sighs. "My God," she would exclaim, "dost Thou not see that thus I cannot live? Without Thee I die. Remember that I am a poor orphan. I have none but Thee, and yet, wilt Thou depart from me?" If indeed this excruciating suffering had not been sometimes momentarily suspended, Gemma would have ceased to live. But the God of Compassion, when her struggle was at its fiercest, hastened to her assistance. Then, with words of divine efficacy, this tender-hearted Father consoled her and encouraged her to persevere in the way of the Cross. A few examples of these divine words as told me by the child herself will be acceptable to my readers. They are words of Divine Wisdom that cannot fail to be of great help to many.

"My child," said Jesus to her, "thou complainest because I will to keep thee in the dark; but remember that after darkness comes light, and then thou shalt have light indeed. I put thee to this test for My greater glory, to give joy to the angels, for thy greater gain, and also for example to others.

If thou dost really love Me, thou oughtest to love Me even in the midst of darkness. I delight in and play with souls. I thus play through love. Be not afflicted if I begin to abandon thee. Do not think it chastisement. It is truly My own Will in order to detach thee from creatures and unite thee to Myself. Though it seems to thee that I repel thee, know that instead I draw thee more closely to Myself. When I appear to be far away then I am near at hand. Take courage, for after the battle comes peace. Fidelity and love must be thy necessary weapons. For the present therefore be patient if I leave thee alone. Suffer, be resigned and be consoled.

I am leading thee by rough and sorrowful ways, and thou shouldst consider thyself honored when I treat thee thus and when by a daily and hidden martyrdom I allow thy soul to be tried and purified. Think only for the present of how thou art to practice great virtue. Make haste in the ways of divine love, humble thyself, and rest assured that if I keep thee on the Cross I love thee.

Be not like some, who being attached to consolations and spiritual satisfactions care but little for the Cross. Finding themselves in desolation of spirit, they shorten by degrees the time of prayer because they no longer find in it the consolations they had before experienced."

It is certain that Gemma was not of this number. She had had so many and such charming lessons from her Divine Master, that far from drawing back because of those painful privations, they gave her fresh impulse. And in proportion as she felt herself uncared for, and apparently rejected by God, so much the more earnestly she strove to become pleasing in His sight. She went with greater ardor to the Tabernacle, to the Holy Table, and to the exercise of at least vocal prayer, when she found meditation impossible. Although in her rapid advance she saw not where she put her foot because of the intense darkness in which her soul was rapt, she nevertheless pushed forward, in order, as she used to put it, "to go find Jesus in the *de profundis*." She suffered but did not complain, and with the same alacrity as when full of consolation, she applied herself to all her temporal duties.

Now, let the wise ones of the world look and see if their false maxims, or any force of nature, is able to generate magnanimity such as this.

CHAPTER 19
Attacks By The Devil.

GOD, in order to purify His elect and render them victims of expiation, makes use even of the devils, who because of their hatred of souls and large intelligence become more efficacious instruments than others to the attainment of His ends. The sacred writings assure us of this, and Christian hagiography enables us to prove its existence in the Church of God. Thus Our Lord, when He made known to our holy founder St. Paul of the Cross, that He willed to raise him to an exalted degree of sanctity spoke thus: "I will have thee to be trampled under foot by devils." And in like manner, He said to His servant Gemma: "Be prepared My child, the devil, at My bidding, shall be the one who, by the war he will wage against thee, will give the last touch to the work that I will accomplish in thee." I wish to point out here that this war was general, in that it was waged against all the virtues and holy operations by which this child of grace studied to advance in perfection. They were all hateful to Satan, and he attacked them all with unmitigated rage. One would have said that it appeared to be almost his only aim, to torment this servant of God, by continually inventing new methods of assailing her.

Gemma had early learned that the best way to securely reach God's ends is prayer. So with all the ardor of her soul she practiced it, and derived the most marked advantages from it. What then did not the enemy do to prevent it? He upset her temperament in order to excite within her, at least weariness and disinclination, for he found it impossible to make her lose sight of God. He caused her violent headaches so that she might be obliged to go to bed rather than remain in prayer, and strove otherwise to turn her from the holy exercise. "Oh!" she said to me, "what torment this gives me, not to be able to pray! What fatigue it costs me! How many efforts does not that wretch make to render it impossible for me to pray! Yesterday evening he tried to kill me, and would have succeeded if Jesus had not come quickly to my aid. I was terrified and kept the image of Jesus in my mind, but I could not pronounce His name." At other times he attacked her differently. "What art thou doing?" he said blaspheming, "stupid that thou art to think of praying to a malefactor. Look at the harm He does thee, keeping thee nailed to the Cross with Himself. How then canst thou care for Him, for Him Whom thou dost not even know, Who makes all who love Him suffer?" But these and other equally iniquitous suggestions were as dust before the wind, and only served to afflict her at hearing her Jesus outraged by such blasphemies.

In the midst of so much suffering the servant of God found some comfort in letting her spiritual father know what she was undergoing and how she was acting, so as to have his direction and advice. Even this the wicked enemy could not bear, and in order to turn her away from her spiritual guide, he tried to circumvent her in a thousand ways. He depicted her director in such vivid colors to her imagination, as an ignorant, fanatical, deluded man, and with so many arguments stove to convince and terrify her, that the poor child thought herself all but lost. Hence on one of these occasions she wrote:

> *"For some days Chiappino (a name she called the devil) has pursued me in every guise and way, and has done all in his power against me. This monster keeps on redoubling all his efforts to ruin me and tries to deprive me of whoever directs and advises me. But even should this happen"* (notice here her virtue of detachment) *"I am not afraid."*

That was not enough to make the enemy desist. Seeing that with all his arts he could not succeed in shaking her confidence in her director, he resorted to acts of violence, and assaulting her while she persevered in writing, he snatched the pen from her hand, tore up the paper and dragged her from the table, seizing her by the hair with such violence that it came away in his brutal claws. Then withdrawing he shouted in his fury, "War, war, against thy father, war as long as he lives!" And the fiend has known right well how to keep his word. "Believe me, father," she said, "to hear this despicable wretch one would say that his fury was against you more than against me." He carried his audacity so far as to feign to be the priest to whom Gemma used to make her confession. She had gone one day to the Church and while preparing herself before the confessional, she saw that the confessor was already in his place awaiting her, at which she wondered, not having seen him pass. At the same time she felt very much disturbed in spirit as generally happened when in the presence of the evil one. She entered the confessional however and began as usual. The voice and ways were indeed those of the confessor, but his talk was foul and scandalous, accompanied by improper gestures. "My God," she exclaimed, "what has happened?" At such a sight and such words the angelic child trembled from head to foot, remaining aghast. Then her presence of mind returning she hurriedly left the confessional and saw as she did so that the pretended confessor had disappeared. It was the devil who by his coarse and fiendish ways had sought to deceive her, or else make her lose all confidence in the minister of God. Once however he counterfeited the priest so successfully that, God permitting it, he was able to make the poor child believe that he was really her confessor. Fortunately I happened at the time to be passing through Lucca, and hearing of the case, I was able, but not without great difficulty, to undeceive her. I was obliged to interpose a formal precept in order to make her regain the peace she had lost and her esteem for the holy priest who was in reality her confessor.

Failing in this attempt the enemy made another. He appeared to the servant of God in the form of an angel, resplendent with light, insinuating himself with most subtle cunning so as to throw her off her guard. Then, as with Eve in the Garden of Eden, he depicted things in falsest colors. "Look here," he said, "I can make thee happy if only thou wilt swear to obey me." Gemma, who this time did not feel in her soul the usual disturbance indicating the presence of the demon, stood listening with her wonted simplicity. But God came to her aid. On the first wicked proposal of the miscreant her eyes were opened. She started up, exclaiming: "My God! Mary Immaculate! make me die rather!" And with these words she rushed at the feigned angel and spat in his face. At the same moment she saw him vanish in the form of fire.

Gemma relating to her director what had happened on another occasion wrote as follows:

> "*A fresh assault; listen, father: Yesterday after confession, on my return to the house and as soon as I had a moment to myself, for it was the time of my prayer, I knelt down and began to recite the Rosary of the Five Wounds of Jesus. At the fourth Wound I beheld before me a figure like Jesus, freshly scourged all over, with his heart laid open and bleeding. He began by saying: 'Is it thus my child that thou repayest me? Look at me. See how much I have suffered for thee. And now instead thou canst not give me the consolation of those penances' (those that had only recently been forbidden her). 'Ah! they were not much. Thou canst very well continue them as before.' No, no, I replied, I wish to obey, and if I do what thou desirest, I disobey. And he: 'But after all, it is not thy confessor who has forbidden it– it is that...' (and he meant me, as in reality I had disapproved of those excessive austerities), 'and thou art not in the least obliged to obey him. Do as I tell thee,' and many other things. At last I was on the point of taking the discipline, as before the prohibition, but no, Jesus helped me. I rose, took holy water, and became calm, not however without receiving a blow or two— not an infrequent gift of Satan. And you know, father, it was he without doubt.*"

With a view to protect her from these satanic apparitions, I enjoined on her, under whatever form persons of the other world might appear to her, to begin at once to repeat the words *Viva Gesù!* I was unaware that Our Lord Himself had given her a similar remedy in the words: "Blessed be Jesus and Mary!" And the docile child in order to obey both, used to repeat the double exclamation. The good spirits always repeated her words, *Viva Gesù!* Blessed be Jesus and Mary! Whereas the malignant ones either did not reply, or else pronounced only a few words, such as *"Viva,* Blessed," without adding any name. By this means Gemma recognized them, and scorned them accordingly.

In order to move her to vanity, Satan sometimes caused her to see in sleep or awake a crowd of spirits clad in white who placed themselves around her bed to offer her homage. At other times he showed her that letters to her spiritual guides were religiously preserved for some important end. Other representations were tried with similar aim. But all in vain. Gemma was not so easily to be seduced by vainglory, being solidly grounded in humility, as has already been shown.

This spirit of darkness also made an attempt to shake her immense confidence in God. He strove accordingly during her periods of desolation and abandonment to renew in her mind the fear that she would be lost. "And dost thou not see," he said to her, "that Jesus does not hear thee, and does not want to know anything more of thee? Why weary thyself running after Him? Give it up, and resign thyself to thy unhappy lot." This was the most terrible temptation that agonized many of the greatest saints of the Church. Gemma too felt all its force. But yet, she overcame it, either through the constant habit she had acquired of turning to God with lively faith in every spiritual trial, or because of the special assistance given her by God Himself. Thus she was able to say to me on one occasion: "The devil, contemptible wretch that he is, tries his best…But Jesus, by His words gives me such tranquillity that, with all his efforts, he has not been able to shake my confidence, not even for one moment."

Satan finding all his machinations set at naught by this child, became furious. Throwing off the mask, he took to waging open war against her. He appeared to her repeatedly in horrible forms. At one time as a savage dog, at another as a hideous monster, again as a man in a fury. He used to begin by terrifying her with his horrible and threatening appearance. Then he rushed on her, beat her, tore her with his teeth, threw her down, dragged her by the hair, and in other innumerable ways tortured her innocent body. No one can attribute these things to mere hallucinations, for their effects were but too real—her hair scattered about the room, the bruises and livid marks that remained for days, the excessive pains she felt in all her members, etc. So also were but too real the noises that were heard of blows and of the shaking of her bed, lifted and then thrown down, as remained to be seen. Nor were these assaults and annoyances things of a few moments. They lasted for hours together without cessation, and even during the whole night. Let her give some particulars of them herself. The simplicity of style, and the sincerity with which this candid soul was accustomed to explain things to her spiritual father, will of themselves serve as a commentary on what she says:

> *"Today I thought I was to be entirely free from that nauseous animal, and instead he has knocked me about greatly. I had gone to bed with a full intention of sleeping, but it turned out otherwise. He began with certain blows that made me fear I should die. He was in the shape of a big black dog and put his paws on my shoulders hurting me greatly. I felt it so much in all my bones that sometimes I thought they were broken. Also, when I was taking holy water he wrenched my arm so violently that I fell from the pain. The bone was dislocated, but went back, because Jesus touched it for me and all was remedied."*

And in another letter she writes:

> *"Yesterday, too, the devil knocked me about. Aunt told me to draw a bucket of water with which I was to fill the room jugs.*

When passing with jugs in my hands before the image of the Heart of Jesus, to Whom I offered fervent acts of love, I got such a strong blow of a stick on my left shoulder that I fell, but nothing was broken. Even today I feel very unwell and everything I do seems to give me pain."

Again she writes:

"Once more I have passed a bad night. The demon came before me as a giant of great height. He beat me fiercely all night, and kept saying to me: 'For thee there is no more hope of salvation. Thou art in my hands.' I replied that God is merciful, and that therefore I feared nothing. Then giving me a hard blow on the head he said in a rage, 'Accursed be thou!' and disappeared. I went to my room to rest a little and there I found him. He began again to strike me with a knotted rope, and kept on because he wanted me to listen to him while he suggested wickedness. I said no, and he struck harder, and knocked my head violently against the ground. At a certain moment it came to my mind to invoke Jesus's Holy Papa" (thus she used to name the Eternal Father), "I called aloud: Eternal Father through the most Precious Blood free me! I don't quite know what happened. That contemptible beast dragged me violently from my bed and threw me, dashing my head against the floor with such force that it pains me still. I became senseless and remained lying there until I came to myself a long time afterwards. Jesus be thanked!"

It would take too long to recount all these painful scenes. They happened very often and sometimes continued for days. The poor victim had become in a certain sense inured to them, and, beyond the bodily sufferings they caused her, she ceased to be alarmed at them. She regarded the hellish monster with a serenity like that of a dove looking at any unclean animal. Until I forbade it, she used occasionally to answer him contemptuously. When finally overcome by the invocation of the Holy Name of Jesus he was forced to leave, shuffling precipitately away, the simple child followed him with jubilant laughter. "If you had but seen him, father," she wrote to me, "how he ran, and how often he tripped as he fled, and gave vent to his rage, you too would have laughed at him. My God! How fetid he is, and how horrible to look at! But Jesus has told me not to fear him."

Once I was assisting her when she was ill and in danger of death, and as I sat down in a corner of the room to say my office I presently heard and saw passing me a large dark-colored and furious-looking cat. After rushing round the room it jumped upon the end of the iron bedstead, directly in front of the sick girl, and there crouched with savage looks. I felt my blood curdle at the sight, while Gemma remained quite calm. Dissembling my trouble I said to her: "What is the matter now?" And she: "Don't be afraid, father, it is that vile demon who wants to annoy me. But don't fear, as he will not do you any harm." I approached her trembling with holy water and sprinkled her bed. The demon vanished leaving her in perfect serenity as if nothing had happened.

What really frightened her was the fear of offending God by yielding to Satan's malicious suggestions. Although she was aware of having always so far resisted, the danger nonetheless seemed to her to be always imminent, and kept her almost beside herself with fear. There was no remedy that she did not use in order to defend herself against those satanic assaults—crosses, relics of saints, scapulars, special prayers and, above all, filial recourse to God, to His Heavenly Mother, to her Angel Guardian and to her spiritual director.

> *"Come quickly father," she wrote, "or at least repeat the exorcisms at a distance. The devil is doing all he can against me. Help me to save my soul, for I fear I am already in the power of Satan. Ah! If you only knew how much I am suffering! Last night how contented he was! He took me by the hair and tore it away saying: 'Disobedience, disobedience! Now there is*

*no more time to amend. Come, come with me,' and he wanted to
take me to hell. He remained more than four hours tormenting
me, and thus I passed the night. I fear so much that listening to
him I may displease Jesus."*

It happened at times, though very rarely indeed, that the evil spirit
was allowed so to invade her whole person, fettering the powers of
her soul and disturbing her imagination, that she seemed almost
obsessed. On such occasions it was most pitiable to see her. She
herself had conceived such a horror of this deplorable state of being,
that the bare thought of it made her grow pale and tremble, "Oh!
God," she said to me, "I have been in hell, without Jesus, without
Mary, without my Angel. If I have come out of it without sin, I owe
it, O Jesus, to Thee alone. And yet I am contented, because suffering
thus and suffering ceaselessly I know that I am doing Thy most Holy
Will." Doubtless if attacks of this kind were often to be repeated, or
were to last for a considerable time, the poor sufferer, though perfectly
resigned, would die of anguish.

To the above torments may be added bodily ailments that we
conclude were caused her directly by Satan. Also the pains to which
I have repeatedly alluded of her participation in the Passion of Our
Savior during the periodical piercing of her hands and feet and side,
in the crowning with thorns, scourgings, wounds and other torments.
Gemma indeed had good reason to be contented at having, by so
much suffering, attained her object and accomplished her mission.
The object was to become like the Divine Man of Sorrows, and attain
to the most perfect love of God. Her mission was to serve in our
Lord's hands as an instrument of expiation for the sins of the world.

Exult then, chosen spouse of Christ, purified, tempered, ennobled
by the distinctive marks of all the true followers of the Crucified, and
be prepared to receive the crown of thy virtues that He has held
prepared for thee from Eternity.

CHAPTER 20

Assistance Of St. Gemma's Angel Guardian. A Great Help To Her Sanctification.

ONE of the most consoling dogmas of Holy Faith is that of the assistance of the Angels. After the fall, man had need in his misery and weakness of being specially helped and protected, in order to attain the end for which he was created. And God in His love, wishing to give him assistance, deputed for this purpose the ministering spirits of His heavenly court. He accordingly assigned one of these holy spirits, rightly called "our good angels" to each one of us. They take us by the hand on our first entrance into life and never leave us while life lasts. "Behold," says the Lord, "I will send My Angel, who will go before thee, and guard thee in thy way, and introduce thee into the land that I have prepared for thee."

But while God loves all men He takes special care of some and ordains degrees of preference according to their merit. Hence it happens that in each one the kindly mission of the Angels may differ greatly. Thus Gemma having been destined by God to an exalted place among the elect, it followed that the Angel assigned her by heaven should take special care of her. Divine grace willed to manifest itself towards Gemma in extraordinary ways and if we had not in the Sacred Scriptures the touching story of Tobias, and in Christian Hagiology instances of angelic intercourse with many canonized Saints, one would be tempted to doubt much of what I have to say in this connection about this favored Servant of God.

She was well prepared to treat with Angels by her many striking virtues. They were innocence, purity, candor, child-like simplicity, and at the same time a most lively faith that enabled her to see, as it were without veil, the sublimest heavenly truths. Her holy Guardian must have found in his consoling charge something partaking of the angelic nature, which enabled him to hold familiar intercourse with her.

What assuredly will be thought most singular in this angelic intercourse, is what I may call the sensitive as well as the constant presence of the Angel. Gemma saw him with her eyes, touched him with her hand as if he were a being of this world, remained talking with him as one friend would with another. "Jesus," she said, "has not left me alone. He makes my guardian angel stay with me always." She thanked God most earnestly for this benefit, and also declared her deep gratitude to the Angel. "If I am sometimes culpable, dear Angel," she said to him, "don't be angry with me, I wish to be grateful to thee." And the Angel to her: "Yes I shall be thy guide and inseparable companion. Dost thou not know who it is that gave me charge of thee? It is the merciful Jesus." At this the angelic girl unable to restrain her emotion, stood rapt in ecstasy with her Angel. What happened then is told by Gemma herself in the following simple words: "We both remained with Jesus. Oh! father, if you also had been there!" And for her to remain with Jesus meant being engulfed mind and heart in the immense abyss of God's Divinity, there to behold and hear and learn secret things.

As a rule during those intimate meetings, a considerable time was spent in praying together and offering praise to the Most High. The Angels, according to a holy Doctor, delight in assisting the Saints while they pray; and the Archangel Raphael assured the elder Tobias that, while he prayed, he himself was offering those prayers to the Lord. Now as Gemma all day and during a great part of the night was intent on prayer, and that with great ardor of faith and extraordinary devotion, must not the Angel of the Lord have greatly rejoiced thereat? He let her see him sometimes raised in the air with outspread wings, and his hands extended over her or else joined in attitude of prayer. At other times he knelt beside her. If they were reciting vocal prayers or psalms, they did so alternately. If aspirations or ejaculatory prayers, "they rivalled one another" (these are Gemma's words) "as to which would say them more emphatically—*Viva Gesù!* and Blessed be Jesus! or such-like beautiful words. And Jesus showed His pleasure at it." When it was the time of meditation the Angel inspired her with sublimest ideas and moved her affections so that the result of the holy exercise might be perfect. And as the subject of these meditations was, for the most part, the Passion of Our Lord, the Angel, like a good master, laid open its profound mysteries to her soul. "Look," he would exclaim, "at what Jesus has suffered for men. Consider one by one these wounds. It is Love that has opened them all. See how execrable sin is, since to expiate it, so much pain and so much love has been necessary." These and other such exquisite reflections, like rays of light and fire, went straight to the heart of the fervent child.

I myself have many times assisted at these meditations of Gemma with her Angel, and from what I beheld in her exterior only I could vouch for what I have stated, even if she herself had not repeated it to me in the account she gave me of it after the meditation. I remarked moreover that every time she raised her eyes to look at the Angel, listen to him, or speak to him, even out of the time of meditation and prayer, she lost the use of her senses. And during those moments one could prick, burn, or shake her without her feeling it. As soon however as she turned her eyes from him or ceased to speak with him, she immediately came to herself; and if this was frequently repeated, even within a short space of time, the same phenomenon of alienation from her senses was as frequently renewed. I wish to emphasize this fact now, although later on I shall have to speak more at length of the ecstasies of the servant of God. My object is to remove at once any idea that this intimate dealing with the Angel can be attributed to any delusive fantasy. The same thing happened to her while walking in the street, seated at table, working in the kitchen. Always and everywhere the Angel was ready to show himself, and Gemma was ready to receive him. In her exterior nothing remarkable was to be seen except the superhuman brilliancy of her eyes. She remained immovable and it was only when she was touched that it became evident that she was in converse with beings of the other world.

Very often, as has already been shown by examples, those interviews were of the most simple and sociable kind, and so great was her familiarity with the holy Angel, that its parallel can only be found in that of the Archangel Raphael with young Tobias. "Tell me, my Angel," these are her words, "what was the matter this morning with the Confessor who was so very serious that he would not listen to me? And will the father write to me from Rome, and when, in answer to the letter I wrote him, asking him how I should act in a certain case? And that sinner for whom I am striving, tell me dear Angel, when will Jesus convert him for me? And what answer should I give that person who has come to ask my advice? And what do you think of me? Is Jesus contented with me, or what must I do to keep Him so?" And similar things, all bearing on spiritual matters, for nothing else was thought of. The Angel with ineffable condescension adapted himself to such child-like candor, answering all her questions, and the result invariably showed that the answers were given by a celestial spirit. I have such a quantity of information on this subject, (of Gemma's angelic intercourse) that it would fill one volume, and another volume might be filled with proofs of the credibility of such extraordinary things against the blind assertions of modern rationalism.

The Angel Guardian was to Gemma, so to say, as a second Jesus. She made known to him her own wants and those of others. In her sufferings she wished to have him always by her side. She charged him to lay several matters before the throne of God, before the Divine Mother and her Patron Saints, giving him also letters closed and sealed, for them, with a request to bring her back the answers in time, and those letters, as a matter of fact, disappeared. Oh, how many steps and measures did I not take to ascertain if such an extraordinary fact had really happened through supernatural intervention! Yet every one of my efforts convinced me that in this, as in many other extraordinary events, heaven, so to say, had willed to play with this simple and divinely favored girl. But when she sent her holy Angel on any special errand to someone in this world, as often happened, great was her surprise if she was not answered. "And yet," she wrote to me, "so many days have passed since I sent the Angel to tell you of it. How is it that you have not done anything? At least you could have let me know through the Angel that you did not intend to act in the matter. At all events don't be vexed, if I write again to insist. It is a very serious matter."

It was thus she kept the heavenly messenger continually on the move, and he most gladly favored her. Even without being invoked he hastened to her in every need and danger. He restrained the power and malicious artifice of the devil who on all occasions seemed quite as vigilant in his efforts to do her harm. Instances are not wanting of this blessed Guardian's constant watchfulness. Once when Gemma was at table with the family one of those present did not hesitate to blaspheme the Holy Name of God. She no sooner heard him than horror-stricken she fainted, and falling would have dashed her head against the ground had not the Angel hastened to her aid. He took her hand, sustained her, and with a word only restored her. At another time when she had remained to a late hour in church without noticing it, because engaged with Jesus, the Angel came to call her and taking charge of her accompanied her visibly to her home. She had once been cruelly beaten by the devil during her evening prayer, and being unable to move, the Angel coming lifted her to her bed and there stood watching by her pillow. At other times he was at hand to warn and advise her, so that she might not fail to use the necessary precautions.

The most important mission of the Angel with Gemma was in what concerned her spiritual advancement. Thus while on one side he acted as her watchful guide, on the other she found in him a perfect master of Christian perfection. He lost no opportunity of admonishing, instructing and directing her in lessons of heavenly wisdom that

Gemma herself has preserved to us in the manifestations she made from time to time to her spiritual father. Nay, once, in order that a syllable might not be lost, the holy Angel wished her to take pen and paper, he standing and she seated before him at her desk, like a child at school writing at the dictation of a teacher, he thus began: "Remember, child, that one who truly loves Jesus, speaks little and endures much. I command thee on the part of Jesus, never to give thy opinion, but be silent at once. When thou hast committed any fault accuse thyself of it at once without waiting for others to do so. Punctual obedience, without reply to thy Confessor, and to others when he enjoins it. Also, sincerity with him and with them. Remember to guard thine eyes and reflect that the mortified eye shall behold the beauties of heaven."

When needful the holy Guardian knew how to show severity. She one day told me of this in the following words: "My Angel is a little severe, but I am glad of it. During the past days he brought me to order as often as three or four times a day." And indeed sometimes it almost appeared as if he had gone too far. "Yesterday while at table," it is Gemma who is speaking, "I raised my eyes and saw the Angel looking at me with a severity that would frighten one. Later when I went to rest a little, O my God, how angry he was! I looked at him but lowered my eyes immediately. 'Art thou not ashamed,' he said, 'to commit faults in my presence?' He cast such severe looks at me! And I did nothing but cry and recommend myself to my God and to my Blessed Mother, that they might take me away, because I could not bear it much longer. Every now and then he repeated: 'I am ashamed of thee.' I prayed also that others might not see him so angry; for if they did no one would come near me. I suffered a whole day and could not recollect myself. I had not courage to say a word to him, for whenever I raised my eyes he was looking at me with severity. I should have so liked to ask pardon, but when he is angry there is no chance of his granting it. Yesterday evening I found it impossible to go to sleep, and at last about two o'clock I saw him approach. He put his hand on my forehead saying: 'Sleep my poor child,' and disappeared."

It is impossible to explain the great fruit this holy child derived from such angelic teaching. She was attentive to every word that was said, and with great joy did the many penances that were given her by the Angel. She once wrote to me as follows:

> *"I felt great repugnance to the obedience he gave me as a penance, to go and say certain things to the Confessor. But you know, father, I obeyed, doing myself violence, and went early in the morning, to give the message. In this way I overcame myself, and the Angel has been greatly pleased, and has come back to his kind way with me."*

Gemma seeing the great charity lavished on her, loved her Angel immensely, and his name was always on her tongue as well as in her heart. "Dear Angel," she would say, "I so love you!" "And why?" he asked. "Because you teach me to be good, and to keep humble, and to please Jesus."

What wonder then that love so strong in a soul, so simple and ingenuous, should lead to a familiarity that sometimes seemed almost excessive? To hear her speaking with her dear Angel, it seemed as though she were almost treating with an equal, going so far as to contend with him earnestly in order that he might yield to her wishes. I myself in the beginning wondered greatly at it, and warned her against it. Nay I went so far as to accuse her of pride, because instead of trembling before the heavenly messenger she treated him with such familiarity. And in order to try her virtue I ended by forbidding her, when treating with him, to exceed certain defined limits. Gemma hung her head and with all humility answered: "You are quite right, father, I won't do it any more. From this day forward, I will always use the right terms when speaking to the Angel, and I will show him every reverence, and keep at a respectful distance when I am allowed to see him." And she kept her promise while the prohibition lasted, although in the proper terms of address she often got confused, and corrected herself even when in ecstasy. As soon as she saw the Angel she explained everything to him with perfect freedom. "We must have patience, dear Angel, father wishes it, so I must change my way." On one occasion having a scruple she wrote about it to her spiritual father as follows:

> "The holy Angel tried my patience. I did not want him in the least, and yet he wished to speak to me of several things. Then I said to him: 'Holy Angel, listen to me: go away, because I don't know how to act.' In a word I explained myself. He then said: 'What dost thou fear?' 'To disobey,' I answered. And he: 'No, because I am sent by Him Who has power to send me.' Then I let him talk. If I have done wrong forgive me. I won't listen any more to the Angel."

It happened also occasionally that her holy Guardian appeared to her with other Angels in order—let me put it so —to keep joyous company with their angelic sister. As soon as I knew of it I showed my disapproval, having the same object in view, and said to her that this must end. Now hear her reply: "Indeed, father, I understand very little about it all. Others when they pray see their Angel. But if I see mine you scold and are displeased. At any rate yesterday—that was their Feast day—I told them all to go away. Mine however did not go, nor did that other whom you know of. Now, what am I to do? Don't get angry again. I will be good and will obey, and you must not get put out any more."

I will add particulars of two other apparitions, among many, and so end this chapter.

> "I was in bed," she writes, "suffering greatly, when on a sudden I became absorbed in prayer. I joined my hands and moved with heartfelt sorrow for my countless sins, I made an act of deep contrition. My mind was wholly plunged in this abyss of crime against my God, when I beheld my Angel standing by my

bed. I felt ashamed of being in his presence. He instead was more than courteous with me, and said, kindly: 'Jesus loves thee greatly. Love Him greatly in return.' Then he added: 'Art thou fond of Jesus's Mother? Salute her very often for she values such attention very much, and unfailingly returns the salutation offered her. And if thou dost not feel this, know that thus she makes a proof of thine unfailing trust.' He blessed me and disappeared."

Here the reader has an idea of the kind of intimacy that existed between Gemma and her Angel. So simple, spontaneous and full of profound humility. The other apparition was very similar, but I must not omit it.

"The Angel Guardian, while I was making my evening prayer, came near and touched me on the shoulder saying: 'Gemma, why such great distaste for prayer?' No, I answered, it is not distaste. I have not been well for two days, and he added: 'Do thy part assiduously and Jesus, thou wilt see, wilt love thee still more.' I begged of him to ask Jesus for leave to pass the night by me. He disappeared at once, and when he got leave from Jesus to stay he returned. Oh! he was so kind, and when he was about to go I besought him not to leave me yet, but he said: 'I must go.' Go then, I replied, and salute Jesus for me. He gave a last look at me and said: 'It is my wish that thy conversation be no longer with creatures. When thou dost wish to speak, speak with Jesus, and with thy Angel.'"

Of this kind are almost all the apparitions of which Gemma has given an account, or that have been gathered from what she said while in ecstasy. Hence it is easy to form an idea of how dear to God this young girl must have been when found quite worthy to be thus visited, helped and guided by His holy Angels.

CHAPTER 21
St. Gemma's Gift Of Supernatural Prayer

BY means of prayer the soul is enabled to lift itself near to God, and thus live a spiritual life–that of Christian perfection. This spiritual life has various degrees, and the soul that is enabled to pass through all of them will assuredly come to a full union with God. The first degrees are those of ordinary prayer and meditation by which we consider the eternal truths and apply them to ourselves so as to excite corresponding heartfelt sentiments. Many souls stop at these first degrees which are those of the so-called ascetic life. Others pass from meditation to contemplation, which belongs to the mystical life.

Contemplation is an elevation of the soul to God and heavenly things, by means of a simple intellectual-loving gaze that brings an absorbing peace and light into the mind and heart of the contemplative.

In meditation the soul must often labor much in the exertion of its powers-memory, understanding and will. In contemplation she has only to gaze and admire the beauty of the object that God shows her. She does not then exercise herself in reflections, applications, reasonings, etc., but remains, as it were, in mental suspense before the great things that draw her out of herself in admiring wonder. We may say that the contemplative does here on earth in a limited degree what the blessed do in heaven.

Having made the above remarks on prayer in general in order to be better understood in a matter concerning which many have not clear ideas, we come now directly to Gemma. In the first place we shall consider her spirit of prayer in general, then the lofty flights of her soul by the ways of contemplation.

From her earliest years Gemma attended with great diligence to the exercise of prayer, thus meriting a constant increase of grace. We have noticed her earnest entreaties to her saintly mother and to her mistresses in order to be taught how to pray, and how, when she came to know something about it, avoiding the company of others she used to pass long hours of the day working and praying alone. To this source we must trace her great dread of all that outside God could occupy her mind or heart, or distract her thoughts. Hence that absolute detachment from all created things; that rigid watchfulness over her senses; that extreme delicacy of conscience; that continual mortification of her will and inclinations, and all those rare virtues that she practiced without ceasing. Thus she prepared herself to enter into converse with her Lord. Such efforts could not rest without reward from God's own Heart, and soon she came to fix her gaze on Him as the eagle gazes at the sun and is not dazzled. Now if the object of prayer is to stand before God and treat with Him alone by faith, we must needs conclude that this chosen soul attained all the ends of prayer in a most exalted degree.

Generally speaking, in order to commune with God she had no need to use effort, to concentrate her thoughts such as others must resort to. Our Lord was always present to her, and nothing could turn her attention from Him, while at the same time she was most exact and attentive to every duty. Once only, and for a moment, can I remember her to have been distracted from her actual attention to God. This is how it was: "Signor Lorenzo," she said, "gave me some accounts to make up for him, and as they were rather difficult, I applied such attention to them that I lost sight of God. Father, you see here how imperfect I am. Because of a few figures and a material interest I left our Lord. This thought disturbed me greatly for a short time. I asked God to pardon me and He did so at once."

It was enough to see this girl, even at a distance, in order to be convinced that she was absorbed in God. Her dignity of countenance, gravity of bearing and moderation of words; her angelic modesty beautified by a spontaneous smile that always played around her lips. All went to show the beholder that Gemma was only in body a dweller in this world. This uninterrupted attention to heavenly things had become so natural to her, that she would have had to do herself violence to think of anything else. Finding myself one day at table with the family, who are benefactors to our Institute, on seeing Gemma, who was sitting opposite me, all absorbed in God, I used my authority as her spiritual father and told her to distract herself, that not being the time or place for prayer. At my words I saw that she turned pale and seemed to tremble all over. She continued to eat as if her manifest mental suffering was nothing. After table calling her aside I saw that she was perspiring profusely. "Now what is this?" I said to her, wondering. "You know it, father," she answered with her usual candor. "Oh did you not take Jesus from me at table? And can I live without thinking of Him?" I turned the subject, and with an air of reproof sent her to change her things. In about an hour I renewed the precept and the strange phenomenon repeated itself. Once again I renewed the same precept with the same result. After this I left her free, as it pained me greatly to see how much suffering my prohibitions caused her.

Gemma's constant attention to God did not consist merely in a recollection that many souls may have who feel themselves in the Divine presence. It was an exercise of exalted supernatural prayer, spontaneous and full of sweetness. She saw her God, spoke and listened to Him, found her whole delight in Him, and, passing with marvelous ease from the most abstract contemplation to the most obvious and commonplace ideas, she laid her doubts before Him, asked graces for this or that soul, and thanked Him for those already received. Thus we learn the nature of this holy child's recollection and of her spirit of prayer. Thus she occupied twenty-four hours of her day. I say twenty-four hours, because taking as she did very little sleep and at short intervals, her prayer was scarcely interrupted. On awakening she immediately took it up where she had left off. She rose from bed without weariness or heaviness of brain, and whoever might be present as she got up would have seen her sign herself devoutly with the Crucifix, that she always kept in her hand while sleeping, kiss it and then smile with heavenly grace. Making allusion to her nocturnal interviews with her Lord, she was once, when in ecstasy, heard to exclaim: "See, O Jesus, even at night, those hours, those hours! I sleep, but O Jesus, my heart does not sleep. It watches with Thee at all hours."

The reader will observe that formal vocal prayers were little used by this angelic soul. The Rosary was said in the family. Sometimes she recited that of the Seven Dolours and of the Passion as an introduction to meditation on the Sorrowful Mysteries, and nothing more. Being helped much better by the light she received from above she formed her own prayers according to her wants. "It does not help me," she said to me, "to read prayers from books, nor to repeat Our Fathers and Hail Marys. They don't satisfy me and I get tired. So I do for myself as best I can."

It will, I am sure, gratify my readers if I give them here some more examples of Gemma's improvised prayers such as were gathered faithfully from her lips when taken unawares as she prayed aloud. Possibly they will not be found inferior to the soliloquies of St. Augustine. "Praise to the unbounded love of Jesus, Who moved to pity by my misery, offers me every means of coming to His Love! Thou Jesus art a treasure not known to me before, but now Jesus I have known Thee. Thou art all mine, specially Thy Heart. Yes, Thy Heart is mine, because Thou hast so often given It to me. But Thy Heart, Jesus, is full of light, and mine is full of darkness. When, oh, when, shall I pass from this darkness to that clear light of my Jesus?

But how shall I be able, my God, to praise Thee? When Thou didst create me, Thou madest me without me. So likewise, even without me, Thou hast the praise Thou deservest. Then, let all Thy Works, done from the sublimity of Thy majesty, praise Thee. My mind has beginning and end, but the praise that God possesses shall never have an end. And when we praise Thee, O Lord, it is not we, it is Thou Who praisest Thyself in Thyself." And praying for herself: "Jesus I come to Thy feet, to ask of Thee a grace. If Thou wert not omnipotent I would not ask this favor. Oh how is it that Thou dost not cure my soul so insatiable in its desires? Wouldst Thou despise the desires that Thou Thyself hast put into my heart? This grace I will have, and Thou wilt grant it me. Is it not so? O Jesus, have mercy on me, whose prayers Thou hast so often heard for others. Have mercy on a sinful creature that has cost Thee Thy life. Pardon me, my God. I am an orphan, without father, without mother. Have pity on poor orphans. They are the fruit of Thy Passion." Of tender colloquies like these I have enough by me to fill a volume.

Sometimes Gemma gave vent to her love in short heartfelt aspirations, and these likewise were all aglow with love: "O Jesus! O God of my heart! O Father! Alone with Thee alone! When, oh when, shall I see Thee face to face? O earth how vile thou art to me? O Cross of my Jesus, how dear Thou art to me!" These and such ardent expressions coming from her intellect to her heart, passed from her heart to her lips when she believed herself alone and unheard. Sometimes they were verses from the psalms, the best adapted to her sentiments; and she used these more particularly during great spiritual desolation, when the flood of mental agony rendered her mind and heart emotionless. During times of ordinary dryness of soul the action of her mind and heart remained perfectly free; perhaps more so than during periods of consolation, with this difference, that then her prayer was sorrowful and pitiable to such a degree as to be heart-rending to those who heard it.

Among her writings I found a little book into which she had copied some of the above-mentioned aspirations taken from the psalms, entitled: "Prayers, Aspirations, Ejaculations, a short collection from the Psalms, to be repeated during the day, particularly at those times when Jesus hides Himself." Thus we have already heard her call that state of spiritual martyrdom: "When Jesus hides Himself."

Treating of Contemplation, mystical doctors divide it into infused and acquired. The first is purely the gift of God, independent of any human industry. The second, less elevated, less luminous and sweet, can be acquired by our own efforts aided by divine grace, and by the exercise of more or less assiduous meditation. By this exercise the soul grows more and more accustomed to think of heavenly things. The mind and heart become, so to say, more subtle and spiritualized until there is no longer any need of the discourse and reflections of the intellect as a means of being united to God. Then a single thought, an image, represented to the mind, detaches and holds her in suspense in the simple, tranquil, attentive gaze of contemplation. Gemma knew both these kinds of prayer, and it is manifest from what has been stated, that in the ways of the spirit she was not merely passive but labored strenuously to become holy and thus rendered herself worthy of the most exalted gifts of divine grace.

She began to practice ordinary meditation while quite a child and applied herself to it with her whole being in the morning when in church, and in the evening before going to rest. Besides these special hours, she devoted every other spare interval of free time to this holy occupation. In her eagerness to know how to meditate she aimed at following the rules commonly laid down by masters in spiritual matters. Such rules are: Remote preparation by recollection and choice of subject; proximate preparation consisting of the acts of faith, sorrow for sin, etc., that precede the devout exercise; then other more detailed and technical rules are added by some, such as preludes, composition of place, representation by the memory and imagination, consideration by means of the intellect, application of the subject of meditation to oneself, exciting the affections through the will, etc. All these rules are useful to many, and may be necessary to some, but not to all. Gemma can scarcely ever have gone into them, having been lifted far above them from the beginning. Her ordinary subjects of meditation were the attributes of God and the Passion of our Savior. And even when others offered themselves she always ended with these two: God and Calvary. She entered so eagerly into them that she would have been able to occupy herself in them for many hours at a time without feeling tired, and even without suffering the least distraction. Indeed, she never had distractions while meditating, no matter how long the time of prayer might last. As she began to pray the world vanished entirely from her thoughts, and she remained free to treat with God as if this earth no longer existed. We know only of a few Saints who enjoyed this privilege.

Now anyone can see how easy it must have been for Gemma to pass from such attentive meditation to the form of contemplation that we have called acquired. And in fact she passed to it very quickly. I will here repeat the very words in which, at my request, she gave me a written account of her prayer:

> *"When I place myself to meditate, I use no effort. My soul immediately feels itself absorbed, in the immense greatness of God, now lost at one point, now at another. But first I begin by making my soul reflect, that being made to the image and likeness of God, He alone has to be her end. Then in a moment, it seems that my soul flies away to God, loses the weight of the body, and finding myself in the presence of Jesus, I lose myself totally in Him. I feel that I love the heavenly Lover of His creatures. The more I think of Him the more I come to know how sweet and lovable He is. Sometimes I think I see in Jesus a divine light and a sun of eternal brightness, a God so great that there is nothing on earth or in heaven that is not subject to Him; a God in Whose Will is all power. I recognize God among all kinds of goodness as the supreme Infinite Goodness–that which exists of itself; and Jesus, being Infinite Perfection, I find everything in Him. I lose myself also in His Goodness and here almost always my mind flies to paradise. Jesus is infinitely good, and in Him I hope to enjoy all good. And I end by begging of Jesus to increase His love in me, so that I may be perfected in heaven."*

And in another account she writes:

"In prayer I feel as it were out of myself. I do not distinguish where I am, if I am out of my senses, or in a peace and tranquillity that cannot be explained. I feel myself drawn by a force. But it is not a force used with effort, it is a sweet power. And when I find myself in the fullness of the delicious happiness that I experience in possessing Jesus, I forget entirely if I am in the world. I feel that my mind is full and has nothing to desire because it possesses an immense goodness, the Infinite Good, to which no other can be compared; a goodness without measure, without defect. Not even after prayer does it happen to me to willfully seek or desire anything, because of the exquisite contentment that Jesus in His Infinite Goodness and Charity gives me. It is not always, however, a love of contentment. Sometimes during prayer such great sorrow for my sins takes possession of me that it seems to me I must die."

In answer to a doubt that I designedly proposed to her, she thus replied: "On entering into prayer I behold Jesus not with the eyes of my body but I recognize Him distinctly, because He makes me lapse into a blissful abandonment and in this total surrender I know Him. His voice is heard by me with such force that, as I have often said, it cuts more than a double-edged sword, so deeply does it enter into my soul. His words are words of eternal life. When I thus see Jesus and hear Him I don't seem to perceive beauty of body, nor figure, nor sweet sound, nor charming song. But when I see and hear Him, I see an infinite Light, an immense Good. His voice is not an articulate voice, but it is stronger, and makes itself more felt in my soul than if I heard pronounced words."

From prayer so exalted there is but a step to that which we have called infused contemplation. But we must not imagine that this infused contemplation is merely a more perfect degree of prayer which the soul may reach by its own efforts. It is something quite separate. Still when such splendid dispositions exist in the soul, as we have seen in Gemma, it may well be supposed that God will not allow her to slacken in her progress, but will call her to more lofty elevations and to more sublime communications. I will call this infused contemplation a supernatural drawing of grace, that wills to introduce the faithful soul into the secrets of celestial things. It is a purely divine light that comes suddenly when least expected and takes possession of the mind and heart. For which reason this form of prayer can easily be distinguished from all others, being vastly more sublime, more penetrating, more rapturous than the others. It is so precisely because it is purely divine. This infused contemplation is based on a fullness of the gifts of the Holy Ghost, more particularly of the gifts of *Understanding* and *Wisdom*. To the first in fact belongs the enabling the soul to penetrate the hidden things of faith through sublime ideas, and to the second, the appreciating their value whence such joy, sweetness, and contentment inundate the soul in contemplation.

It is evident from all Gemma wrote in her letters, and in her manifestations of conscience to her spiritual director, from what she said particularly while in ecstasy, and from what she did, that she had those gifts of the Holy Ghost in a more than ordinary degree. Everything goes to show that the mind of this girl, more angelic than human, was endowed with a power of refined and penetrating vision that enabled her to plunge without effort into the abyss of Infinite Goodness and draw sublime conceptions therefrom. She was also endowed with a clear discernment and rare prudence that made her prefer the things of heaven to anything created, seeking them with avidity and loving them with unspeakable love. Thus raised by such exalted gifts above the infirmities of nature, and invigorated by celestial light, that at certain moments was given her by the Divine Spirit Himself, she beheld the Unity of Nature in God, the Trinity of the Divine Persons, the ineffable Union of the Word with human nature in the Incarnation, the mystery of the Divine Wisdom, Justice and Mercy in the government of creatures, and other inscrutable truths of our holy faith that God found her fit to receive. She saw them almost without a shadow, as if they were not mysteries but evidences.

She beheld and was not satiated, and desired to see more clearly. She rose in daring flights and still she felt that there were greater heights to be reached and greater depths to be penetrated. The end at which she aimed was to see God face to face. Hence on one of many occasions she was heard to exclaim: "Oh! who will give me the wings of the dove that I may fly to Thee, my God? Give them to me Thou, the wings of contemplation. How am I to fly to Thee? Break, break these chains that hinder me from flying to Thee. There are other things, O Jesus, in contemplating which my soul seems to be nourished, but in none of them can it rest. In Thee alone can my soul find rest."

She used to say that if human speech could possibly give expression to what God made her understand in these contemplations, she would be able to write volumes on every one of the mysteries of our holy faith. And in her desire to be understood by her spiritual father from whom she did not wish anything concerning her soul to be hidden, she used, as we have already seen, to attempt an explanation by means of material figures and similitudes. "Imagine," these are her words, "that you see a light of immense splendor, that penetrates everything, surrounds everything, enlightens everything, and at the same time gives life and animation to all, so that whatever exists has its being from this light and in it lives. Thus I see my God and creatures in Him. Imagine a fiery furnace, great as the universe, nay, infinitely greater, that burns everything without consuming anything, and burning, illumines and strengthens, and those who are most penetrated by its flames are happiest, and desire more ardently to be consumed. Thus I see our souls in God." And on the subject of the Blessed Trinity: "I seem to behold three Persons within a boundless light, all three united in one essence. Trinity in unity and unity in trinity, and as the essence of the Trinity is but one, so one only is its goodness, one only its beatitude." The ordinary confessor once asked her in confession to explain to him in detail what she understood of the august mystery of the Trinity. Gemma tried to comply, and, as God enlightened her mind, she went so deeply into those divine truths in what she said that, as she told me afterwards: "When we had well entered into it we both remained unable to go any further."

It is difficult to give any idea of the greatness of Gemma's veneration for these adorable truths, and of the torrent of spiritual delights that, while she contemplated them, inundated her soul. It is enough to know, that very often she was unable to resist this flood of consolation, and either swooned away or remained rapt in ecstasy. "How could I explain to you," she said to me, "what I feel in those moments? It is all heaven that pours itself into my poor soul. First one wonders, then is overwhelmed, the mind becomes confused, and remains as it were stupefied. The heart beats strongly, oh, so strongly! and one knows not what to do. One enjoys and suffers at the same time, and would not like to turn back. And when the prayer is over, if you were to know how one remains! I don't know if you have ever experienced it. My God how good Thou art to me!"

Such sublime light as this was very often granted her, either while she was at prayer or engaged at some work that of itself was calculated to distract her. All of a sudden her mind seemed to become dazzled by a mysterious light, everything else disappeared from around her, a profound recollection followed and Gemma was in heaven to contemplate God and His infinite beauty. She herself not knowing how to explain this superhuman phenomenon, with her usual candid simplicity put it thus: "My senses leave me. I was in the kitchen by the fire speaking to the servant, when lo! I felt the usual thing come on me without giving me time to run away. Then immediately I lost my senses and found myself with Jesus."

Infused contemplation is of three kinds: intellectual, imaginary and mixed. The first proceeds by the way of abstract species, in other words, is purely intellectual. The second, by that of sensible pre-existing images, or else is divinely impressed on the imagination. The third partakes of the first and second, either divinely so disposed, or because of the natural nexus existing in man between the intellect and the senses. When the mystery contemplated is of itself sensible, such as the Passion of Our Savior, it is clear that this imaginary contemplation is not objectively less noble than the intellectual, and is exercised equally by beginners and by the more advanced in this divine faculty. The intellectual, strictly understood is, according to the unanimous opinion of theologians, most rare, because grace corrects and restrains nature, when it may hinder the divine action, but does not force it. Hence the more common form of contemplation is the mixed, in the second sense in which we have explained it, inasmuch as sensible images enter into the contemplation not as its precise instrument but only by a natural adaptability.

Now this was generally the form of Gemma's contemplation, and of that we are assured, because after her prayer she remembered perfectly what she had contemplated, and she was able, though very imperfectly, by the help of sensible images to give an idea of each mystery. She would not have found this possible if in the contemplation her imagination had not taken any part. Then this faculty which in her was always so well regulated that even in her ordinary prayer it was not perceptible, could not possibly be a hindrance to her when, under the direct action of the Holy Spirit, those sublime mysteries entered into her prayer. The formal exercise of her imagination would seem to have been only in the contemplation of mysteries that were objectively sensible, specially those of Our Lord's Humanity. But even then, with what delicacy! Thus this faculty of imagination showed her the Divine Beauty of Jesus. It depicted the flames of love in that Heart, His deep wounds, His Body all bleeding, His Head crowned with Thorns. And then, so to say, withdrew, leaving her mind, and still more her heart, moved by increased lights and impulses to plunge deeper into the ocean of Infinite Love. So it had to be, because in contemplation the fantasy is neither casual nor arbitrary, but regulated by God. Enough has been said so far to make it quite clear that Gemma's contemplation was from God.

When this blessed child was a beginner in mystic ways, the Holy Spirit, adapting Himself to her youthful simplicity, led her on my means of purely sensible and imaginative contemplation, even with regard to mysteries that of themselves are intellectual. He showed her, for example, the Eternal Divine Father in the form of a venerable old man clothed with all the honor of paternity, and all the majesty of a just judge; the goodness of God like a sea without bounds, without depth; Divine Grace like a refreshing shower that, filtering gently through the soil, reanimates and vivifies the plants and bids them bloom and fructify. Nay, though she made most rapid progress to the very highest contemplation, even then it sometimes happened that her sublimest abstract contemplations alternated with imaginary ones. And this likewise is conformable to the doctrine of mystical theologians, who teach that contemplation, being purely a gift of divine liberality which God bestows when and where He pleases, it not infrequently happens that the most advanced souls are made to descend for a while to the lowest grades of beginners, even passing from the delights of the unitive to the labors of the purgative way. It would seem that the rare simplicity which in Gemma instead of growing less as she advanced in years and perfection of soul, became greater, must have moved the Sacred Heart of Him Who delights to play with simple souls, to treat her as a child. And this will explain how, together with the most sublime conceptions of the Divinity that came from her pen and lips when already an adult in spiritual ways, we find her from time to time making mention of the "Holy Papa of Jesus," of the Angel, "who spies after her," of the "Heavenly Mamma," who embraced and pressed her to her heart. Let the lives of the Saints who had to pass by these ways be read, and it will be seen how conformable to theology were the contemplations of the Virgin of Lucca.

All Christians are not called by God to the heights of contemplation. It is however true, that if those whom He selects for these sublime degrees of prayer are in our days so few, sound reason finds in this fact the result of there being so few who render themselves worthy of this grace. Oh! let us learn from Gemma how we are to correspond to Divine Grace, and how we are to reach that sanctity to which all without exception are called. And the Holy Spirit will give, even to us, at least as many of His Gifts as are needed to enable us to know Him and love Him: *Spiritum Sapientiae et intellectus.*

CHAPTER 22

St. Gemma Is Raised On The Wings Of Contemplation To The Highest Degree Of Divine Love.

IN the foregoing chapter we have treated of contemplation in general, without distinguishing the different degrees by which the soul ascends to its perfection. These degrees, or grades, as determined by theologians may be reduced to nine, and are named differently according to their results. And as contemplation is the soul of the mystical life and this is centered in Divine Love and union with the Infinite Good, to every degree of contemplation from the lowest to the highest there corresponds a distinct degree of love and union. The highest degree is that of perfect charity which is called the mystical espousal of the soul with God. In the present chapter I shall have to allude to these degrees one by one in order to show how this favored servant of God passed through them all, thus deserving the glorious title of Seraphic Virgin. The subject is not easy, and I confess I feel nervous about it. Human language can but poorly explain such sublime things, and then how is one to succeed in making himself intelligible to the general reader, as mystical theology is little less than an enigma to the majority at the present day, even among Catholics? However, I will try, encouraged by the thought that I have not gotten to prepare the matter, but that Gemma herself will present it in perfect order. In her own simple and expressive words she will make known and give us to understand the hidden things that grace wrought in her soul.

The first degree of contemplation is that called *Mystic Recollection*, which consists in an extraordinary light by means of which God communicates Himself of a sudden to the intellect, wholly absorbs it, and by its reaction on the interior and exterior senses, this light concentrates them, quiets them, and holds them sweetly in attendance on the soul. It is not ecstasy, which suspends the use of the senses, but it is a gentle attraction that, causing forgetfulness of all else inclines one's whole being towards the Infinite Good, as, in the words of St. Francis de Sales, the magnet attracts the needle placed near it. The very members of the body put themselves in an attitude of recollection and remain immovable as long as the soul is visited by that unexpected light. That this grace was truly vouchsafed by God to Gemma is evident from what we have already seen in the preceding chapter, and I do not repeat it, as I wish to speak here only of the love and union that in her corresponded to this first degree of contemplation. Doubtless, to see God by means of an infused supernatural light, feel oneself in His presence with all the faculties of the soul, and not taste His sweetness, not love Him, not unite oneself to Him would be impossible, at least so it was with Gemma. And as from her earliest years she was favored by God with this first degree, she began then to feel herself united to Him by a sweet attraction, and to love Him alone with tenderest affection. And has she not often assured us of this herself? "No, don't speak to me of anything else," she would say, "He alone is enough for me, and I wish for Him only. Thou knowest it, O Jesus, that I love no other outside Thee. Tear me in pieces, but leave me Jesus and I shall be content."

In sacred writ we are told how sweet and meek is our God, and that it is enough to see and taste Him only once to be captivated by Him. What then must not have happened to Gemma who not only once but continually was illumined by God with those clear and strong lights of contemplation, and made partaker of the Divine Sweetness of His presence? We must say that she was as a spouse wounded with love, who living for no other than her Celestial Spouse kept her mind, heart, senses and whole being reserved for and intent on Him, and with the Royal Prophet kept exclaiming: "For what have I in heaven? and besides Thee what do I desire upon earth? For Thee my flesh and my heart have fainted away. Thou art the God of my heart, and the God that is my portion for ever." And it was quite enough to glance at her, at any time or place, to feel convinced that in the depth of her heart those acts of love were being ceaselessly repeated. And how much more did not this become evident when anyone succeeded in getting into conversation with her? Her words were few, concise and full of fire. "Oh," she was heard to exclaim, "if all were to know how beautiful Jesus is, how amiable He is! They would all die of love. And yet how comes it that He is so little loved? Oh! it is time lost to be with creatures! Our heart is made to love one thing only, Our Great God." And after having said some such words as these she immediately re-entered into herself, and was lost in her habitual recollection.

The second degree of contemplation and of love is the *Spiritual Silence*, so called because in it the soul illuminated by a stronger light than in the preceding degree, and by more deliciously sweet attractions, is held riveted in astonishment before the Majesty of the Lord, not daring to address Him, but only to love Him while remaining enraptured in His Love. The imagination itself wonder-stricken at what it experiences abstains from every act that may disturb the sweet peace reigning in the intellectual faculties. The soul is in silence while God is allowing her to taste delights of Paradise. In Gemma's case this more perfect degree of contemplation and loving union alternated very often with the first. And while in this state of mystical recollection she treated with her God, listening to and addressing Him in acts of gratitude, humility, etc., all of a sudden, as the force of the Divine Light increased, illuminating and attracting her, she became enraptured and motionless. Again, after a little, she returned as at first to affectionate outpourings. This change was visible in her exterior while in prayer. For while in the first degree the various movements of her soul were partially depicted on her countenance, in the second her face remained unchanged. Once when she was giving me an account of this degree of prayer, she said: "I have been in the presence of Jesus. I said nothing to Him, and He said nothing to me. We both remained in silence. I looked at Him and He looked at me.

But if you only knew, father, how delightful it is to be thus in the presence of Jesus! Have you ever experienced it? You would wish it were never to end. But then, all in an instant Jesus says: Enough, and that Light disappears. But the heart, you know, does not grow cold so quickly."

And that heart within the breast of God's servant most assuredly did not grow cold. Nay, although she ceased from the act of contemplation, which in the less perfect degree is always of short duration, still the flame continued to consume at least in part for a long time. One would not be wanting in truth who would assert, as I believe I am entitled to assert, that the habit contracted by this holy girl of remaining silent during the course of the day in an uninterrupted recollection, was the result of the frequent recurrence of that supernatural silence in which God placed her contemplation.

Doubtless with her great ardor of soul, and the constant thought of the Infinite Beauty that she was so often called to contemplate she must have had little wish to stay talking to creatures.

The soul now accustomed to remaining in spiritual silence in the Divine Presence, and to the enjoyment of Its sweetness, is quite disposed to pass to the third degree of Mystical progress, which is the *Contemplation of Quiet.* It consists in a more intimate and almost habitual union with God based on a vivid sentiment of His Divine Presence. Hence results a great spiritual peace that keeps the soul in tranquil repose. Its faculties do not remain suspended while in this state. On the contrary, once it has become habituated to this degree of prayer by frequent experience, it can occupy itself in organizing works to please and glorify Our Lord without being in the least distracted from the Divine Presence. Then are seen in the soul the parts both of Magdalene and Martha wonderfully represented and united. The first in contemplation enjoying delights at the feet of Our Savior; the second working for Him. Thus it was with Gemma, who reached this degree of Mystical perfection nearly three years before her death. The external habitual recollection that we have wondered at and admired in her is a proof of the first of the aforesaid prerogatives in an eminent degree. The readiness and energy by which she was moved in the practice of virtue to please the God she so loved, her zeal for the salvation of souls, with the assiduous prayers and penance's that she offered for the conversion of sinners, and the fervor with which she took part in good works, all assure us of the second. The example of this happy girl shows us by contrast how certain souls deceive themselves, who as soon as they begin to taste some sweetness in the above-mentioned prayer of Quiet, would wish always to remain alone, always in Church, always in search of confessors and directors, neglecting meanwhile the duties which their state of life requires of them. It is impossible, as the Mystical Doctor Scaramelli rightly says, for these souls to make any seriously steady advancement in the interior ways of the Spirit.

I shall have to devote a special chapter to the subject of Our New Martha's singular material activity, and I must refer my readers to it so as to speak here only of the repose of Magdalene and its marvelous fruits. Listen to Gemma's words: As long as I had so many desires my soul was without rest. Now that I have only one, I am happy. But let me act, O Jesus. Though Thy love be inaccessible, I will see to it, I will reach it. Here Jesus, here in my heart, I will raise Thee a pavilion all of love. Thou alone must enter into it. I will keep Thee always with me, always here a prisoner. I won't leave Thee any more liberty, no, not until Thou hast given me the consolation I so long for. And what do I so long for, and what do I ask Thee for, O Jesus? Ah! Thou seest it. In that we are agreed. I ask Thee for that which Thou Thyself willest, and desire that which Thou Thyself desirest."

Is not this effusion of love supernaturally sublime? What I have here said of the third degree will do for the present, as I must return shortly to speak of Gemma's abandonment, peace, tranquillity of spirit, and loss of self in God.

The *Mystic Sleep*, fourth degree of union, is allied to the preceding degree of *Quiet*, but is more perfect. The difference consists in this, that the Mystical Quiet is caused by the celestial light making the soul feel and taste in delicious calm the presence of God, whereas the sleep is caused by love which by its soothing influence on the soul, together with all her intellectual and sensitive faculties, lulls her to sleep and tranquil repose in the bosom of God. In this state the soul knows to a certainty, but without reflection, that she ardently loves her God. It is enough for her to love, caring for nothing else, and even not knowing how this state of happiness has come about, because she sleeps and is lost in God. The Seraph of Lucca was enriched with this gift shortly before she was raised to the much more eminent degree of the ecstatic union. God gave it to her frequently, and for a considerable period, even several times a day. And as in this state the external senses are asleep, she was easily discovered while thus absorbed either standing, seated, on her knees or lying down. She then seemed to be asleep, and used the term "sleep" when referring to the mysterious phenomenon. But her heart was not asleep although her mind was quite alienated from everything, even from itself. When she returned to herself she knew not what to say, except that she had been in the bosom of God. "Imagine a baby," she once said, "in her mother's arms asleep. She is then forgetful of herself and of everything else. She thinks of nothing and only rests and sleeps, not even knowing how or why. That is the way with my soul during this time. But believe me, father, it is a most sweet sleep."

Wishing however to thoroughly satisfy myself regarding her, by a practical trial, and also to mortify her, I said to her once that such a sleep in the daytime seemed to me a mere act of sloth, and told her to desist from it. Strange to say! although in this entirely supernatural sleep the human will can do nothing—neither enter into it, nor come out of it, nor in any way hinder its happening—Gemma besought Our Lord to make her obey and He did so. The mystical phenomenon never happened again. But instead, another of a far higher order was very soon manifested in her, no doubt in reward of her goodwill and obedience. It was that of the ecstatic union which I must treat of in a special chapter. "You see," the simple child said to me, "Jesus has made me obey, and I have not slept any more. Now you will be satisfied, and you won't be displeased with me if again I happen to give you some annoyance. I will be good and do what you tell me." And these are facts in which it is quite evident artifice has no part.

Placed in the midst of so many flames, and so close to that ardent furnace which is the bosom of God, it is easy to understand how the favored soul cannot always sleep, nor always repose tranquilly. The very sleep itself and repose must inflame it more, and rouse it now and then from its rest, by exciting in the heart almost a delirium of love. Theologians call these loving impulses *Spiritual Inebriety*, which, when clearly proved to be supernatural, constitutes one of the mystical grades, more or less perfect in particular cases than the degrees already named. In this state the soul would fain exhaust itself in praising the Lord and making its voice heard to the ends of the earth, to induce all men to glorify Him and love Him. It would wish to suffer great things to please God, and would undertake everything for Him. Those who have read the Psalms of Holy King David, and the lives of St. Francis of Assisi, St. Teresa, St. Mary Magdalene de Pazzi and other Saints equally favored by God will understand what is meant by this divine inebriety.

Gemma too experienced it, as is made known by the words she spoke and wrote while in that state. On one or two occasions only was she seen to give vent externally in positive acts, nervous words and earnest gestures. One would almost have said that Divine Grace wished thus to respect that modest reserve so carefully practiced by this humble girl. Even during the most burning overflow of her heart's love while in this state, she knew how to contain herself, and all the external commotion seen in her (on the few occasions that this phenomenon was witnessed) reduced itself to some slight acts of exuberant joy and loving yearnings that yet were very moderate and full of dignity. Feeling that she had all Paradise in her heart, she made sign to those around her to come near and place their hands upon it, so that they also might be assured of it, and then exclaimed: "Oh God! Oh Love! Oh Paradise!" Apart from these few exceptions of external manifestation, the spiritual inebriety of this seraphic girl was indeed perceptible, but mainly confined to her soul, so that her state of ineffable bliss then only became known through the radiancy of her countenance and the accents like darts of fire that came from her heart. Listen to her words: "The snares of Thy Love, my God, are so strong, that I cannot get out of them. Set me free, give me full liberty. I will love Thee everywhere. I will seek Thee always. Oh, whatever hast Thou done, Jesus; oh, what hast Thou done to my poor heart that makes it incessantly so yearn for Thee? Ah! would O Jesus that my voice could reach all the bounds of the earth. I would call all sinners and tell them all to come into Thy Heart! Oh! if all poor sinners were to come into this Heart! Come, come, sinners, don't be afraid. The sword of Justice will not reach you here. Ah! I cannot bear it. I must give vent, I must sing, I must exult. Increated Love for ever! Heart of my Jesus for ever!"

These and such-like outbursts of exuberant love were the most frequently repeated during Gemma's ecstasies, and they often came from her pen when writing. Here is an instance of this from one of her letters:

> *"I have such a great longing to fly away to my God! Oh if I could but hear from you, father. For days Jesus has been making me a victim of Love. He is making me die, ah! only of Love. What a precious death! I am not quieted if Jesus does not inflame me a little with His Love that I may be consumed in Him. I would have my heart become ashes, that all should say: Gemma has been burned to ashes for Jesus."*

Let not the reader imagine that this degree of union is less estimable because the senses take part in it, inasmuch as that which the senses here make manifest is nothing more than an overflow of the inner joy of the soul produced by the torrent of light with which the Holy Spirit inundates the mind, and by the love that He excites in the heart.

Sometimes also this overflow is so great, that pouring like a torrent of fire into the purely material heart, it inflames it in a most extraordinary way. And this ardor, understood as above explained, constitutes a sixth degree of perfection called by mystics the *Flame of Love*. In the seraphic Virgin of Lucca this flame was so intense, that if it had continued for more than the two or three months that it lasted, her heart would have been consumed in her breast. I am not narrating fables but facts that have been verified. Her heart was like a furnace, and the hand could not approach it without feeling it burn, even though it was outside the clothing. Wishing to make quite certain of this, I gave an order to the lady who looked after her, to examine it during her ecstasy; and, wonderful to relate, the whole of the skin over the region of the heart was found, on several occasions, to be burned, just as if red-hot coals had been applied to it. This mysterious phenomenon lasted during the time I have already mentioned, and when it ceased, the marks of burning and the cicatrix caused by it remained for a long time. Let Gemma herself describe this phenomenon to us:

> *"For the last eight days I have felt something mysterious in the region of my heart, that I cannot understand. The first days I disregarded it, because it gave me little or no trouble. But today is the third day that this fire has increased. Oh so much, as to be almost unbearable. I should need ice to put it out, and it hinders my sleeping and eating. It is a mysterious fire that comes from within to the outside. It is, however, a fire that does not torment me, rather it delights me. But it exhausts and consumes me. 'Jesus, father, will have made you understand all about it.' Great God! How I love Thee, O how I love Thee!"*

When I questioned her about it, Gemma herself had to acknowledge that the suffering she felt from this mysterious fire, although it was a joy to her, was really very painful. She said to me: "In order to form an idea of it, imagine that into the very center of this poor heart a red-hot iron, kept constantly heated in a furnace, has been introduced. Thus I feel myself burning." And yet she would not have exchanged this excruciating torture for all the delights of the world. For while she thus suffered in her body the sweetness it caused in the depths of her soul was truly beyond all description. Hence rapt in ecstasy she exclaimed: "Thou art on fire, Lord, and I burn. O pain, O infinitely happy Love! O sweet fire! O sweet flames! And wouldst Thou have my heart become a flame? Ah! I have found the flame that destroys and reduces to ashes! Ah! cease, cease, I cannot withdraw my heart from so much fire. What do I say! No, rather come Jesus, I will open my heart to Thee. Put Thy Divine fire into it. Thou art Flame, and let my heart be turned into flame." At other times, as if she had never had such experience she kept saying with restless yearning: "Oh what is this great fire that I feel within me? Are they the flames of Thy love O Jesus? Yes, they are the flames of Thy love." It was by these outpourings of love that she sought some vent for the inner flames that were consuming her. "Poor Gemma!" thus wrote the lady who adopted her, "how she suffers! She is consumed with love for Jesus. She is continually saying that she feels herself burning, but does not see the fire. That she feels herself tightly bound but does not see the chains that bind her. Ah! if you but heard what bursts of love, what expressions come from her lips when she is in ecstasy!" I would like to be able to write one by one the expressions that it has been possible to collect in great numbers from her lips and pen, but that is not allowed me now.

Even during the withdrawal of spiritual consolation the ardor of her spirit found a new impulse, nay, it then impelled her all the more. In one of her ecstasies she was thus heard to lament and exclaim: "What peace, what quiet, even though Thou hidest Thyself! Yes, Jesus, even keep far from me if Thou wilt. Enough for me that Thy love does not fail me. Set me on fire. Thy Love is enough for me. I would that all were to say, that Thy love has consumed me. Love! Love! But I want to come to Thee." Again, becoming still more daring, impelled by the Love that burned within her soul she exclaimed: "Why didst Thou show me so much love at first, and then leave me so desolate? It is my love for Thee, Jesus, that makes me speak thus. But if Thou dost not return, my God, I shall die. O Jesus, sustain me. Let everything fail me, but not Thy love, then fly from me as much as Thou wilt."

Our holy father St. Paul of the Cross, who also experienced this degree of burning love, used to exclaim: "I feel my entrails parched, I thirst and want to drink, but to extinguish this burning I would wish to drink torrents of fire." Whoever has tasted of the sweetness of Divine Love must feel and speak thus. For when the fire of charity comes to this, it can no longer contain itself. The Spouse of our souls, Jesus Christ Himself, first gave us an example of this when, satiated with sorrow and love on the Cross, in agonized accents He exclaimed: "I thirst: *Sitio,*" whence Mystical theologians have come to call the next or seventh degree of Mystical Union the *Thirst and Anguish* of love. Father Scaramelli gives the following definition of it: "The anguishes of love are a living and ardent desire of God, loved and tasted, but not yet possessed by the soul. The continuance or duration of these pangs which form and establishes themselves, so to say, in the very marrow of the soul, is called the *Thirst of Love.*"

The possession of God was the one desire of this angelic girl from her very earliest years. And we have seen from what has been said up to the present that it was truly the passion of her heart. By degrees as her soul grew apace in perfection undergoing the severe so-called purgations of sense and spirit sent her by our Lord in great number and severity, this one desire likewise went on increasing. And then, from the state of an unquenchable fire consuming her whole being, it became a burning thirst that had to be satisfied and could only be so by fully possessing her God and her all. In such a state of loving agony this dove found no relief except in sighs and longings, and in truth she sighed and yearned night and day. "For me," she exclaimed, "Jesus is what I want. Oh! give me, give me Jesus." And turning to Him, "Make haste Jesus. Oh dost Thou not see how this heart longs for Thee? Oh dost Thou not see how it languishes? Does it not pain Thee, O God, to see it thus languish in desire? Come! come, Jesus, make haste, come near, let me hear Thy voice. O God, when shall my whole being be satiated with Thy Divine Light. Oh when? Jesus, food of strong souls, strengthen, purify me, make me divine. Great God, Jesus, help me. God begotten of God, come to my aid, I thirst for Thee, Jesus. Dost Thou not see how I suffer every morning until I feed on Thee? Grant at least, that thus nourished I may remain satisfied."

Being then in the center of such a fire was it possible for the heart of this seraph not to blaze forth? I have told how it blazed so fiercely that it burned the flesh that surrounded it, even to the outside skin. Here I add, that as the spiritual flames continued, the mysterious physical phenomenon increased, and, little by little, that fire which at first was confined to the sole region of the heart spread itself over her whole body, which thus became, so to speak, a furnace. Thus after having given me particulars of it, she added: "My heart, father, is the victim of Love, and I shall soon die of love. These flames of love consume my body as well as my heart, and I shall be reduced to ashes. Yesterday as I drew near to Jesus exposed in the Blessed Sacrament I felt myself burning so violently that I was obliged to move away. I was burning all over. It rose even to my face. *Viva Gesù!* How happens it that so many who are standing close to Jesus do not burn to ashes?" This prodigious phenomenon was several times verified by me, by the use of the thermometer, and no sooner was it applied to the part affected than the column of mercury instantly rose to the summit of the tube as if it had been exposed to burning heat. The next chapter will contain what remains to be said on this subject.

CHAPTER 23
Continuing The Subject Of Contemplation.

THE seven degrees of contemplation and union which we have explained are nothing more than a preparation for the last. This as I have also said, consists in perfect union with the Infinite Good and is called the "Mystical Espousals." God, by Mystical *Recollection*, makes the soul attentive, and in the *Spiritual Silence* it listens to His Voice. The Mystical *Quiet* disposes it to generosity of action, while by the *Sleep* He renovates it. The Mystical *Inebriety* quite vivifies the soul. Then by the *Flame* God sets it afire, and by the *Thirst* attracts with longings and consumes it. The happy Soul, thus having reached such great perfection, both sees and feels how near it is to God, and tastes the sweetness of His Love, still knowing well that it does not yet possess Him intimately. It is like the fly that, attracted by the light of a flame, goes round and round and then dashes into it, but without penetrating so far as to become one with the flame and remain consumed therein. Thus the poor soul sighs and yearns with all the greater anxiety, in proportion as the light received in the various degrees of prayer, showing the beauty and loving-kindness of God, has been more vivid and intense. All this has been clearly stated by Gemma, in a few heartfelt words to her director, when making a manifestation of the state of her soul: "Jesus is in me," she said, "and I am all His. I am, however, awaiting the grace to be entirely transformed into Him, and I am consumed by the desire to be able to plunge into the infinite abyss of Divine Love."

As a general rule this immense favor is not granted all at once to the soul, who thus would be unable to bear it. Therefore it is that the Heavenly Father disposes and accustoms it, so to say, by little and little, making it pass first through another lesser degree, that is the eighth degree of Mystical theology. In this degree, from time to time, He communicates Himself to the soul, touching it, as it were, in flight and allowing Himself to be touched by it substantially. O great God of Love, how I would wish to better understand and better explain these sublime things! But it is not in my power. Mystical theologians call these exquisite delicacies of Uncreated Love *Divine Touches*, precisely because they are instantaneous and so to say, superficial. They define them thus: "Spiritual impressions, analogous to that of the bodily touch, by which the soul feels the Divine action and God Himself in the very center of its being, and tastes Him in an ineffable way."

Now that the yearnings of this heaven-favored child had increased to the extent that we have shown, and that the ardor of the fire within her had also increased and brought that loving heart to the point of bursting, God willed to take pity on her and render her life bearable. He, therefore, began again to communicate Himself to her, allowing her now and then to come close to His Divine Heart. I cannot say precisely when this happy state began, having found her in it when I undertook her spiritual direction, although those divine touches were then less perfect and of rare occurrence. They were granted her, as a rule, during the time of contemplation. By degrees a supernatural light displayed the Divine beauties to her mental vision, and her heart warming in her breast began to palpitate while she consumed herself in desire to be united to the Infinite Good. With the increase of these ardors the wall of separation, I will put it thus, between the Creature and the Creator, grew gradually thinner, until at last falling down it left the happy soul in contact with the Divinity.

Then she could say but little: "O Angels, Angels, I can do nothing. Praise all of you the Love of my God. Behold, Jesus, I give myself up to Thy Holy Love." Then her natural strength being unable to stand it, she would fall as one lifeless to the ground. Once this happened while she was in church after Communion. When she came to herself she felt grieved at this, and so besought the Divine Majesty, that the same thing never again happened to her in public. In her simplicity she attributed this grace to the continual violence she did herself in order to avoid singularity, and rejoiced at her success. She wrote of this to her director as follows:

"Jesus continues to make Himself felt at all times and in all places. May He be blessed for ever! Oh, what violence I have to use in order to hide myself from others, particularly when I am in church and out of doors! It goes so far that I sometimes pass the entire day trying to suffocate these yearnings to cast myself into the infinite abyss of the Divine Love. I cease doing myself this violence only for a few moments after Holy Communion, and these moments are hurried because I fear being noticed. In the evening I feel a touch of fever, caused by my efforts to keep in restraint. But always advancing because Jesus tells me that He is pleased at my acting in this way. Shall I be always able to restrain? I fear not, because these impulses keep growing stronger and more frequent, so as to come to surpass my power of resistance. When I can do no more, I must let it take its course. Jesus always and for ever!"

Sometimes the senses were called to take part in these Divine Touches. The Incarnate Word appeared to her in visible form, of which we have already had an example, and after having by His Divine Presence inflamed her heart, He invited her to approach the Wound in His Side. She kissed it with lips on fire and then fell senseless at His Feet. Here is how she describes one of these celestial interviews: "Having been to Holy Communion, I felt Jesus coming, and do you know how I felt Him? At first, when I had scarcely received Him into my heart, He began to make it beat, oh so violently, that I thought it would leap from my breast. Then He asked me if I really loved Him. I answered Yes. 'And dost Thou love me?' I said. Then Jesus touched me, kissed me and I remained as if reduced to ashes in His presence."

In the course of time, these seizures of love, if I may so term them, became very frequent, particularly during her ecstasies, and it was easy to know of them, because their effects became evident. "Those little faintings," she writes to me, "that happened to me in the presence of Jesus, are becoming more and more frequent. But if Jesus continues thus, He will soon be left alone. Ah! the love of Jesus is irresistible. How is it possible not to love Him with all one's soul? How can one cease to long to be all absorbed in Him, and consumed in the flames of His love?" During her musings, in the same ingenuous way, turning to Our Lord, she was once heard to exclaim: "My beloved Jesus, but if Thou makest all others feel like this, on fire, and unable to live in Thy presence, people can no longer exist, and Thou will be left all, all alone." Thus this seraphic girl thought that all Christians must be on fire, as she was, with heavenly love, whereas hers was the rarest privilege and might be called unique. She even thought that she of all others failed most in love, and with ceaseless prayer entreated of our Lord to grant it her. These frequent Touches of the Hand of God enkindled greater fires of love and increased her burning thirst. Hence, the following ardent utterance: "My heart is always united to Jesus, who more and more consumes me. O my most sweet Jesus, I would wish to be all dissolved in the midst of the flames of Thy Love. Ah! how can I correspond, my God, since Thou hast so immensely benefitted me? Who will help in this? To Thy Mercy alone I owe the little love there is in this poor heart for Thee." Another time, on her asking our Lord how it could possibly be that in the center of her whole being she should feel such a longing to please Him and be united to Him in bonds of Eternal Love, He answered: "Because I have been victorious." And she: "Ah! yes, I am happy at being conquered by such great Goodness and by so much Love."

And it was precisely so. Jesus had conquered, and in order to glorify Himself in this, His beloved Servant, after thoroughly purifying her for so many years, and after having prepared her by such an abundance of grace in all the degrees of the Mystical Life, He willed to crown

His work by the most exalted gift of perfect union. I have said, when speaking of her profound humility, that this modest Virgin did not dare to call Jesus her Spouse, it being enough for her to be His servant and His child. Even when in ecstasy, she abstained at first from giving Him that sweet title, and from calling herself His Spouse. But as the fire of Divine Love increased in her heart, and with love, courage and confidence, she began to utter occasional aspirations, such as the following: "If I experience, O my God, such consolation every morning, when Thou makest me call Thee Father, oh, what will it be when I shall be able to call Thee my Beloved? Yes, Jesus, console this Thy poor child and promised spouse." And on another occasion, being likewise in ecstasy, she was heard to speak thus to her God in ardent accents: "O Jesus, but always child? Nothing more? and yet I would wish...O Jesus! Yes, I know it, it would be too much, Jesus, for me. Shall I tell Thee what it is that I desire? I would wish, Jesus, I would wish to be, Jesus, Thy Spouse. Yes, Thy Spouse, O Jesus." And saying this, she fell fainting, and remained several hours on the ground as dead. And now, O Divine Spouse of souls, hasten Thou, and say that the time has come. Say to this innocent soul, arise and come—*Veni Sponsa Christi accipe coronam quam tibi Dominus preparavit in aeternum.* The desires of this holy soul were satisfied, and the Divine Word united her to Himself in indissoluble bonds of love. Rich presents were not wanting to these espousals. Jesus appeared to her in the form of a lovely child in His Mother's Arms, and the Holy Mother, taking a ring from His finger, put it on that of His fortunate servant.

From that day forward Gemma did not seem to be a human being. That majesty of countenance which had always been admired in her, that splendor in her eyes, that sweet smile on her lips, and whatever else up to then had adorned her, now assumed a heavenly mien that exacted reverence and made her appear an angel from paradise. "You may believe it, father" so those who lived with her wrote to me, "you cannot look her in the face, she seems a seraph, and when you have looked at her for an instant, you are forced to lower your eyes through reverence. She is more retired than ever, more silent, more grave. Yet on the other hand, she takes part as before in every domestic work. When she is alone at prayer, she passes all the time in ecstasy. If you were to see her, you would be moved to tears. If you only heard the words of fire that come then from her lips! Our dear Gemma!" This holy girl herself describes her new happy state to me in the following few eloquent words: "Jesus continues to love me but *not in the same way as before,* by uniting me to Himself in recollection, but in *another way.* From that day a new life began in me."

From the lowly idea and imperfect similitude offered in earthly espousals the reader can form some conception of what Mystical Writers intend by this most sublime degree of union and love to which the Seraphic Virgin of Lucca was raised. For, as in earthly matrimony, two persons give themselves to each other with all they are and have, so as to become, as it were, one and the same person, so in this spiritual and Divine Matrimony the soul gives herself with her whole being to God and God to the soul. And this union, like the other, through an infinitely more perfect way, is intimate, continuous, indissoluble. Intimate, because it takes place in the center, and as the same writers say, in the substance itself of the fortunate soul. Continuous, because it is not subject to suspension or interruption on the part of God who is its true Author. Indissoluble, because, according to the ordinary law, it never happens that such a soul loses sanctifying grace by mortal sin, so as to be separated from God.

This most perfect union is, therefore, clearly distinguished from that of the eight preceding degrees, in which Our Lord communicates Himself in His gifts, but not in Himself. He is communicated to the powers of the soul, but not to the soul itself, and at intervals more or less frequent, but not in a permanent form. Let Gemma herself, who had the happy experience of this sublime union, describe it to us: "Today I am no longer in myself. I am with my God, all for Him, and He all in me and for me," which is the saying of the Spouse in the

Canticles: *Ego delecto meo et ad me conversio ejus:* "Jesus is with me, He is all mine. He is alone, alone, and I am alone to bless Him, alone to pay Him court. He dwells in the miserable cell of my heart and His Majesty disappears. We are alone, alone, any my heart palpitates continually with that of Jesus. *Viva Gesù!* The Heart of Jesus and my heart are one and the same thing. A moment does not pass without my feeling His dear presence always manifesting Himself in the most loving way."

From these and like words very often spoken by the new spouse, it is easy to understand how great must be the happiness of a soul that has arrived at this height, while yet a pilgrim in this vale of tears; also, how abundant must be the supernatural fruits that she gathers and tastes in her intimate union with the Infinite Good. Nor could it possibly be otherwise, if it is true that all the goods of the Spouse also belong to His bride. Therefore, with good reason Gemma was able to exclaim: "Oh, what precious moments these are! It is a delight that can only be compared to the heavenly beatitude of the Angels and Saints. Yes, I am happy, because I feel my heart beat with Thine. I am happy because I possess Thee, O Jesus. O Jesus, with what joy it fills me to know that I possess Thee! But, my God, if Thou dealest so with us on earth, what must it not be in Heaven!" And, writing to her director:

> *Oh, father! If I was only able to feel and taste more fully the gifts that Jesus grants me! Oh, how good Jesus is! I ask Him to cease and put bounds to so many graces, because it is too much for me. Help, help! and bless me.*"

It would be quite impossible even for Gemma to explain all the gifts that she received at this time from our Lord. They were sublime graces that day by day ennobled, beautified, adorned and rendered her more acceptable in the eyes of His Divine Majesty. She felt herself transformed in God with all her powers and all the operations of her soul, and submerged in an abyss of light, serenity and peace. In this happy state her ecstasies, and out of them, how intimate the secrets that the Divine Word told her! How sublime those intellectual visions, and those others, alternating with them, in which her sense took part! How clear those lights in which He revealed to her the glory of heaven that He held prepared for her, and the greatness of the mysteries of Faith, and the perfection of His own Divine attributes! Ah! now I see why this perfect Servant of God showed herself then, more than ever, weary of the things of this earth, so that she was often heard to exclaim: "In this world everything wearies and weighs me down. I desire nothing, only to love, to love, to love. I give vent as much as I can in aspirations and ejaculatory prayers. Thus I pass my days." I do not wonder at her looking at all the graces she had received as little in comparison with those reserved for her in paradise, and at hearing her cry out: "Oh! to Paradise, let us go to Paradise where we shall see God as He is, in all His entirety, and possess Him perfectly and to satiety. When, O my God, wilt Thou take me to Paradise?"

I understand also now the terror that the mere mention of sin caused Gemma; and that ardent zeal that would have carried her so far as to make "bits of herself," in order to hinder the very least offense against God; and that intense desire to give Him satisfaction by every kind of suffering and by doing great things for His glory. She would say with vivacity: "But what is done for Jesus? Oh! what would I not wish to do! Would that I could give my whole life at once! But no, I wish to live always, if it pleases Him, always to work and do penance for Him, to suffer, O so much! and so much! to love Him, O so much! and so much! Oh! if I could but possess, as I always ardently desire, the fervor and the love of all holy souls! Even more, that I might be able to equal the Angels in purity, and I would go as far as our most holy Mother, Mary!" And it was natural that she should think and feel thus. The spouse lives only to please the beloved and give him pleasure. She never thinks of herself, and there is no inconvenience or pain to which she would not willingly submit in order to gratify him. The dishonor and insults that she sees offered to him are dishonor and insults done to herself in the most sensitive part of her being.

In proof of this, as regards Gemma, I give the following fact. She was returning from church and was overtaken by one from their house, who, blinded by furious passion on account of something that had happened, began giving expression to horrible blasphemies. At hearing him, she shuddered and raised her voice to stop him, but her strength failing, she fell senseless on the spot. Meanwhile, her heart throbbed violently, and unable to resist the pressure of such grief drove the blood through her veins so forcibly that, oozing through the pores of her whole body as a profuse perspiration, it saturated all her clothes and even the very ground. A spectacle, surely, this to be compassionated, and I do not know that Christian hagiography has registered anything like it, except what we know of Christ, Our Lord, Who, to show us what a horrible thing is the offense against God caused by sin, fell in agony in the Garden of Olives and sweated Blood! Now, let the reader say if it is possible to imagine a love for God more tender, fervent and sincere, than that which this young girl has here shown us. When she recovered from her faint and her anguish had lessened, she rose, and not knowing what had passed, so distracted was she by her grief, she went home. The first to meet her was her Aunt who, not knowing what to think of her pallor, asked her what had happened. Then, seeing her covered with fresh blood, and thinking that she had thus punished herself with a discipline or otherwise, she upbraided her sharply. The holy girl, finding herself discovered, blushed, did what she could to get out of the embarrassment, and not succeeding, with tears and sobs confessed ingenuously that what had happened had been caused by blasphemies she had heard. Her friend, greatly moved, tried to pass it off, saying: "Oh! is this the first time that you have heard blasphemies in this unhappy city of ours? How is it that only today they have had this effect on you? And Gemma, continuing to cry said: "It is not the first. It is not the first time. It has always this effect on me when I cannot run away or otherwise distract my thoughts." She might have added that at other times it was still worse, and that the intensity of her affliction had caused her to shed tears of blood. This extraordinary phenomenon, also the only one of the kind we know of, was often witnessed, and by many persons, after Gemma had been raised to the perfect love of which we are treating. The blood ran down those innocent cheeks in streams through her deep sorrow at the insults offered to the Divine Spouse, and sometimes had to be removed in clots.

Another fruit of Gemma's perfect union with her God was a certain impassibility in the midst of the greatest sufferings. Either she did not feel their effects or paid no attention to them, and while all around her were seen to be in great trouble, she alone remained undisturbed. "Don't be uneasy," she used to say, "Jesus won't allow any harm to happen to us. Oh! is not Jesus with us? Why be afraid?" During physical pains that tormented her greatly, she was even cheerful. In the past, when our Lord withdrew His sensible presence, she suffered great anguish of soul and trembled all over, fearing that she had lost her beloved Lord for ever. Now, having become His spouse, she is no longer distressed. She knows that the bond which unites her to Him will never be broken. God can, indeed, try her by depriving her of the sweetness of His Divine presence, but He cannot separate Himself from her heart. Observe how different her language now is from what it was formerly: "Who knows if Jesus will let Himself be seen any more? But, if He does not look at me any more, what matter? I look at Him always, and if He does not want me with Him any longer, I, on my part, am always seeking Him. I will think of Him without ceasing, and in the end He will return. Fly from me, fly far away, O Lord, if Thou wilt. I will continue to follow Thee, being certain that neither heaven nor earth nor hell can ever separate me from Thee. If it please Thee to make me suffer a martyrdom by hiding Thy dear presence from me, it will be the same to me only to know that Thou art satisfied. Thou being satisfied, all should be satisfied. Jesus hidden, Jesus for all Eternity!"

What more? Even the diabolical assaults which we have described elsewhere were no longer able to make her lose her peace of soul. Hence, in the last letter she wrote to me shortly before her death, she was able to say: "Be assured, father, that I have no longer any fear of the devil. He beats and cuffs me, but I am sure that, if Jesus permits him to molest me, He will not allow him to do me any harm."

The conclusion, that all I have said leads to this: that Gemma's will, owing to the closeness of her union with God, became totally transformed into His Will, and in It reposed. And this perfect abandonment in God is one of the most excellent fruits of the Mystical Union in a soul. I should have much to write, were I only to allude here and there to all that I have in my notes on this subject. But the reader will be able to form a right idea about it from what he has already learned of the Servant of God's perfect conformity to the Divine Will. As this young girl from her very infancy willed only what was purely the Will of God, and in its fulfillment always found peace and happiness, no sooner was she raised to the dignity of spouse, than the Divine Will became truly the passion of her heart and a real necessity. Therefore, she was able to say to me one day: "Father, be quite content, for now I have given myself entirely into God's hands. I have surrendered myself totally to His Divine Will. I seek Jesus, but only that He may help me to do His most Holy Will. So, also, I have learned another thing, in my spirit I no longer go seeking or thinking, and I live in silence and peace of heart. Oh! what great joy there is in remaining totally united to His Most Holy Will! His pleasure only, that is enough." Hence, her indomitable courage in facing difficulties and obstacles, which has already been mentioned, her heroic fortitude in bearing up under every kind of trial, and her unfailing cheerfulness, that, passing from the spiritual or superior part to the lower, made her always bright and rendered her enviable and dear to all! But what strikes me most, and what I wish here to emphasize in this happy state of God's faithful Servant is the immense increase in the ardent yearnings of her heart towards the Infinite Good.

From what I know of this for certain, I am able to assert that very few souls among those commonly known have given proof of similar inner burning fire of the love of God. Gemma herself, who for so many years had been incessantly palpitating with love, was heard to exclaim: "But what is this I feel? I cannot, O my true God, abandon myself to this sweetness, to this happiness. What is it that I feel, my God? Ah! I feel Thee in my heart. I feel Thee so living. What a mystery! I feel in paradise. Sooner or later, my Jesus, Thou wilt make me die, when I feel Thee thus palpitating in my heart. O Jesus, what if I could someday be able to say that I have been consumed by Thy Love? No, no, Jesus, don't command me to love Thee. No, no, I will not ask Thee for more love, because I cannot contain any more. Don't continue to consume me, as I am unable to bear it."

And that was true. The natural organ of love, that is the heart, itself gave indubitable proofs of it. For as soon as this young Saint was raised to the highest and most perfect degree of charity, her heart, finding itself unequal to the fervor of her soul, reacted in an extraordinary way. "My heart," she said to me, "beats with the greatest violence and seems to want to leave my breast. It is too weak and cannot stay quiet. It is most trying to me to be obliged to remain sitting in bed, and the whole bed shakes. At certain moments it appears to me that my heart is coming out of my breast and I am obliged to put my hand on it. Oh! how I would wish to have someone to help me to moderate the fire and flames by which my heart is constantly agitated!" Do not imagine, reader, that these words are exaggerated, for I have had many proofs of what Gemma has stated. That overflowing heart in reality beat so strongly, that anyone trying to resist it with both hands joined, felt forcibly repelled. I myself have often seen Gemma's chair and bed vibrating greatly during those strong palpitations, while she remained tranquil, and, what is more wonderful, without the slightest sign of oppression or trembling. She spoke freely and was quite at her ease, as if she felt nothing strange, and seemed not to suffer the least inconvenience, her heart alone was thus agitated. Once I asked her what she thought of such a strange phenomenon, and she with her accustomed simplicity answered: "O! don't you see it? Jesus is so great and my heart is so small! There is no room for Him in such a little heart; and yet wishing to dwell there, He shakes it in this way. And things will be badly remedied, father, if Jesus does not remedy them. Oh! that this heart were dilated! that Jesus might stay there at His ease!"

Her heart was indeed dilated, and expanding, it forced out three ribs on that side, as we read to have happened in a strong impulse of love to St. Philip Neri, and to our Holy Father, St. Paul of the Cross. In Gemma's case, as this mysterious occurrence lasted a considerable time, there was the facility of observing and studying it. Those three ribs were greatly bent, almost at right angles–thus forming a large protuberance on the outside and a cavity within that allowed the heart to palpitate more freely. Here this chapter must end.

CHAPTER 24

Ecstasies And Apparitions
Of The Servant Of God.

THEOLOGIANS put Ecstasy and Rapture among the degrees of Mystical Union, and rightly so. The ecstasy is but a stronger and sweeter drawing of the soul to God, which, while rendering it incapable of attending to the government of the senses, causes these to remain, as it were, abandoned and spent. And when this drawing and consequent inaction of the senses happens rapidly, and with an impulse, then the ecstasy is called a rapture. Although in the last chapter I spoke of the highest of all mystical degrees, namely, that of perfect and permanent union, yet much remains to be said of Gemma's ecstasies and raptures, of which I think it advisable to treat in a separate chapter. Here I must repeat that, although, according to the general rule, the soul advances in the mystical ways by passing from lower to higher grades, nevertheless the Holy Spirit, who is not bound by these rules, very often changes the order and communicates Himself by means of the most sublime graces to certain souls who have not been prepared for them by lesser gifts.

It was certainly so with the Virgin of Lucca, who began to have ecstasies and raptures before her contemplations had risen to the other degrees of perfection already described. And, when I undertook the direction of this privileged soul, I found that she had already received the gift of ecstasies. This went on increasing as she advanced in the other degrees, until it became so frequent that it seemed to be natural to her. Without distinguishing here between ecstasy and rapture, as both these endowments from above alternated continually in Gemma, and the very impulses of the second preserved all the evenness of the first, I will designate them by the same name.

Having made the above remarks, I must call attention to the fact that the ecstatic state in this child of heaven, as seen when treating of her contemplation in general, showed itself at any time or place, when and where she least expected it—while at table, working in the kitchen, in conversation, when walking out of doors, and so on. She generally felt it coming on, but only a few minutes before. It came in a sudden state of recollection. This was followed by an ardent desire to be united more intimately with God, and then her heart began to beat violently. At these forewarnings she tried to distract and rouse herself, or else to get away, so that others might not become aware of her state, and in this she generally succeeded. But sometimes the Divine visitation was quite instantaneous. It came on her wherever she was, and there she remained in ecstasy, that is, absorbed in God, mind and heart, with all the powers of her soul, while her external senses lost all their use and exercise. I say her senses, and not her body, for this continued to maintain its flexibility, liberty of movement, and generally the strength to remain standing or kneeling.

In this our miserable age, when rationalism moved by impulse or desire to disbelieve, signalizes itself by casting doubt on all that is supernatural, and yet remains the dupe of charlatans, of spiritism, hypnotism, etc., one would say that God has willed to show a special regard for this His Servant, modifying in her the form of certain phenomena which, in many other ecstasies, gave occasion to sophistic criticism. It has been well ascertained that Gemma in her ecstasies showed all the signs of one in perfect health, and in a perfectly normal state, according to physiological rules. No death-like paleness, no agitated movements, no strange postures, no muscular contortions. Her exterior senses only, as I have said, ceased to act. One might puncture her hands, head or arms with a pin, apply fire to her skin, make deafening noises, all without effect. While this holy child was with her God she felt nothing whatever, and noticed nothing that was said or done around her. When her ecstasies were sorrowful, and this was the case very often, those innocent limbs, without ceasing to be as usual perfectly healthy, became weak, and it was necessary to support her, in order to prevent her falling. When in bed, she remained like one perfectly prostrate. In other ecstasies her body seemed to take part in the joy of her soul, according to what is written: *Cor meum et caro mea exultaverunt in Deum vivum.* And that became quite evident from the light that lit up her eyes, which in her ecstasies appeared to shine like the sun; also, from the color in her cheeks and from her whole face, which seemed like that of an angel come from heaven. "If you had seen her yesterday," wrote one of the family, "my God, one could not look at her. She did not seem to be a mortal. Her countenance was that of a seraph, and moved one to devotion and tears. How short that hour seemed to us, while our Gemma was in ecstasy!" This wonder was most frequent, seen and admired over and over again in that family, and yet it always seemed new. So true is it that mortal man can never have enough of such supernatural things. Towards the end of her life sickness had emaciated Gemma's face and taken away its beauty, but her ecstasy not only brought it back at once, but increased it, giving her a certain dignity of mien that inspired respect and veneration.

With a view to better the order in what I have to say, I will distinguish three forms of ecstasy in the Servant of God: the smaller and less perfect, the greater and the extraordinary. The small ecstasies which were also the most frequent, even occurring several times a day, were at the same time the most spontaneous and simple. Whenever the least ray of infused light illuminated her mind, or if even one of the most ordinary celestial visions was represented to her, she immediately lost sight of the world of sense, an intense recollection came over her, and in an instant she was in the region of the blessed with her whole being, without any movement preceding or accompanying her flight. It was purely spiritual. In order to make sure of it, one should look at her eyes that were then full of light and fixed on heaven, and in order to see that her senses were not in exercise it was necessary to prick or pinch her. How often have not I shed tears, while praying near her or saying the Divine Office with her, she being in ecstasy! Once we were sitting at table, Gemma at one side with her breviary in her hand, I on the other. We recited alternately, and she read the lessons of the nocturns and answered the responsories and versicles with admirable exactness, turning over the pages regularly. But how could she do this? I confess that I have never been able to understand it. She was in ecstasy and dead to every impression of touch. Though she used her eyes when reading, yet she was quite insensible to the heat of the candle, when I held it close to them, as I have done repeatedly. During this devout recital of the Office she was unable to see or hear anything else. No sooner was it stopped for any reason, than she returned to the use of her senses, to lose them again immediately on resuming the Divine Praises where they had been interrupted. Many times it happened that, on my asking her if the dear Angel Guardian was at his post looking after her, Gemma, with her charming ease of manner, turned her eyes in that direction, and beholding him, remained in ecstasy, alienated from her senses, as long as she continued to contemplate him. The same sort of thing happened repeatedly on other occasions that were daily offered her by the Divine Spirit, who thus gave evidence of the delight He found in the company of His faithful Servant. I call these ecstasies of Gemma the smaller ones, precisely because they were less perfect, lasted a shorter time, and for the most part, allowed the exercise of the senses. They were also much less profound, because the senses, excepting that of touch, were not entirely dormant. Consequently, it happened now and then that, while in that state, she was able to occupy herself, not only as we have seen in reading but even in writing letters or conferring with her spiritual father. And what letters! And what enchanting conferences!

The greater ecstasies, on the other hand, besides being less frequent, more intense, and more sublime, although at the same time equally simple and spontaneous, also lasted longer, varying from half an hour to an hour and more. In these the loss of her senses was entire and continuous. To recall her there was need of a formal precept, and sometimes not even that was enough, as the Holy Spirit is not bound to yield to the will of a man, even though he be His minister. There were times when at a purely mental precept Gemma was seen to come out of her most sublime ecstasies, and she did so without showing the slightest sign of regret. At other times, when the return to her senses was spontaneous through suspension of the Divine influx, it was charming and at the same time most touching to see her come to herself. No yawning or stretching, no movements that could indicate weariness, distress, confusion of mind, or disturbed imagination; but a sweet smile as if having had a talk with one person, she was turning to speak to another who was waiting for her. This was Gemma's usual way of coming to herself. Sometimes she was seen to cover her face with both hands, as if ashamed to have been found in that state; or, perhaps it was because of her regret to see the earth after she had been contemplating heaven. These greater ecstasies used to take place in church at the time of Holy Communion. Also when she came to visit Jesus solemnly exposed during the *Quarant 'Ore*, and on other such occasions when her fervor of spirit was liable to be more easily moved.

Finally, the extraordinary ecstasies were of more or less frequent recurrence during the year, without any fixed rule, but as it were periodically, that is, every Thursday evening about eight, and on Friday afternoon about three o'clock. These periodical ecstasies came on generally while she was at supper with the family. Those who lived with her were well-able to say what was coming, from the greater recollection that was seen to preoccupy her, from certain indescribably celestial glances that she gave at intervals towards heaven, and from a sort of immobility of person together with a violence that she seemed to do herself in order to resist. As soon, however, as she became aware of what was going to happen, she hastened to take what little food she was accustomed to, and, seeking to be unobserved, she rose from the table and ran off to shut herself up in her little room. A few moments later one or other of the family followed her and found her kneeling near her bed with her hands joined, her eyes raised to heaven, lost in God, and deprived of all use of her senses. When, however, the loving assault of the Divine Spirit indicated its approach with greater vehemence, the wise child, fearing want of strength to stand against it, hastened to recline upon her bed, where also she was found in full ecstasy, and generally sitting in an Angelic attitude. This ecstasy lasted about an hour.

I call these ecstasies extraordinary, although so frequent, on account of the intensity of the Divine Light that caused them, of the great things that in them were shown her, and of the marvelous effects they produced in her. One of these effects was a participation in Our Savior's bodily pains during His passion, even to the extent of the sacred Stigmata, of which see full particulars in Chapters seven and eight. How truly wonderful were these and other effects produced in Gemma's soul, and how sublime were the communications she received, may be gathered from what she herself manifested during those precious moments while speaking aloud to her God. The devout friends with whom she lived, sometimes one, sometimes another, were charged by me to take down those discourses in writing, omitting nothing. And this was a most fortunate provision, as otherwise they would have been lost in great part, or else much less faithfully reproduced from memory. By this means, taking into account those ecstasies only in which she spoke and could be understood, we have been able to preserve what she said in a hundred and fifty of them, accurately reproduced. Their subject matter is very varied, the ideas are the most exalted, the doctrine, theologically and mystically, is exact, and the expressions, full of majesty and sweet heavenly unction, sink deeply into the minds and hearts of those who read them. Imagine what it was to hear those words from the mouth of the Ecstatic herself! I, for myself, must acknowledge that when listening to those words so full of fire, I could not refrain from tears. The theme of each ecstasy was generally one—it consisted sometimes in a hymn of praise to a

Divine attribute, at other times in expressions of love to the Divine Spouse, or again in a loving contest with God's infinite Mercy for the conversion of some sinner. But it generally turned on the Passion of Christ, and on her desire to be transformed in Him Crucified. I intend soon, if God wills it, to publish as many of these precious documents as I can. My difficulty would be where they are not complete, either because of the many reticences of the Ecstatic–unable to repeat in words what in her soul she saw and felt, or because of the answers given by her Celestial Interlocutor being such that she alone could understand them. The reader will be gratified, if now I give part of one of those discourses written by Gemma herself after the ecstasy, in obedience to my wishes. It was on the 19th of March 1901, at ten o'clock in the morning, and was as usual between Jesus and His holy servant. For brevity's sake I only give the end of it.

> *"O Jesus!" she said, when He had finished speaking, "when I hear Thy Holy Name repeated, my soul is lifted up. Thy Name only, only Thy Name, O Jesus, soothes my life. O Jesus, I have detached my heart from this earth and reposed it in Thee. But the soul, O Jesus, longs ardently and takes courage, seeing itself loaded with so many continual favors. And not being able to repay them, as it ought, with heroic deeds, it finds relief in thoughts and outpourings of love. And Jesus (it is Gemma that still speaks) in answer to my words, made me hear His voice with greater force than ever, and His words had such effect upon me that I would gladly have died, to go to heaven, and exclaimed: O Jesus, this poor soul, thus fettered in this miserable, vile body, unable to fly to Thee, spreads its wings and lifts itself as best it can to come to Thee, to be more close to Thee. It lifts itself with the spirit (she means by thoughts and affections) because this is not tied down as is the body. Then, beside myself with consolation, and full of tears, I turned to my Angels in paradise, witnesses of all the wonders of God's works. 'O say,' I called to them, 'are not these acts of God's omnipotence all*

wrought by Infinite Love?' Then, turning to Jesus, I asked Him whatever He had done to my poor heart that makes it quite impossible for me to restrain it. It always wants to go to Him and I cannot hold it back. Already, of its own accord, it has resolved not to belong to me. It has given itself to Jesus! And Jesus, with His loving, and at the same time penetrating voice, said to me: 'I have carried the day.' Ah! yes, I am happy to be worsted by such infinite Goodness, by so much Love. Jesus now and forever!"

This thought of mine to make Gemma put the subject of some of her ecstasies in writing was not an idle one. By such a step I was able to ascertain that she remembered in order and detail what had happened in her ecstasy, because the words that she repeated to me agreed perfectly with those that had been taken down in writing by members of the family during each ecstasy. A clear proof of this is in the passage just quoted, where Jesus declares Himself to be victorious over Gemma's heart. Let the reader compare it with the words already mentioned in another chapter that were written by persons present as she spoke them while in that ecstasy.

But by far the most tender outbursts of this seraphic girl's love were those that regarded the Passion of Our Savior. Here is a sample of them: "Who has slain Thee, Jesus? Love! Ah! those nails, that Cross, that Blood, are all works of Love!" And, while the Divine Lover of Souls was pouring floods of light into her mind, thus unveiling to her the ineffable mysteries of Redemption and fire into her heart, inflaming it with His Love, she gave vent thus: "O Jesus, what would it be, if some day...? Ah! victim of love for Thee! Do grant O my Lord Jesus that when my lips approach Thine to kiss Thee, I may taste the gall that was given Thee. And when my shoulders lean against Thine make me feel Thy scourgings. And when my flesh is united with Thine in the Holy Eucharist, make me feel Thy Passion. And when my head comes near to Thine make me feel Thy Thorns. And when my heart is close to Thine make me feel Thine Embrace.

O what shall I ever return to Thee for all Thou hast bestowed upon me, in having loved me and lifted me up? What couldst Thou want or expect from me, vile creature? I will give Thee that which Thou Thyself hast given me." Then turning to herself she spoke thus: "O my soul, bless Jesus. Never forget the many graces He has given thee. Love that God Who so loves thee. Lift thyself up to Him Who has so lowered Himself for thee. Show thyself as He shows Himself with thee. Be clean of heart, be pure. Love thy Jesus Who has lifted thee out of so much misery. Love thy God, bless thy Lord." And Jesus, showing Himself pleased with her, insisted on her loving Him more and more, and on her knowing that love is shown by sacrifice, said: "Then Jesus, to learn how to love one must first learn how to suffer. Ah! now I see well that Thy Blood is the work of Love. Oh! then Jesus, if Thou wilt have me, I offer myself as victim. From that Chalice to which Thou hast put Thy Lips I also wish to drink. I thank Thee Jesus that Thou keepest me on Thy Cross."

What shall we say of the ineffable simplicity that we find so very often, nay, almost always, in these sublime outpourings of love? Even at the cost of some slight repetition, let us listen again to this seraphic child, as she begs of her God to take from her those external marks of the Stigmata which, as she could not conceal them from others, troubled her so much. "What dost Thou say, Jesus? Dost Thou grant me this consolation? Thou hast given me so many graces, and now the most necessary, (mark, the most necessary) wilt Thou not grant it me? If Thou actest thus, when Thou sayest to me: 'Gemma, dost thou love Me?' shall I have to answer Thee 'No'? At last, when I shall have wearied Thee and Thou wilt be tired by my importunities, Thou wilt say: 'Yes, I grant thy request.'" At these words her loving Lord seemed to smile, and she, become more daring in her love, subjoined: "Thou smilest Jesus, but I do not smile. Listen Jesus, dost Thou grant me this favor? If not, things will go badly. Come, say yes. Do not look at what I deserve, look at the merit of the one who asks it for me" (Fr. Germanus). Then Our Lord, having assured her, at least in part, that He would satisfy her, as in fact came to pass, she thanked Him thus: "It seemed to me impossible that Thou wouldst not do it for me. How good of Thee dear Jesus!" And, having said this, smiling and joyous, she came out of the ecstasy. There are many others like those from which I have quoted. For ardor and fullness of elevated ideas, they can be compared with those of St. Mary Magdalene di Pazzi and other noted Saints. For simplicity carried to such a degree they are unique in mystical hagiography, and go to show to what a height grace can raise a child, and how the majesty of the God of innocence takes delight in simple souls, and values their homage: *Ex ore infantium perfecisti laudem.*

It sometimes happens that the impulse by which ecstatics are drawn to God is so strong that the body also is moved by it, and assuming, as it were, the agility and lightness of a glorified body, it follows the soul, or rather, is carried by it and remains suspended in the air. This kind of mystical flight is the culminating point of rapture, although rapture can take place without lifting the body from the ground. Now, among Gemma's frequent raptures that were always, as has been said, so calm, spontaneous and dignified, the above-mentioned form, while it was seldom seen by others, was not wanting. This child of heaven, on the pretext of doing some domestic work in the dining-room, where hung a large crucifix venerated by her with great devotion, was seen to go in and out of that room many times a day. And, finding herself alone, she used to stop before the sacred image, standing or kneeling with her eyes fixed upon it. But, when she felt her heart becoming moved at that sight and still more by the deep thoughts it inspired, fearing to remain there in ecstasy, she affectionately kissed the foot of the Cross and hurried away. Sometimes, however, it happened that, outdone by her fervor, she did not get away in time. Moved by the desire to do more, and imprint a kiss on the Sacred Side of her Crucified Lord, she yielded to it, and while thinking how she could reach up there with her lips, the rapture seized her, and, lifted without any human aid in the air, she found herself in the embraces of her Savior. I cannot say how often this happened, simply because I had not the courage to ask her to tell me. Enough for us that the fact remains established, that of all the degrees of sanctity enumerated in Mystical Theology as known by their effects, there is not one to which this humble child of God in her short earthly pilgrimage did not attain.

But I have still more to say on this point. In one of those loving visits to that Crucifix, in September 1901, Gemma, who was preparing the table for dinner, had plenty of time, and being alone she kept continually moving, so to say, like a butterfly about the Holy Image. The more she looked at Him the more her heart beat in her breast and yearned. She would fain have flown to His embrace, and at last exclaimed: "O Jesus, let me come to Thee, I thirst for Thy life-giving Blood." Wonderful to relate! As happened to St. Francis of Assisi, and to our Holy Father St. Paul of the Cross, the Image transformed itself into the Divine Person it represented. Jesus detached His right arm from the Cross and called her to Him. She in an instant was with Him. He pressed her to His Side and she, standing as if on a cloud and embracing Him with both arms, in blessed rapture drew from His Sacred Heart long draughts of love. How gladly would I have been present, thus to have been another witness and to have another proof of the love of Jesus for His creatures, and of their happiness in being united with Him.

The ecstasy, which after all is only a more perfect degree of contemplation, implies of its nature having visions. For the soul is ravished out of its senses through something given it to see or hear that satisfies, attracts and makes it blessed. After all that has been seen up to this of Gemma's contemplation it is needless to further explain the precise nature of her visions while in ecstasy. I will only add here that nothing could ever be discovered in them, either unbecoming, exaggerated, or incoherent, which could leave the least suspicion of their being the result of her imagination. There was nothing in them at variance with the holiness and majesty of the teachings of our holy religion. On the contrary, there was always to be found dignity, order, propriety, and clear dogmatic truth. Surely clearer proofs could not be given that her visions were supernatural and divine. For a girl as simple as Gemma, who had only learned what is ordinarily taught in elementary classes, and who never indulged in reading or listening to lectures and sermons, could not possibly by the aid of her imagination have fabricated things so successfully as never to have made a mistake. It suffices to have thus briefly touched on this matter here, as I shall have to treat of it more fully in a dissertation in the form of an Appendix to the Life, so as to put it in clear evidence. I may, however, add, if indeed it be necessary after all we have seen when treating of the humility of the Servant of God, that she knew how to keep the strictest silence on all she had seen and heard when in ecstasy. How different from many deluded souls, who would wish heaven and earth to know whatever happens to them of an extraordinary nature, and make a boast of it. Gemma would not have manifested what happened to her, even to her directors, if she had not felt the need of their guidance. And this likewise is a most certain sign of the genuineness of her visions and ecstasies.

What has been said applies also to her celestial "locutions." These are certain vibrated words which God speaks to the Soul while in ecstasy with such vivacity and clearness that they effect what they signify in the very center of the spirit. St. Paul calls them "hidden words": *Audivi arcana verba,* and says they are so sublime and elevated that it is not given to human language to express their meaning; *quae non licet homini loqui.* Gemma was largely favored with these locutions, there being scarcely an ecstasy in which our Lord did not make her hear His Divine Word. Nay, in those intimate colloquies, what she said was the least part. The greatest and the best was the words of His Divine Majesty. We have seen some of those discourses those of which the object was to manifest to her the greatness of God Himself; others, which made known the designs of His Providence; others again, referring to the state of some particular soul, or to some work that He wished established in the Church; or even to some abuse He wished removed. And she, docile to the voice of the Divine Spouse, immediately on coming out of the ecstasy, set herself to do all in her power to carry out the Divine Will, appealing to whomsoever it concerned, in order to obtain the fulfillment of the order received. Hence, those letters of hers, so full of fervor. "Monsignor," she wrote in one, "Jesus has said that He wishes you to interest yourself in this matter and prevent that other. Also, that if you desire to please Him, you must act at once." After Communion on a certain occasion, Our Lord, as often happened, appeared to her when in ecstasy and said: "My child, listen to Me. Thou hast to make known great things to thy director in My Name." The simple girl, thinking that He meant her former confessor answered: "My Jesus, do me a charity. Do not send me to him. Thou knowest well, Good Jesus, that he has no faith in my fantasies" (so he called them). And Jesus: "No, I send thee to thy father. He for certain will give My Heart this satisfaction that I so desire. Say to him that if what I command is not done, so and so will happen, and then there will be no time to remedy it." Of the matter here referred to I will speak in the twenty-seventh chapter. There is scarcely a letter written by Gemma to her directors in which mention is not made of locutions such as these that happened in her ecstasies; and facts, which she could not otherwise have known, and much less have foreseen, always came to verify them. Very often also these locutions took the form of teachings in which the Divine Master instructed His beloved disciple in heavenly things, and directed and urged her on in the path of virtue. Of these I have already given examples in many places; but only one example at a time because, owing to the quantity of information at my disposal on these subjects, it would be endless were I to attempt to bring it all forward. Blessed Gemma, who like the Apostles deserved to be taught by the Incarnate Wisdom Himself! It is thus I explain to myself how in so few years she rose to such perfection of sanctity.

Now we come to her apparitions. Visions and apparitions are objectively one and the same thing. They differ, however, in this, that visions generally take place in ecstasy, whereas apparitions occur at other times. But the soul who sees an apparition may easily pass into ecstasy, as always happened with Gemma. Our Lord willed to be glorified in all His dealings with His faithful Servant, and in the most extraordinary ways, and it was to be expected that in her heavenly apparitions He would likewise show forth His magnificence. So it was, whether we consider their frequency, their cordiality, not to say familiarity, or finally their efficacy in their salutary effects on her. We have already seen the sweet, familiar guardianship of her Angel, that may be said to have been continual. I have likewise made mention of apparitions of other Angels, and of Saints, in particular of Blessed Gabriel of the Dolours, as also of the souls in Purgatory, and I shall have to do so more opportunely elsewhere. I say the same of the Saint of saints, Jesus Christ, especially when He appeared as our Suffering Redeemer. Let not the reader lose sight of these touching apparitions of Jesus as already described, and let him be prepared to see others still more beautiful. Now I am going to speak particularly of the apparitions of the Blessed Virgin.

Gemma always loved with warmest love this Heavenly Queen of the Angels whom, with sweet confidence, she called "My dear Mother." Left orphan by the death of her earthly mother in her tenderest years, she accustomed herself thenceforward not to recognize any mother but Mary, and towards her ever afterwards she acted as her devoted and loving child. After Jesus, all her heart was for Mary. "Oh! how I love my Mother," she used to say. "She knows it and then Jesus Himself gave her to me, and told me to love her so much. And what great goodness this Heavenly Mother has always shown me! What would have become of me, if I had not had her? She has always helped me in my spiritual wants. She has preserved me from countless dangers. She has freed me from the hands of the devil who was ceaselessly coming to molest me. She pleaded my cause with Jesus when I sinned, and she soothed Him when I moved Him to anger by my wicked life. She has taught me to know Him and love Him, to be good and to please Him. Ah! my dear Mother, I will love thee always and ever." These and similar expressions of tenderest affection were ever in the heart and on the lips of this holy child and were continually occurring in her letters. Was it possible then for our Holy Mother not to repay such tender love a hundredfold? Gemma gave herself all to Mary and Mary to Gemma. And to show her how much she loved her, besides the favors without number and without measure that she obtained for her from Jesus, she very often deigned to come to her visibly and allowed her to see her face to face, caressing her and pressing her to her maternal bosom. Let us leave it to Gemma herself to describe these delicacies of love.

"Whoever could have imagined," thus she wrote in a manifestation of conscience, "that this evening my dear Mother would have come to see me? It was not even to be thought of because I believed that my bad conduct would prevent it. Yet she had compassion on me. Her presence quickly put me in a state of recollection and then, as often happens, I lost my senses and I found myself, I think, with Our Lady of Dolours. Oh! what happiness! What sweetness of heart I felt during those delicious moments! Let whoever can, explain it. It seemed to me, after some moments of emotion, that she took me in her lap and made me rest my head on her shoulder and keep it there for a short time. My heart during that time felt perfectly happy and contented without any other desire. "Dost thou love only me?" she asked me now and then. "Oh no" I answered her, "before thee I love someone else." "And who is it?" pretending not to know. "It is one so dear to me! more dear than all else. I love Him so much that I would now, this moment, give my life for Him. For His sake I regard not my life." "But tell me, who is it?" she asked me impatiently. "If thou, Mother, hadst come the evening before last, thou wouldst have seen Him with me. I instead go to Him

every day (she meant in Holy Communion) and I would go oftener if I could. But dost thou know Mother," I continued, "why I do so? Because I know that He wishes to see, by His keeping so far away from me, if I am capable of ceasing to love Him. But quite the contrary. The farther He keeps away the more I feel drawn to Him! No," I replied, I won't tell thee. If thou didst only see Him, Mother! He is like Thee in beauty. His hair is the color of thine." Mother then embracing me, seemed to say again: "But my child, tell me of Whom are you speaking?" I then exclaimed aloud, "Dost thou not understand me? Of Jesus, I speak of Jesus." "Repeat it still louder," she said. Then smiling she looked at me and pressed me closely to herself saying, "Yes love Him, but love Him greatly; mind, love Him alone!" "Don't be afraid," I said to her, "no one in the world shall taste my affections! Jesus alone." Again she pressed me to her. She seemed to kiss me on the forehead. Then I awoke (meaning that she came out of the ecstasy) and I found myself stretched on the floor with the crucifix near me."

Although six years have passed since I first received that statement from Gemma herself, I have read it over and over again and it always seems to me more exquisitely touching. Here is another. The form is always the same.

"I was sitting in bed, not having yet gone to sleep. It seemed as if a beautiful lady drew near me and moved to kiss me. I was taken out of myself and no longer in the world. I immediately made a thousand protests, according to the instructions given me. My heavenly Mother" (and it was truly she, although Gemma showed doubts of it at first) "looked at me, smiled and said: "Dear child!" Father, (Germanus) forgive me if I yielded too quickly, but I let my Mother do as she pleased and she took me in her arms. I nearly died, yes died, of sweetest consolation. Oh! how many loving caresses! She loves me so much! She said

she had come for my bouquet, don't you know? She found me so poor, and she encouraged me to practice virtue, particularly humility and obedience. She said some words that I did not understand, and then added: "My child, labor to refine thy spirit and become perfect quickly." What happened then I do not know. That "Quickly" caused such a violent movement in my heart, on which my Mother placed her lovely hand, that I could not speak. But mentally I asked her for an explanation. I opened my eyes and made my request through them. She answered me thus: "Tell thy father, (the director) that if he does not see to thee, (to enclose her in a convent) I will take thee soon to paradise!" She kissed me saying: "If not quickly, we shall be together more quickly than he imagines."

It happened precisely as she said, and I still feel remorse because of it. In less than a year Gemma quite unexpectedly fell sick and went to heaven.

"O father, O father!" she continued, "after such things how contemptible the world appears! I don't know if you have ever had this experience. Oh! how beautiful our heavenly Mother is! Have you ever seen her? Although I have already seen her very often, yet my ardent desire to see her again remains."

On another occasion the Holy Mother appeared with her Divine Son as a beautiful child, and with her own hands placed Him in Gemma's arms. She, trembling, pressed Him to her heart and kissed Him with much love. The Divine Infant did the same, and having instructed her divinely, ended by giving her His blessing. She gave Him to His Mother and the vision vanished. I cannot say how often that happened, but I have a distinct recollection of three instances. On four other occasions Our Lord appeared to her alone, but likewise as a tender infant. She will tell us how that came about:

"Yesterday evening at the hour of guard, I went to my room and was left all alone. Then the Infant Jesus came to visit me. Oh!

how beautiful Jesus is! If all were to know Him, how immensely
they would love Him! He came in my lap, kissed me, petted me,
and asked me if I loved Him. I kissed Him with ardent affection
and felt how intensely I loved Him. He asked me if I would be
all His, and I was so overjoyed that I knew not what to answer,
but I held Him more tightly."

This young girl is a poor child of Adam. He Who comes to her in
the humble semblance of a baby is the God of Majesty, the Incarnate
Word. He lowers Himself so far as to embrace and allow Himself to
be embraced by His creature, asking her love in return. O depth of
the mystery of God's Love in the Incarnation!

The Ecstatic of Lucca, I venture to say, has measured this sublimity
and yet she does not seem to be dazzled by it. Nay, quite the contrary.
She goes on to say:

"Then I began to talk to Him in all confidence. I told Him to
make things well known to you and the confessor, and not to let
me be troubled any more." And Jesus smiled and said to me: "I
will do it," but He said it slowly and gently. Then I asked Him
not to wait so long, as I did not want any further delay. And He
replied: "But if I have loved thee more than so many others of
My creatures, though thou mayest be worse than they? As for
the truth of these things, he who should know it (Fr. Germanus)
knows it already. With regard to the other (the confessor) it is
not yet time, but the time will come for him to know it. I am
Jesus Who am speaking to thee!"

This colloquy lasted a whole hour. Now, see how the simple child
ends her narration:

"Jesus went away, and here I am again all alone. Tell me, father,
are you willing that Jesus should come back to me? If you are,
He will surely return. Give me a big blessing. Send Jesus back
to me. I cannot do without Him."

I did not answer this touching letter. But, deeply moved, I said to myself: Love has made this seraphic girl become happily foolish. She knows that she is espoused to her God in an indissoluble bond and still she yearns. Only one who truly loves can so think and speak.

CHAPTER 25

St. Gemma's Singular Devotion
To The Blessed Sacrament.

THIS faithful Servant of God, guided as she was in the way of sanctity, knew how to choose in it that which was most solid and perfect. All the devout practices commonly in use among the faithful pleased her, and she rejoiced at seeing them taken up by many. But she confined her own choice to very few. First, devotion to the Sacred Humanity of the Word Incarnate, and to His Passion. Then devotion to the Mother of God, specially in her Dolours. Finally, devotion to the Blessed Eucharist. The first touched the very center of her heart and stimulated her to sacrifice. The second comforted her and filled her with filial confidence. The third fed her soul, and satiating it, enabled her to lead a heavenly life on earth. We have already treated of her extraordinary fervor in the two first-mentioned devotions. It now remains for me to speak of the third, and here also I have to relate great things, things so singular as to lead us to believe that God by a special providence raised up this child of heaven at a time of so much falling away in piety, as an example and stimulus to Christians to venerate and love the most Holy Sacrament of the Altar. The Blessed Eucharist is by excellence the Mystery of Faith: *Mysterium fidei*.

Gemma had such a vivid faith that in her it seemed to be changed into evidence. She had indeed a pure heart, and our Lord has said that He allows Himself to be seen by those who are pure and clean of heart. She was humble and simple as a little child, and our Lord has said that to such souls He manifests the hidden things of His Wisdom and Goodness. Thus then with the clear and penetrating glance of virginity, of simplicity, of immaculate purity, and with the vivid light that faith infused into her during her sublime contemplations, she was able to see clearly into this Sacrament and measure the width and the depth of Its mysteries. For us, in order to enter into communication with the hidden God in the Blessed Eucharist it is necessary to collect our thoughts and excite our faith and devotion by repeated acts, with Gemma it was enough to recall it to mind, if indeed that was needed, as her thoughts were continually with It. So much so, that turning to the altar in thought she at once beheld our Lord exposed thereon, felt Him present with her, and with her whole being and almost, I might say, with all her bodily senses she rejoiced in the presence of that sweet Majesty.

In order to form a just idea of the great ardor of her devotion it would be necessary to have heard all that this blessed child said on the subject, and read all she wrote about it in her letters, as well as what others gathered from her lips during her ecstatic colloquies. It would be impossible to give all Gemma's inspired words regarding this mystery in this biography. But I cannot withhold from my readers a selection of edifying extracts that I have collected from her thoughts as expressed in writing, her sayings to others, and the outpourings of her soul while in ecstasy. I begin with her ideas of the Blessed Eucharist.

> *"My father," she once wrote, "you will find a letter without sense. It does not matter. Let me speak of Holy Communion. I cannot contain myself. Is it possible that there are souls who do not understand what the Blessed Eucharist is? Who are insensible to the Divine Presence, to the mysterious ardent effusions of the Sacred Heart of my Jesus? O Heart of Jesus! Heart of Love!"*

She writes to a Roman lady, her intimate friend:

> *"How sweet the Spirit of Jesus is! Oh what is it that ever induced Jesus to communicate Himself to us in such an enchanting and wonderful way? Just think—Jesus our food! Jesus my food! At this moment what would I not wish to say to you? But I fail in*

the attempt. I succeed only in crying, and in repeating: Jesus my food! And in thinking that Jesus has done this through the immense love He has for us."

And that weeping of hers was continuous as it was also spontaneous and sweet. To put it in her own words it was "a weeping in silence, with tears of gratitude and heavenly happiness." In an ecstasy, speaking with her God she was heard to express her happiness and thankfulness as follows: "I know that Thou hast not given me temporal and passing riches, but Thou hast given me the true wealth that is the nourishment of the Eucharistic Word. What would become of me if I did not dedicate all my affections to the Sacred Host? Oh! yes, I know it, Lord, that in order to make me deserve a paradise in heaven Thou givest me Communion here on earth." It seemed almost that she made no difference between the delights of heaven and those of the "paradise of Jesus" that are tasted on earth at the Holy Table. At other times, speaking likewise in ecstasy, she called the Eucharist the "Academy of Paradise where one learns how to love." And explaining this thought she added: "The school is the supper-room, Jesus is the Master, the doctrines are His Flesh and Blood." From these words and others like them it is easy to gather some idea of how many treasures of celestial wisdom she discovered in the mystery of the Blessed Eucharist. As we go on we shall find at every step fresh proofs of the sublime idea that Gemma had of this Divine Sacrament.

Although this blessed child was always deep in thought, and always found herself in spirit before the sacred Tabernacle, yet she was not fully satisfied unless she could go to church, and there adore her hidden God. In order to avoid singularity, which she always detested, she contented herself with going to the Church only twice a day. In the morning when she went to hear Mass and receive Holy Communion, and in the evening for the public Adoration. "I am going to Jesus," she used to say, "let us go to Jesus. He is all alone and no one thinks of Him. Poor Jesus!" On entering the sacred building she turned her first anxious gaze towards the Tabernacle. Then devoutly recollected and as if quite alone before the Altar of the Blessed Sacrament she remained kneeling motionless in prayer. She never turned her eyes from where they were first fixed, and except for the glow on her face and occasional tears that trickled down her cheeks, you would not have distinguished her from any others attentively engaged in prayer. "Oh! what immense happiness and joy," she has said, "my heart feels before Jesus in the Blessed Sacrament! And if Jesus would allow me to enter the sacred Tabernacle where He, Soul, Body, Blood and Divinity is present, should I not be in Paradise?" And turning to Our Lord Himself in His Sacrament, "Jesus," she exclaimed, "Soul of my soul, my Paradise, Holy Victim, behold me all Thine. I felt that Thou wert seeking me and I ran." And then with filial confidence she continued to say that she had come to keep Him company, and offer herself wholly to Him, and present Him some little acts of virtue practiced for His love, and to receive any orders He might wish to give her, or at least to listen to some sweet word. But above all, to ask His Love, Love, Love.

And with what an impulse of faith did she not make these acts! Here are some of her words spoken in ecstasy: "O Jesus! Behold me before Thee. Before Thee I present my soul. Soul, O Jesus, that Thou hast created not from Thy substance but by means of the Word which Thou art Thyself. Not from any other elementary matter. Ah! this spiritual soul that Thou hast created, that must live for ever, that Thou hast sanctified, purified in Thy holy Font. Ah!" And here she ceased to speak, continuing mentally to unfold her thoughts. Then she went on: "If down here that which is good gives such delight, what sort of bliss must not come with Thee Who art the King of all that is good? The pleasure afforded on this earth by created things is totally different from that which is found in Thee Who art the Creator. See, O Jesus, when a creature desires anything even though she succeeds in obtaining it she is not content, she is never satisfied, she dies without obtaining all that she desires. Thou alone dost satisfy. Thou alone dost purify. Thou alone renderest immaculate those who live in Thee, and in whom Thou livest." This thought excites her love and she exclaims: "Ah! I have found out Thy habitation, O Jesus. Thou dwellest in the soul that Thou hast created to Thine own image, in the soul that seeks Thee, that loves Thee, that desires Thee. Oh! my poor soul has understood the riches of Thy love!" And humbling herself as she always did, even in the midst of the most ravishing heavenly communications, she continued: "I am Thine. I am Thine O Jesus. Thou wouldst have good reason to complain of me, yes, because I have offended Thee. And undeserving as I am I should be obliged to give back to the Altar so many stolen Breads, and so much precious Blood. But I promise Thee amendment. Only do not cut short the current of Thy favors. Rather make me die, than that I should be wanting in fidelity and love. What dost Thou want O Jesus, what dost Thou want? Is it that my love be unchangeable? To that end I will nourish myself every day with Thy Flesh and Blood."

Thanking our Lord for the victories gained over the enemy, she was once heard to say: "This morning Thou hast conquered O Jesus. After I received Thee I began to think of the hard-fought battles in which with Thy help I conquered the Devil. Oh, I counted many such victories. Who knows how many times without Thy aid my faith, hope and charity would have failed me? My understanding would have been darkened if Thou, Eternal Sun, hadst not enlightened it. And my love, how many times would it not have grown weak if Thou hadst not come to strengthen it with Thy Presence? But Thou with Thy fire didst inflame it. I know it. All was the work of Thy Love. All were victories of this Thine Infinite Love. And now O Lord, ought not I to be grateful?" Then dwelling in more emphatic words on this tender thought she exclaimed: "My God, open Thy Heart to me. O Jesus, open to me Thy Sacramental breast because I wish to deposit all my affections therein. O Jesus, how greatly I love Thee! But why dost Thou act with so much lovingness while I offend Thee with such countless ingratitudes? This thought alone, if I could but comprehend it, should be enough to turn me into a furnace of love. Is it not an irresistible love, to love Him Who is not angry with one who has offended Him? O Jesus, if I but considered attentively Thy immense solicitude for me, how greatly should I not excel in every virtue? Pardon me, O Jesus, so much carelessness, pardon such great ignorance. My God, Jesus my Love, Increated Goodness, what would have become of me if Thou hadst not drawn me to Thee? Open to me Thy Heart, open to me Thy Sacramental breast. I open mine to Thee."

After having thus given vent to the impulses of her heart, repeating always the same ideas, but in ever-changing forms, she lapsed, as if tired, into silence. Then irradiated with heavenly light she was raised to highest contemplation. In these sublime elevations of spirit Jesus spoke to her heart and made her feel how pleased He was by her visits, and told her how they recompensed Him for the disregard of the greater part of men and for the outrages offered Him by sinners. He praised her fidelity, and declared Himself content, and ready to reward her with new graces and enrich her with fresh gifts, encouraging her to remain constant and return Him love for love. Such words inflamed her heart still more and she began again to speak, and after humbly confessing her unworthiness she asked: "Dost Thou wish for love O Jesus? But I have no more in my heart. Ah! I would wish to set all the creatures of the earth on fire with it." And in an effort to make Him know how much she loved Him, with child-like confidence she added: "Supposing, O Lord, that Thou wert I and I were Jesus, dost Thou know what I would do? I would cease to be myself that Thou mightest become me. O God, O Jesus, I behold Thee greater than all the treasures of the earth. How gladly would I unite myself with Thy Angels! How willingly would I spend my whole being in Thy praises and remain for ever before Thee! But what do I say when I speak of Thee? I say what I can, but never what I ought! And if I do not know how to act, must I then be silent? No, because my Jesus must be loved and honored by all. Pay no attention to what I say to Thee with my mind, (she says with my mind because she speaks in ecstasy), but look into my whole being, my every secret is known to Thee O Jesus. Therefore art Thou not convinced that I love Thee more than all else in Heaven and on Earth?"

These and the like were the affections that vibrated in that virgin heart in the presence of her God in the Blessed Sacrament. I could quote hundreds of them, all faithfully taken from her lips and scrupulously put down in writing, but my space will not allow of it. The reader will form an idea of them from those I have given. Owing to such ardent impulses of love her strength often failed her: "Ah!" she exclaimed, "I can bear it no longer. No, I cannot bear to think that Jesus in all the splendors of His most loving Heart, and in the marvelous expansion of His paternal Love, should thus manifest Himself to His lowest creature." On saying these words she fell fainting into the arms of her companion who, being prepared, knew how to dispose things so that no one in the Church should become aware of what had happened, and in this she always succeeded. On one occasion among many, having recovered from her weakness, Gemma said in her own enchanting way: "My beloved Jesus, but if Thou actest in this way with everyone, making them burn before Thee as I do, people will not be able to support it or resist Thee." I once wrote and asked her if when she found herself before Jesus she would present me also to Him, and say to Him that I too wished to love Him. And here is the answer of this simple child: "But will it do, father? For what if things should happen to you as to me? Who would hold a hand on your heart?" (she meant to keep it quiet in impulses of love such as hers); "and if you are alone you will fall to the ground. No, it won't do." Whenever she felt those mysterious impulses coming on she hastened to leave the Church, as already mentioned, particularly when she was alone. "Ah!" she exclaimed, "I don't know how so many who remain near Jesus don't burn to nothing. To me it seems that if I were to stay there for barely a quarter of an hour I should become a heap of ashes."

Once while in ecstasy she was heard to say familiarly to our Lord: "Listen, Jesus, to what the Confessor asks me: 'What do you do Gemma when you are before Jesus?' What do I do? If I am with Jesus Crucified–I suffer; and if with Jesus in His Sacrament–I love." Writing to personal friends, she invited them to come to the Blessed Sacrament, as the place of appointment. "Let us run to Jesus, Heart of Love, Heart full of tenderness. Tomorrow morning I await you with Jesus. Let us remain together before Jesus in His Sacrament, and let us bless Jesus together." She herself was anxious that I should know exactly how she employed her day, in which among other things the first place was given to the hour of her visit morning and evening according to the season: "The morning with Jesus at seven o'clock. In the evening before Jesus at six o'clock during the whole winter, come and join me and help me to love our Great God. She had also made an agreement with her more intimate friends to interchange their daily communions and her humility led her to believe that she was the gainer. She remembered the bargain faithfully, and writing to those friends she reminded them of it. "Good-bye until Saturday. Remember the Communion on Friday." Surely blessed are those friendships whose trysting-place is at the Feet of Jesus their Father and God!

Let us examine more closely the culminating point of Gemma's devotion—Holy Communion—in which precisely the Mystery of the Love of Jesus is accomplished. Would that she who so often disclosed to me the secrets of her soul on this subject would now enable me to relate adequately and exactly what she then told me of the fire that the Divine Spouse enkindled in her heart at the Holy Table. It was her hunger and thirst for Holy Communion that made this young girl hover like a butterfly near the Tabernacle. Her heart longed for this Divine Food only. And we have seen that even when quite a child her ardent desire to make her first Communion almost brought her to death's door. Now I add that this hunger and thirst, far from being satisfied by her daily Communion, kept on increasing until they consumed her whole being. "Every morning," she said to me, "I go to Holy Communion. The greatest and only comfort I have, although I am in no wise provided with what is needed to worthily approach Jesus. The loving treatment that Jesus bestows on me every morning in the Holy Communion excites within me an unutterable sweetness and draws to itself all the weak affections of my miserable heart." And then she exclaimed: "Behold O Lord, my heart and my soul. Come Lord, I open my breast to Thee. Send in Thy Divine Fire. Burn me, consume me, come and delay no longer. I would fain be the dwelling of all Thy fires."

This desire grew stronger every evening, and, increasing every hour, sweetly tormented her all the night so as even to make her faint. Let us hear her describe it: "Last night and the night before while thinking of Holy Communion, I felt myself growing faint, and my heart was in commotion. Yesterday evening also before going to supper I said some prayers, among others this ejaculation: 'Grant, O Lord, that from this small supper, I may pass to enjoy Thy immense supper'" (the Blessed Eucharist). "I stopped a few minutes to think of this and, there and then, I felt forced towards Jesus" (that is rapt in ecstasy). "The same thing happens to me whenever I think of Jesus, particularly when He invites me to receive Him, and when He tells me that He is coming to repose in my heart." This went so far that her confessor, in order that she might have a few hours' sleep, and that her health might not suffer, felt bound to forbid her stopping willfully during the night to think of her Communion of the following morning.

In the morning, at break of day, already beside herself, she jumped out of bed, dressed in a few minutes and was ready to go to Church. Very often when I was receiving hospitality from that devout family, who are benefactors of our Institute, I was moved to tears at seeing Gemma standing with her hat on, absorbed in thought, at the door of her companion's room, that they might go to Church together. "And where are you going my child?" I said to her. "To Jesus, father." "And what to do?" Then with a modest smile she answered, "You know." "To see her," these are the words of the same companion, "she seemed each morning as if she were getting herself ready for her nuptials, or as she put it, 'to go to the Feast of the Love of Jesus.'" There certainly was not the least affectation in her manner, and I often caused her to be watched by others. It was observed however by the one who was generally with her that the dear child's mind and heart at that time were in extraordinary activity. It was impossible then to get her to speak except when it was fitting or necessary. And I have shown in another place how she avoided speaking even with her angel guardian when he appeared to her visibly, telling him confidentially to leave her alone as she had something better to think of.

She was so strongly impressed by the greatness of the action to be performed at the Altar that every other thought vanished from her mind. That will explain why she prepared so carefully for it. "It is a question," she said, "of uniting two extremes. God Who is everything, and the creature who is nothing. God Who is light and the creature who is darkness. God Who is holiness and the creature who is sin. It is a question of taking part at the Table of the Lord. There cannot be then enough preparation for it." Such thoughts made Gemma tremble. So much so, that if her great faith had not given her courage, although full of burning desires she would never have approached the Divine Table. In time of spiritual desolation as well as of heavenly unction, and even in the midst of the most intimate communication of the Divine Lover, this struggle agitated her incessantly, causing her intense suffering so that she even complained of it lovingly to our Lord. "Yes I know, Jesus, it is better to receive Thee than to look at Thee, but I am afflicted because I feel that were I to prepare myself for years and years like the Angels, yet I should never be worthy to receive Thee. O Jesus, it is sweet to confess my misery before Thee. Help me, O Lord! Ah! I can still cast myself at Thy feet. I still love the Faith, and a thousand times I repeat and will continue to repeat, it is always better to receive Thee than to look at Thee." This phrase was suggested to her by Jesus Himself, as is easily gathered from the context. By this means, confidence tempering fear and fear moderating confidence, there came to be established in Gemma's heart that balance of faith and of love so necessary for worthily receiving the Holy Communion.

One morning, Feast of the holy Martyr St. Lawrence, she who knew how to draw spiritual profit from everything was heard to speak thus to Our Lord: "But, dear Jesus, what confusion this morning! Thou hast wished me to turn my thoughts to St. Lawrence, and I feel embarrassed looking at him in the midst of torments, while I in Holy Communion am enjoying the delights of Paradise. O Heart of my Jesus, Heart too sweet, if Thou willest me to have a good share in them (in the sufferings of St. Lawrence) be it so. Enough that I come to Thee always with the fear of offending Thee. I have put two souls together–that of a Saint and that of a sinful creature. Could I have felt otherwise than confounded? I wished through this Saint to offer Thee my sinful soul, but I fear, I fear, because I know it is guilty before Thee. I would fain have Thee see it beautiful as when Thy Hands gave it me." And writing to her director she said:

> *"That which makes me feel anxious is that frequent Communion, the Bread of Angels, has not infused into my soul all those graces that It conferred on so many others in abundance. And the evil, I know it, is because my few virtues are weak, and I come to Jesus without merit. Help, help my father! I could by this time have reached advanced degrees of holiness and instead, I have gone back, to the loss of my poor soul. At times, believe me father, I tremble and blush all over when I think that, being so vile, I go to receive Jesus Who is purity itself. But Jesus, dear Jesus, loves me even in this state, and continues to make Himself felt in my soul."*

Behold how Gemma prepared herself for the Holy Communion, and with what sentiments of faith, of abandonment, of desire, of love, and above all of humility she approached It. What wonder then that the fruits she gathered from It were not small, as she said and thought, but abundant and precious? And what wonder that our Lord showed such great complacency in the Communions of His Servant? He made her feel His presence, as she herself used to say "strongly, strongly," in her heart during those blessed moments, loading her with consolations, sweetness and peace, that from her soul flowed even into her bodily senses, and beautified her whole being. The Sacred Species themselves often produced on her palate a most delicious sensation. She felt them descending into her interior as if they were a balm, and sometimes also the Divine Lover made her feel the impression and taste of His Precious Blood in the Holy Communion. "Yesterday, Feast of the Purification," she said, "after Communion I felt all my mouth full of Our Savior's Precious Blood. Oh! how good it was! It did me so much good! and I clasped my arms that it might enter my heart. Oh that you had felt, father, the good it does me to consume Jesus! I felt this (for the first time) in October from Friday at noon until the following Friday (that is for eight whole days), then it left me. This morning it has again returned. It consumes me, and I continually feel that I am about to die. Jesus overwhelms me. But oh what happiness! Have you ever felt yourself consumed? How delightful it is! The fire of my heart this morning spread as far as my throat. O Eternal Divine Fire! Look, father, if Jesus were to continue to make me feel as at present, I should not last more than a month or two, and who knows?"

And if Our Lord took such delight in Gemma's Communions, was it possible for His Sweet Mother, who in her turn so tenderly loved this angelic girl, not to take the same delight in them? After the many marvels we have seen up to this, I do not think anyone will be tempted to doubt the veracity of another fact that I am about to relate. It is of the Blessed Virgin, who sometimes joined the Angels of the Eucharist to assist at Gemma's Holy Communion. At the unexpected vision the good child went into ecstasy, palpitating with joy at her Mother's feet. "How delightful it is," she said to me afterwards, "to receive Holy Communion in company with my Mother of Paradise! I did so yesterday, the 8th of May. I had never before received Holy Communion in her company. Do you know, father, in what all the outpourings of my heart consisted during those moments? In these words: O Mother! My Mother!"

We read in the lives of different Saints, that as sometimes they were unable to go to the Church for Holy Communion, God made use of an angel, who, to satisfy their hunger for the Blessed Eucharist, acted instead of the priest and took the consecrated species to them. It appears that Our Savior Himself willed to take this great gift to Gemma, and that happened quite three times. Here is how it is told us by one who was an eye-witness:

"On the morning of the Friday on which dear Gemma for the first time underwent the cruel punishment of the Scourging, on seeing her horribly lacerated all over, I forbade her to get up. The poor child obeyed, and collecting her thoughts she set to prepare herself for a spiritual Communion, for which she used to make her preparation in the same way as for her sacramental Communion in the Church. She went into ecstasy, and at a given moment I saw her join her hands and return to herself, while her eyes sparkled and her face suddenly lit up as usually happened when she had some extraordinary vision. At the same moment she put out her tongue and soon withdrew it, returning into ecstasy to make her usual thanksgiving. The same thing happened at other times as well, but I was not then a witness. I learned from Gemma herself, who quite candidly told me of it, that it was Jesus and not an Angel Who came to communicate her."

After all that has been said of the hunger and thirst of this fervent Soul for the Blessed Sacrament, it is easy to understand what a terrible affliction it must have been for her not to be able to go to the Church for Holy Communion. This occurred but very seldom and only when she was dangerously ill. She prayed and besought our Lord to make her well enough to get up, and if He willed her to suffer, that her pains might be increased a hundredfold and she would willingly accept them, "rather than remain," these are her words, "deprived of the Bread of Life." And in order to prevail with Him more surely she added: "To an ardent Lover as Thou art O Lord, so many entreaties are not needed. He understands at the first word. Then say yes, and I come." And as a rule that most ardent Lover said yes, and Gemma, strengthened by her great faith was able to rise, although a little time before her temperature had gone up to 104 degrees. When, however, Our Lord disposed otherwise, this good child bowed her head saying, *Fiat* and contented herself with a spiritual Communion only. In this as well, the spiritual communications she received were so many and such, that they amply repaid her for the sensible privation of the Divine Food. On one occasion her ordinary confessor, with a view to try her, feigned to deprive her of Holy Communion. See now in what terms she told me of her misfortune.

"O father, father, today at 5 o'clock I went to confession, and the confessor said he would deprive me of Jesus. O father, my pen refuses to write, my hand is shaking and I am crying."

These words in the letter I am copying are certainly written with a trembling hand. However, entering quickly into herself as was her way she continues:

"Jesus be thanked! for I have one who knows me and will help me to gain Paradise. No, father, I am not in any way worthy to receive Jesus. How very many times has He not willed to come into this foul heart, that is worse than a cesspit! At this moment I see my misery so clearly that I would, I would...O father, father!"

She wished to say: "You understand me without my adding more." At the same time I must add that it became quite clear from what that enlightened confessor said to members of her family, that he was very far from depriving Gemma of Holy Communion. "Do all you possibly can," he said, "to accompany the poor child to the Church even though she be ill, for otherwise, without Holy Communion, how could she live?"

Once it seemed to her that she ought not to go to Holy Communion without confession, because of some great fault that the devil persuaded her she had committed. She suffered and cried all night at not seeing it possible to find her confessor in time. In the morning she went to Church and without going to Communion came back in tears. She had scarcely got home when she was rapt in ecstasy, and the enemy feigning to be Jesus appeared to her with the intention of tempting her to despair. The scene was most affecting and drew tears from those present. Through the penetrating light of the ecstasy Gemma discovered the snare. "No," she exclaimed with feeble and labored voice, "I don't want thee. Oh! where is my Jesus gone? O Jesus, where art Thou? It is true Jesus has not come to me this morning, but neither shalt thou enter in. I will not have thee. Jesus, drive him away from me. But how, O Jesus, dost Thou allow the Demon to come near Thy place in false guise? Conquer Thou O Jesus in my heart that longs for Thee. Be quick Jesus for my heart desires Thee. O dost Thou not see how he would fain make me fall into sin? Why leave me thus? It is true, I have been the first to leave Thee, but I yearn for Thee. Never again leave me." Here it would seem that Our Lord reproached her with not having yielded to an invitation He had given her that morning to come without fear to the Holy Table. And she pleading her excuse with her usual candor answered: "Yes, Jesus, I have resisted, but it has cost me suffering. I heard this morning's invitation, but oh! Jesus, how should I have acted in order to receive Thee? Look, Jesus, if the Confessor had told me to go to Communion I would have gone, but he said that I cannot trust myself. And so I left Thee, because I thought I had sinned. Then Jesus forgive me, and come, come now into my heart, there Jesus, behold it is Thine! My heart is all Thine. Come and make Thyself felt. O dost Thou not see how I languish?" This argument and colloquy, which, for brevity's sake I have shortened, lasted nearly an hour and ended with a complete victory of the child over the tender Heart of her Savior. To judge of it from the earnestness of her attitude and the agitation of her whole person, one would have thought that she must come out of it weary and exhausted, but it was otherwise. And when the ecstasy was over, she was calm, smiling, refreshed, and able to return immediately to her domestic occupations. See then from this fact what Holy Communion meant for Gemma.

Having treated of how the servant of God prepared to receive her Lord in the Blessed Eucharist, I ought to say something in particular of her thanksgiving after Communion. But this would entail much repetition, because the same varied impulses of faith, love, confidence, humility, abandonment, of which we have had examples in this chapter, as they went before and accompanied the solemn action, so they followed it in her thanksgiving. This began in Church and lasted as long as her companion allowed her to stay there. She afterwards continued it all through the day in the midst of her home duties. Gemma's heart was filled by her Communion and kept overflowing. It had to give vent and her body unable to resist so many impulses, from time to time lost the use of its senses. This explains the frequency of her ecstasies from the time of her return from Church till the evening, and the repetition in them of the stimulating impressions received in the morning from the Bread of Life. Her saying was that "she would have wished to bury in her heart for ever" that dear Jesus Who had come to her at the Altar. And she would have wished Him "to make her known in what measure and to what extent her love ought to excel in order to repay His infinite Goodness." And here not knowing what else to do, she poured out her soul exclaiming: "My God, my Jesus, my Father, my Sweetness, Consolation of all Thy creatures, Love that sustains me, Fire that burns never to be extinguished." Then she implored of Him that it might be His Will for her "to be consumed in that Fire." She turned to the Angels, to her heavenly Mother, to her patron saints, that they might help her to bless, praise, thank, and love Jesus in the Blessed Eucharist. And in this way also one can understand those ardent letters that she often wrote during the course of the day. Whatever chanced to be the subject of them, the thought of the Blessed Sacrament was found to have a place if indeed it was not the chief thought. When writing on this subject so affectingly sweet to her heart she generally lost the use of her senses, and yet thus in ecstasy she continued to write. She was full of Jesus, and the mouth speaks and the hand writes from the fullness of the heart: *Ex abundantia cordis.*

When speaking of the painful trials to which Our Lord willed to subject His faithful servant, I mentioned that of spiritual aridity or desolation, remarking that it was the most torturing of all. And surely to seek Jesus and not find Him, to call on Him and receive no answer, this for a soul who lives for Him alone, and takes pleasure only in Him is a torment of which no one can form any idea who has not experienced it. We have seen that this Sacrament of Love was Gemma's Heaven. Jesus on the Altar was everything to her. She lived in this ravishing Mystery, and found in It all her happiness. But God Who knows the work He is doing in the sanctification of souls subjected His handmaid to this trial from time to time. Then He not only withdrew the joy she felt before the Sacred Tabernacle and at the Holy Table, but He hid Himself from her behind a dense veil. "O father, father," she exclaimed when revealing her anguish to me, "all those consolations that I felt every morning after Holy Communion and that lasted me all the day, have turned into so many agitations of soul. I know not what has happened." And another time after having spoken to me of certain extraordinary communications she had in Communion, she added: "But there are days when it is not so. For the last three mornings after I have received Him Jesus has hidden Himself and remained silent, making me die of desire. Thus I have passed the time, and can do nothing else." So this tender lover expressed herself through a sense of humility, but in reality she never was more active and fervent than in those times of desolation. She ran to the Church and whether her God saw her or not, heard her or remained deaf to her prayers, she sought Him always with ardent anxiety while almost dying with desire, with a longing, as she expressed herself, that "consumed" her. What has been related in this chapter goes far to show how wonderfully God manifests Himself to faithful souls in the Divine Eucharist.

CHAPTER 26

St. Gemma's Apostolate And Zeal
For The Salvation Of Souls.

WHEN I asked my Superior's leave to write and publish this story of Gemma's life, he, having already heard much of this marvelous young girl, highly approved of my doing so. And while encouraging me in the task, he advised me to bring out in relief the fact that God entrusts to certain singularly favored souls a double mission: that, namely, of sanctifying themselves by the practice of heroic virtue, and of doing good service in the Church by their works as well as by their example. Thus in a few words an enlightened and holy man had traced for me the plan of the life I was about to compile. Now having in many chapters dealt with the first part of my work, I should be wanting if I did not devote at least one chapter to the second part, and thus give a completeness to my task.

Gemma had this mission to labor for the good of souls, and specially for the conversion of sinners, thereby cooperating, as far as in her lay, with the work of the Redemption. This mission was not given her in the usual way by which Our Lord, through His Church, ordinarily confides it to others; but by a particular explicit, and, I may say, a solemn investiture. She herself will tell us about it:

"Some days ago I had scarcely received Jesus in Holy Communion when He asked me this question: 'Tell Me My child, dost thou love Me greatly?' What could I answer? But my heart answered Him by its throbbing. 'If thou lovest Me,' He rejoined, 'thou wilt do whatever I want of thee.' And then sighing, He exclaimed: 'What ingratitude and malice there is in the world! Sinners continue pertinaciously to live in crime. Weak and heartless souls will not do themselves violence to overcome the flesh. Those in tribulation lose courage and despair. Indifference

keeps increasing daily, and no one amends. I cease not to dispense heavenly graces and favors to all My creatures: life and light to My Church, virtue and strength to him who rules it, wisdom to those who direct souls that are in darkness, constancy and fortitude to those who have to follow Me, graces of every kind to all the just. I send My light into the dark dens of sinners and even there soften their hearts, doing all I can to convert them. But notwithstanding all that, what do I ever gain? What correspondence do I ever find in My creatures whom I have loved so much? No one any longer cares for My Heart and for My Love. I am forgotten as though I had never loved them and as though I had never suffered for them. My Heart is always in sadness. I am left almost alone in My Churches. If many assemble there it is for other motives than worship and I have to suffer the pain of seeing My House become a theatre of amusement. Many through hypocrisy betray Me by sacrilegious Communions. I can bear no more.'"

This loving Lord of all, had previously made similar complaints to His servant to move her to offer herself as a victim of expiation for the sins of the world, and we have seen with what generosity she corresponded. Later on He will renew the same complaints to induce her to sacrifice even her life for the same end and Gemma will, as we shall see, offer herself with equal readiness. Now He wishes to lead her to spend her whole being for the conversion of sinners. "If thou lovest Me," He says, "thou wilt do what I want of thee," and with a clear light He lets her see the form of her Apostolate in its smallest details. "Thou knowest, O Lord," she answered, "how ready I am to sacrifice myself in everything. I will bear every sort of pain for Thee. I will give every drop of my blood to please Thy Heart and to hinder the outrages of sinners against Thee." Let us see her in action. Of torments we need not speak for she has suffered them in every way beyond measure, and shed her blood, I may say, in torrents from her feet, hands, side and from her eyes and whole body, so as almost to leave no blood in her veins. But what works can this young girl perform to fit her to be an apostle of Jesus Christ? Let us have no doubt. By means of the Spirit with which Our Lord has filled her she will achieve her mission perfectly. And what she does not reach by action she will certainly attain by prayer and tears. I am able to assert that from the first day that I came to know Gemma up to that of her death I always found her exercising her zeal for the conversion of sinners. I say from the first day, alluding to a fact already mentioned in Chapter twelve.

Other authentic facts relating to similar conversions are registered in my copious repertory and omitted here for brevity's sake. Gemma had found the secret of moving the Heart of her Jesus, and those innocent tears, those burning desires, that force of argument that she managed so well, were always successful. On the last day we shall know how many souls have been dragged in this way from the clutches of the enemy by this humble virgin. It is certain that not a day passed without her praying for sinners. A proof of this is to be found in the register of her ecstasies through which, without being aware of it, she laid open her whole soul. "If Thou wouldst give me one a day," she was heard to say, "think Lord, what that would be." And again: "O Jesus, do not abandon poor sinners, think of sinners and of me. I want them all saved." And as she had always some particular sinner more especially in mind, "that one," she used to say, "I want You, Jesus, to remember particularly, because I want him saved together with me." Remark my words: "together with me," the persuasive eloquence of love.

This angelic girl often turned for help to her heavenly Mother whose power with Our Lord she had well experienced in whatever she had most at heart. One day when in ecstasy she found the Holy Mother greatly afflicted and at the same time resolved not to take further interest in a soul for which Gemma was pleading. Behold with what earnestness this child of heaven set about dissuading the Mother of God from her determination: "But what do I hear thee say, Mother?

Abandon that soul? Is it not a question of one belonging to Jesus? Has He not shed all His Blood for this soul? Tis true, I myself have forgotten it for some days, but wilt thou abandon it on this account? No, no, be firm, go and appease Jesus." Here it would seem as if the Holy Mother found the undertaking very difficult, for Gemma said: "But Jesus always obeys His Mother. Then wilt thou say that thou canst not do it? But if thou art omnipotent!" And again, "Oh! rather than abandon a soul! O Mother, it is impossible that Jesus would forsake a soul! Why, He even had mercy on the thief!" "But dost thou know," replied the Blessed Virgin, "what this sinner is? I could show thee what a malignant soul is his." Again Gemma, "I know, Mother, what he is, but I don't want to look at it. When he is saved, yes, then I will see him. O my Mother why dost thou treat me like this today, thou who intercedest for sinners? Hast thou perchance ceased to be Mother. Surely it is impossible. But today wilt thou leave me in such affliction? Obtain for me from Jesus what thou didst get for me on Saturday," (she is alluding to the conversion of another sinner for whom also she had prayed very much) "then how contented I should be!"

"Abandon a soul!" These words pierced Gemma's heart and filled her with consternation. I myself wished to have a proof of this, by repeating them to her with regard to a penitent whom I had resolved to give up because so refractory. This is how she answered me:

> *"Wicked father! rather than be discouraged or use that horrible word 'abandon' why not call her to yourself and make her tell you all the truth, and show her affection as you did with me while I was a thousand times worse than she? Be careful. If you can see her, well and good. If not, write to her at once that if she does not return into the right path as Jesus wishes and leave off all sin He will smite her. This is all I say. I know everything, everything."*

But she did not keep her resolve to say no more and soon wrote to me again as follows:

> *"Assuredly father, Jesus is not content with that soul. No, no, there is so much wanting. He has told me terrible things about her! Tell her to reform, otherwise Jesus will strike her down. Act in this way father: when you speak to her say something of me and tell her to come to me. If she had come things would not have turned out as they did."*

I will relate another fact in the words of a most reliable witness who told me of it. "I was asked," said this person, "by a lady acquaintance to recommend her brother, a great sinner, to Gemma. I did so accordingly and she while in ecstasy began to plead to Jesus for him. But He (no doubt to try her faith) replied that He knew not that sinner. 'How dost Thou not know him,' she said, 'since he is Thy child?' Then she turned to Mary, but seeing that even she remained silent, and wept, she began to pray to Blessed Gabriel of the Dolours (Passionist), and he also was silent. But Gemma, for all that, did not lose courage. She redoubled her prayers." At the same time she said to me: "That man must indeed be a great sinner. Jesus says He knows him not, Mother weeps, and Blessed Gabriel will not answer me." After a year of this assiduous praying, one day, while returning from Church with Gemma, I met the servant of the above-mentioned lady in the greatest consternation. The brother of her mistress, she said, was dying. We were greatly pained, but we had only gone about twenty yards when Gemma exclaimed: "He is saved, he is saved." I asked her who? "The brother of that lady," she answered. I learned afterwards that this man breathed his last pressing the priest's hand precisely when Gemma was going home. That coincided exactly with the moment when she said aloud, "He is saved, he is saved."

Gemma was often asked to pray for sinners by friends, owing to their high opinion of her sanctity. But it frequently happened that

God Himself made such cases known to His servant directly, while she was at home, and by providential coincidences while she was out of doors. She was always ready to take charge of them whatever way they came, rejoicing in each one as if she had found a treasure, and devoted herself the more earnestly to them in proportion to their number. "I would wish," she said, "to bathe with my blood all those places where Jesus is outraged. I would wish all sinners to be saved, because they have been redeemed by the Precious Blood of Jesus." The last one that she had in her mind, or, as she used to say, that she carried on her shoulders, was a gentleman of Lucca, a notorious and obstinate sinner, but not personally know to her. The charitable child labored long and earnestly for his conversion, and renewed her assaults on heaven without losing confidence. In her last sickness she said: "I am keeping him on my shoulders for the whole of the Lent, then he will be taken off." On Holy Thursday, the good priest who had recommended him to Gemma, all full of joy told me that a great sinner had been converted in his hands. It was Gemma's sinner. Two days later, freed from that great weight, with another palm in hand, the virgin of Lucca took flight to heaven.

This was the last conversion wrought through Gemma's intercession. The first, an interesting one, took place before she received the solemn investiture of her Apostolate. It was while she was yet in her father's house stricken by the dangerous disease that brought her to death's door. Among those who used to visit and nurse her was a woman who was found to be leading a bad life. Some of the family complained of this to Gemma and she with her face full of animation replied: "O, then perhaps the Magdalene was rejected by Jesus because she was a sinner? Let her come. Who knows that we may not be able to do her some good? Don't take her from me I implore of you." And although in a dying state she took the poor sinner in hand. It was a difficult case as the woman lived by her own infamy. But what cannot the Charity of Jesus Christ effect through a soul inflamed by it as was Gemma's? Her Aunt of Camaiore from time to time sent her money to meet the grave necessities of her illness. And she, not caring for herself, passed it with exquisite delicacy to this woman, paying even the rent of her house so that the want of it might not cause her to offend God. And when any of the family asked what she had done with the money sent by her Aunt she answered: "Hush! I'm not wasting anything you'll see. You shall know the use I make of it." In this way, owing to her repeated attentions and the fervor of her untiring exhortations, she so prevailed with that soul as to wrest her from the hands of the devil. She got her to make a general confession and from that time forward she has been leading a good life.

Certainly Satan must have growled with rage at the zeal of this holy girl, finding how she snatched his choicest victims from him. He often appeared to her with eyes of fire and in threatening tones said: "While acting for thyself do as thou pleasest, but mind, do nothing for the conversion of sinners. If thou attemptest it thou shalt pay me dearly for it." At other times assuming the role of prudent counsellor he would say: "How and whence comes such presumption? Thou art laden with sins and all the years of thy life would not suffice to bewail and expiate them, and yet thou losest time about the sins of others. Dost thou not see that thine own soul is in danger? A strange gain that of thinking for others and neglecting thyself." But all was in vain. Once she was heard to say to Our Lord in ecstasy: "Dost Thou wish to know, Jesus, who has forbidden me to think about sinners? The devil. On the contrary, Jesus, I recommend them to Thee. Think of them, O Jesus, poor sinners, and teach me to do as much as possible to save them."

Whenever it happened that any one of those sinners was hostile to her, then indeed her prayers for such a one were a hundred times more fervent. There are many proofs of this. Here is one example: "Jesus, by order of my Confessor, I recommend to Thee my greatest enemy, my greatest adversary. Guide him and if Thy Hand should have to weigh heavily on him, no, press it on me. Give him every grace Jesus, do not abandon him, console him. What does it matter if I am left in pain? But do not let him suffer. I recommend him to Thee now and for ever. Confer so many benefits on him that they may surpass immeasurably all that wrong. Thou understandest me, Jesus? I mean all that he would have done to me, and to show Thee that I wish him well, tomorrow I offer my Communion for him. He perhaps will think of doing us some harm, and we wish him every good."

Gemma's heart's desire was not only to save the souls of sinners, but to help all to love her Lord, to serve Him faithfully, and to become perfect in the practice of virtue. She seemed unable to give herself peace at seeing so much languor among Christians of the present day, among the secular and regular clergy, and in the sacred cloisters themselves. Besides praying as she did continually for them all, she availed herself of every opportunity to advise, correct, and, if needed, threaten in the name of Jesus, so as to ensure fidelity to duty. "This," she said to one, "let me tell you, does not please Jesus. You must give it up." And to another: "In order to please Jesus you should do so and so." A venerable prelate once came to consult her, and I happened to be present. He asked her if his way of governing others was right, and she who knew him to be too ready to believe stories and inclined to be hard with his subjects answered: "Father, it is necessary that you act more cautiously and more gently, otherwise you will not content anyone." This simple girl had no human respect. She said things as she felt them, with modesty and humility, but without any hesitation. And her frankness when dealing with others was not displeasing to anyone because the angelic candor that accompanied it was manifest to all. She wrote pressing letters to directors of souls with whom she was in correspondence, and to her Confessor, urging them to correct some of their penitents who were known to her. "Speak to her, tell her that things cannot go on thus. That soul loves herself more than Jesus. Warn her of it." Nor did she spare me, but very often admonished me freely for my defects both in person and by letter, and I must confess she was always right.

Although she so hated mixing herself in the affairs of others, and was so concentrated in her inmost thoughts that she seemed to belong to another world, still, because God's glory called for it, she was frequently to be found engaged in this work of apostleship.

Sometimes God Himself sent her as His Ambassadress to admonish even distinguished persons. And she went at once after having the approval of her Confessor or Director, for she never trusted to her own lights. "Several days ago," thus she wrote when asking one of these approvals, "Jesus said these words to me: 'Go to the Superior' (of a certain convent) 'and tell her that if she continues to neglect My inspirations, remaining obstinate in her determination not to yield to the commands of her Superiors, she will very soon realize the consequences, as I have already prepared her punishment. Woe to her, if she does not heed this last warning! Tell her also that if I have withheld her chastisement, I have done so solely for the sake of certain souls who are very dear to Me. But now there is no more time. Tell her that all lies in her hands.'" And again: "On Thursday during the Holy Hour Jesus asked me if I had willingly suffered all that I went through on that night" (referring to another occasion in the usual martyrdom of Thursday and Friday) "for the ill deeds of certain nuns. I answered that I had most willingly. And I heard these words: 'Woe to them, and to the one who guides them, if they refuse to do as Jesus wishes! If they refuse to hear His voice, they will very soon be sorry for it, but it will be too late, because Jesus will no longer grant the peace of the past to that Community. Discord will daily increase among them and they will soon be forced to separate.'" Happily those nuns listened to Our Lord's voice. They looked to their eternal interests and the peace of Christ was established in their midst. All this was due to the prayers, dolorous expiation, and zeal of one who only wished to be called "Poor Gemma."

Our Lord, in order to render His servant's ministry in the interests of souls more efficacious, willed to enrich her with extraordinary graces. Such in particular were the discernment of spirits and the knowledge of hidden and future things. She was in spiritual, as well as epistolary, communication with certain great souls whom she had never seen, yet she knew them so thoroughly that even her Confessors who had directed her for a considerable time marvelled at it. When she met persons casually for the first time she often became aware, through certain spiritual impressions, of their being souls very dear to God or of the ordinary run. And in a marked way she knew if they were in mortal sin. Then she was seen to suffer even exteriorly at finding herself in such company, so repulsive was sin to her. Notwithstanding this, she had no difficulty in admonishing them as I have already said, when social rules gave her an opening. Indeed she knew perfectly well how to use the Divine Light given her in order to help efficaciously whoever had need of it. I myself had frequent recourse to Gemma in my doubts about others, although on principle and in disposition I am not credulous, specially when dealing with women, unless there is positive proof of their spirit. She used to answer me in a few days. Thus for example: "Believe me father, I may be mistaken, but the person about whom you ask me has not good intentions. I don't like to say it, but you will get no good out of her. Therefore you would do well not to attend to her. Ah! how deformed I have seen that soul before God!" Facts very soon proved that it was precisely as she had said, and I had to thank this holy child for having enlightened me in time. It was the reverse on other occasions when she recommended to me a soul of whom, judging from appearances, I had greatly doubted and intended to rid myself. Here again Gemma was always right. She was not less so when predicting the fatal consequences that would ensue if what God had made known to her as His Will was not done. I could give many proofs of what I have said but as there is not space for it I confine myself to the mere statement. Still I ought to inform the reader that Gemma was most sparing in these predictions. She spoke so very little and attended so closely to herself. Nothing less than the manifest glory of God or the good of some soul could induce her to come out of this reserve. With these exceptions she never showed herself to be a prophetess. I say "never," for when she was questioned by curious persons, or even by her director her ordinary modest answer was: "I don't know. Ask Jesus."

The way in which the above-mentioned light regarding hidden and future things was given her by God, is told us in her own words: "Dear father, I mention this to you alone. Sometimes when I am not thinking of anything a light comes to my mind. I pay no attention to it, and after a day or so I see that what flashed before me was from my God. This, you should know, happens very often, but all in silence." Our Lord, according to mystics, is wont to speak in this way to His servants. I pointed this out before when treating of Divine Locutions. Gemma's humility made her slow to believe, but in the depth of her soul she had not a shadow of doubt, and only her spiritual father could persuade her that the thing was not as she saw it. Occasionally feeling a necessity to verify something, she asked Jesus with humble confidence to explain it to her, and our dear Lord was sure to gratify her. "I have asked Jesus," thus she writes to her confessor, "if what you intend to do should be done, and He answered me: 'tell him to do it.' Later on when Jesus came back He desired me tell you to do things so that they be not noticed and so that no one be aware of them. If you wish to bring the father (that you have in mind) Jesus also is satisfied. You will then be convinced of certain things that are now perplexing you. Jesus has told me so." And it was quite time, for that holy and learned confessor, seeing such extraordinary things in his penitent found himself in a state of indecision and was thinking of bringing a Religious from Rome to examine her spirit!

Another matter has its place here. I had instituted in Rome and in several other cities and villages a Society called the College of Jesus. It consists of a selection of generous souls who, without any external display of dignities and offices, without secretary or treasurer, labor to cultivate their own spiritual lives, and under the direction of a good Priest do, according to each one's capacity, some meritorious work in the Church. Such a work would be for the decorum of the Divine worship, particularly of the Blessed Sacrament; in hospitals, prisons and families; in a word, wherever the members knew of disorders to be removed and souls to be helped. The code of regulations that I gave this pious Society pleased many. In a short time a large number joined it, and with God's blessing much good was done. When I went to Lucca I spoke of it to Gemma. She greatly rejoiced at it, wished to be the first to join it, and immediately started to propagate the good work. How many journeys did she not make from house to house, to seek members, animate directors, and organize works! She often spoke of it to Jesus, even during her ecstasies, and Jesus assured her that He was greatly pleased with it, and blessed all those who belonged to it. I have spoken of this work in order to throw clearer light on the apostolic spirit of the servant of God.

Mention must also be made of the zeal of this child of heaven in aid of the suffering Souls in Purgatory. If love when it is true has no bounds, certainly hers that had reached the summit of perfection must have been unlimited. Her zeal for the poor suffering souls was indeed extraordinary. She offered fervent assiduous prayers together with penances and her immense spiritual and corporal sufferings for all of them in general. At the same time, just as was her way with sinners, she always had some particular soul on her mind for whose relief she was specially interested. "Yes, suffer!" she used to say, "suffer for sinners, and more readily for the suffering Souls, and in a marked way for N..." (whom she named). And our loving Lord Who likewise ardently desires to draw those just Souls to Himself moved His servant to an increase of zeal and continually suggested to her new modes of expiation. "The Angel has told me," she said, "that this evening Jesus will let me suffer a little more for a Soul in Purgatory, that is, for two hours beginning at nine o'clock." That suffering was very great as she herself confessed: "My head pained me more than usual and every movement I made was torture." Heaven accepted the expiation of so worthy a creature, and the pains of those blessed Souls from day to day grew less and their suffering was shortened.

Gemma knew by inspiration that in the Convent of Passionist Nuns at Corneto there was a sister very dear to God who was near death, and she asked me about it and on my answering that it was so she at once began to implore of Jesus to make that Religious expiate all her faults on her death-bed, so that breathing her last she might enter Paradise at once. Her prayer, at least in part, was heard. The Sister suffered greatly and died in a few months. Gemma told those of her home of it, in order that they might pray for the deceased, and she gave her name Mary Teresa of the Infant Jesus, as she was not known in Lucca. This soul appeared to her full of sorrow imploring her help as she was undergoing great torments in Purgatory for certain defects. Nothing more was needed to set all the fibres of Gemma's heart in motion. From that moment she gave herself no rest—prayers, tears, and loving contests with Our Lord. "Jesus save her," she was heard to exclaim. "Jesus, take Mary Teresa to Paradise without delay. She is a soul that is most dear to Thee. Let me suffer much for her. I want her to be in bliss." And the dear victim of expiation suffered without ceasing for sixteen days, at the end of which God was pleased to accept her sacrifice and release that soul. This is how Gemma herself told me of it: "Towards half-past one it seemed to me that the Madonna herself came to tell me that the hour was drawing nigh. Then almost immediately I thought I saw Mary Teresa coming towards me clad as a Passionist, accompanied by her Angel Guardian and by Jesus. Oh! how she was changed since the day I first saw her! Smiling she drew close to me and said: 'I am truly happy and I go to enjoy my Jesus for ever.' She thanked me again. Then she made sign of bidding me good-bye with her hand, several times, and with Jesus and her Angel Guardian she flew to Heaven. It was about half-past two o'clock in the morning."

God converted the world through the labors of twelve poor fishermen. And now He continues to save many through the secret tears, penances and pains of humble souls who are discarded by the world, and yet are great in His eyes. One of them assuredly was this saintly Virgin of Lucca.

CHAPTER 27

The New Monastery Of The Passionist Nuns In Lucca

THIS angelic maiden, so enamored of heavenly things, was necessarily out of her element in the world. Hence she was often heard to exclaim: "O how could I remain in the world where everything is so insupportable? Take me, take me from the world where I cannot trust myself any longer." And to her director she said: "I implore of you in the name of Jesus, come and shut me in, the world is not for me." These expressions of her anguish frequently recurred in her letters. God Himself, in order no doubt to try His servant, let her understand that such a step would gratify Him, and spoke to her heart in the sense that she would certainly be a religious, if the persons, on whom the execution of His good pleasure depended, would carry out what He had disposed. And as this child of heaven saw that it was not being done, she toiled for years to bring it about. And towards the end of her life she suffered a veritable agony until our Lord told her to put aside all disquietude and every thought of the matter. The first impulse towards the cloister, sent her from heaven, was in 1899 when she lay near death in her own home. This fact is certified by a certain Letitia Bertuccelli, servant in the Galgani family. I give it just as she told it me after Gemma's death.

"On entering the room of the sick child one night, I beheld her all surrounded by a light and someone standing by her. Terrified, because I thought it was an apparition of her father, who had died a short time before in the same room and bed, I went to awake her Aunt. She did not get up, thinking that I was under a delusion, and I returned trembling to Gemma's room and found her in the same way, and the same person, a lady, with her. I had not courage to look at her, and drew back in fear. Then

hearing them talk to one another I got behind the door to listen, trembling all the while. The lady said: 'Gemma, once thou hadst the intention to become a nun. Wouldst thou become one now?' And Gemma said: 'Yes, certainly, if the Madonna will help me, but I am so poor and sick.' And the lady rejoined: 'If thou dost not find means to enter a convent, persons will not be wanting who will succor thee and enable thee to live.' Then again Gemma said: 'Yes, yes, and then the Will of God be done.' When the vision was over I went in, and Gemma said that the Madonna had been to visit her, and forbade me to say anything during her life of what I had seen. Two days later she recovered."

To avoid needless repetition here I must refer my readers to Chapter six where full particulars are given of Gemma entering the Convent of the Visitandines and having to leave.

Her Confessor thought also of the Capuchin Sisters, the Teresians, the Servites, and other austere Institutes. But she always said: "I go if they decide, but my heart tells me that Jesus does not wish me where they say. Whatever they do they will not succeed. Jesus seems to have another idea." And they never did succeed, as, whatever steps were taken, things always fell through for one reason or another.

The only Convent that seemed to satisfy all Gemma's desires was that of the Passionist Nuns. She came to know these Religious through reading the life of Blessed Gabriel of the Dolours, and it would appear that by this Servant of God she had, in vision, been given hopes of becoming one of their number. Thenceforward she evinced no other desire, and continued to sigh at our Lord's feet for that Institute only. There existed then only one house of Passionist Nuns in Italy—at Corneto, a hundred kilometers from Rome and two hundred and seventy from Lucca. What was to be done? She thought and thought, asked advice, and resolved to go there for a course of spiritual exercises. She accordingly with three companions from Lucca made a formal request to that effect. The Superior, although a woman of very large mind and heart, answered, God so permitting it, in these resolute words: "Let the three come, but not Gemma. And mind, if they bring her with them, we shall not allow her to enter." That good Mother who had heard much of Gemma in a wrong sense, had probably thought she was one of those hysterical and deluded girls who do not do well in communities. The unexpected refusal was made known to Gemma who felt it intensely but was not irritated by it. Nay, on hearing some of the family grumbling about it, she said: "O why should we speak like this? Don't blame the Mother President," (this is how the Passionists name the Superior in their houses) "I instead wish her so well that when I go to paradise she shall be the first I will go to meet and salute." And speaking to a friend of a dream she had she said: "I recognized the Mother President in my dream. She looked at me so severely! I feel so well disposed towards her, and she does not want me."

Gemma however, feeling persuaded that it was her vocation, did not give up the idea of becoming a Passionist. She failed with the President of Corneto, and at the same time formed a close friendship with a Mother of that Community. She wrote letters to her on subjects of exalted mystical theology and always ended them with some emphatic expression touching her great desire. "Take me with you into the convent. I will be good. Make me happy. I have no money. I am very poor, but I will try to do good service as a lay sister. Rest assured I know how to do something." (See what child-like simplicity). "I know how to sweep, and wash the plates, and help in the kitchen, and I have good strength for any kind of fatiguing work. Take me and please Jesus." And in another letter: "I know that the father is at Corneto. Say lots of things to him from me. Tell him to put me in the convent with you. I will obey him always, and do nothing of my own initiative. I will tell you everything and do what you wish. I feel in my wrong place, Mother, in the world. Tell the father to pray most earnestly, and then decide, for in a short time it will be too late." She wrote with the same haste and also in a spirit of greater abandonment to me: "Be quick father. Listen to Jesus, otherwise you will not be in time."

Meanwhile people began to discuss the foundation of a convent of Passionist Nuns in the City of Lucca itself. Gemma was filled with joy at this, and felt almost sure that she was about to realize the object she so long desired. What did she not do to stimulate all who were interested in this holy undertaking to confide in our Lord, and not allow themselves to be deterred by difficulties. Nay, to draw fresh impulse from the difficulties themselves! "Jesus wishes it," she used to say, "and what Jesus wills must succeed. Make haste, set the work in hand." Those however who judged the matter with perhaps too much human prudence, of whom I confess I was one, were not satisfied with such arguments and procrastinated. "How is it possible," they said, "to found a convent of Papal enclosure without money? The house must be purchased, adapted and furnished. And where is the needful for the support of the Religious to be found?" At the expiation of two years of assiduous efforts to find what was necessary only about two thousand francs were collected, and the diocesan rules required a deposit of ten thousand francs for each Sister. At Corneto also it was determined that none of the Sisters should leave that convent for another foundation unless their maintenance was provided for. Gemma, for all that, insisted: "Be careful, father, how you act. Jesus is dissatisfied with your want of confidence, as if He could not provide all in an instant. Begin and you will see that Jesus knows how to act." In the meantime accompanied by her inseparable benefactress, she went through all the streets of Lucca seeking and inquiring to try and find a suitable house for the object in view, or at least a piece of ground on which a convent might be built. In March, 1901, as if she had already done and provided everything she wrote to the already-mentioned Passionist Religious of Corneto as follows: "It gave me such consolation to hear how you also say that Jesus wills the new Convent! That is true, Jesus wills it, and will soon give you this consolation." And again: "Monsignor has said that someone must come and speak to the Archbishop so as to arrive at a settlement. Here we have even eight thousand francs, and there are several buildings that will be sold or let as Superiors think best. But if they go to sleep! Enough, let us hope for the best. May Jesus deign to hide me somewhere, even from myself." And in another letter, alluding to me, she said: "If our good father were to decide and do what Jesus wills (and you know what it is) all would be accomplished. Let us pray that Jesus may give him grace to overcome his timidity. You must also encourage him, for he needs it. Remove his fears. Poor father! He need not fear in the least."

At learning these things I writhed as it were in thorns, and besought His Divine Majesty to open to me some way of acting. But months passed and no light was given me! At the same time our Lord, in order to excite the fervor of His Servant more and more, and move her to prayer and action, showed her the great esteem He had of the Passionist Sisters, the glory He would derive from the new foundation in Lucca, and the good they would do there. On one occasion He appeared to her in the same way as I have described in the foregoing chapter, and, repeating that the Justice of His Heavenly Father had need of victims, added: "How often have I not withheld it, presenting to Him a group of loved souls and generous victims! Their penances, their hardships, their heroic acts have restrained it. Now again I have presented Him with victims, but they are few." She asked Him who they were, and He said: "They are the daughters of My Passion. If thou only knewest how often I have seen My Father relent as I offered them to Him." And He ended with these words: "Write at once to thy father, tell him to go to Rome and speak to the Pope of this desirable work. Let him say that a great chastisement is threatened and victims are needed." Even in her ecstasies this fixed idea of the new convent and her hope to enter it were often manifested: "O Jesus, the Confessor tells me to persist in asking Thee for the convent that he so longs to see founded. Thou must see to this. Thou keepest Thy promise. Is it not so? Then see to it, and be quick."

Thus Gemma had not the least doubt of the work succeeding. Jesus, the Heavenly Mother, and Blessed Gabriel had spoken to her so clearly on this matter that she felt certain of it. They had even explained to her in detail the ways and means by which it was to be accomplished. And now, after her death, all is being verified exactly as she foretold. The foundation, she said, would be completed shortly after the Beatification of Ven. Gabriel of the Dolours, and the Pope, the Bishop, a Consultor-General of the Passionists and their General himself, exhorted by the said Consultor, would combine to effect it. Also another father would be sent by the Provincial of the Roman Province to Lucca to take necessary steps. The devil would use violent and persistent efforts to hinder the holy work by raising such difficulties as to make its success seem impossible. But finally, the work being started, the very persons who previously opposed it would declare in its favor, and all would be glad to see it established. She also made a last prophecy, already referred to, that had to wound her own heart. "Decide at once," she said, "for very soon it will be too late. Jesus will not wait any longer, and He has said that He will take me to Himself, if within six months the work is not begun. My Heavenly Mother cured me of that dangerous illness" (I shall have to speak of this in the next chapter) "but on condition that the convent be built. If it is not started without delay, she will soon cause me to fall sick and will take me with her." Finally God made known to her that the requisite conditions would not be fulfilled and she had to be resigned. "What I have gone through this morning," these are her words, "I cannot explain. I shall only say that I felt a great impulse to cry. I ran away to my room to be more free there and alone, and I cried a great deal. At last I exclaimed: *Fiat voluntas tua!* But those tears were not of grief, they were of perfect resignation."

The *fiat* was spoken. Gemma thought no more of being a Religious. She ceased to speak of it, and occupied herself solely in preparing for death, which came, as she had foretold, in six months. God was satisfied with His faithful servant's desire and with the merit of the sacrifice she had so generously made. She had already as an act of private devotion made the vows of Religious Profession. She was a Religious and Passionist in mind and spirit and bore the stigmata of His Passion on her body. She was then fit to leave this world, well satisfied and full of joy at having perfectly attained the end for which God placed her in it.

No sooner had the seraphic child breathed her last than remorse set in on all sides, and good reason there was for it. Remorse was followed by an awakening, and without further delay the work was begun. I remembered the intimation given me a year before: "Go to Rome, and speak to the Pope," and I went and spoke to His Holiness Pius X, recently raised to the Pontificate. He listened to me most cordially, was pleased with the project of the work, and taking up his pen he wrote his full approval. The precious document runs thus:

> *"We bless with paternal affection the foundation of the New Convent of Passionist Nuns in the City of Lucca. Also our Venerable Brother Nicholas Ghilardi (Archbishop of Lucca) who is praiseworthily promoting it. The Rev. Mother Maria Giuseppa del Cuor de Gesu who is to be its first Superior. All the benefactors who have concurred and who will cooperate henceforth in its establishment and the Religious present and future who shall take part in it.*
>
> *We wish the above-mentioned pious virgins, in all their prayers, penances, devout practices, and other exercises prescribed by the Institute, to hold as a special object of their community, that of offering themselves as victims to Our Lord for the spiritual and temporal needs of the church and of the Pope."*

From the Vatican the 2nd of October, 1903.
Pius X, Pope.

Gemma had told the truth. Jesus had spoken to the heart of His Vicar, and according to what He Himself had made known to His

Servant in vision, He willed that the Pope should solemnly declare it a duty of the Religious of the new convent to offer themselves as victims of expiation for the good of the church.

With this venerable document in hand, I presented myself at Lucca and at Corneto, and made progress. Two other Pontifical letters soon followed to the Archbishop of Lucca and the Bishop of Corneto, to strengthen the measures I had taken, and the foundation was decided upon. It is notable that the Pope himself named as Superior of the new House, precisely that nun of Corneto to whom Gemma wrote those words: "Jesus will give you this consolation." The question of money arose again and was delaying things. Then a third letter came from the Pope to the Apostolic Administrator of Lucca, the see being then vacant, and removed every difficulty. Two Choir Sisters and one Lay-Sister left the convent of Corneto for Lucca in March, 1905, two years after Gemma's death. The enemy has striven in vain to raise obstacles and even persecution on all sides. The work continues to progress, and whereas so many other Communities of old standing in Lucca find it difficult to get novices, this new one increases and multiplies. Up to quite lately the Religious had to put up with a temporary building, not being able, in spite of well-grounded anticipations, to establish themselves in the home they had already acquired. And thus is verified Gemma's prediction that the foundation of the Convent, begun some time before the solemn Beatification of Ven. Gabriel of the Dolours, would be completed shortly after it. This Beatification was celebrated in the year 1908 on the 31st of May, and only two months later, on the 31st of July, full possession of the new convent was given to the Sisters by the former proprietors, precisely as Gemma had foretold.

The Institute of the Passionist Nuns was founded by St. Paul of the Cross, who gave them the same rules and habit, the same penitential spirit and aim of life that he had already given to his brethren the Passionists. Choir, day and night, meditation and work give them constant occupation. Although having Papal enclosure, they may, with the consent of the Parish priest, instruct little children in Christian Doctrine at the Grille. And at fixed times during the year they are allowed to receive into the enclosure young girls in preparation for their first Communion, and others for the Retreat of the spiritual exercises. All these things and the angelic life led by these Religious were immensely pleasing to Gemma and made her regard as blessed those who belonged to such an Institute. Hence a great act of resignation was needed at seeing herself deprived of such a happy lot.

The holy virgins St. Rose of Viterbo and Gemma found themselves in similar circumstances. The former when rejected by the Franciscans of that City said: "They will not have me alive, but they shall have me when dead." Gemma said the same thing when she had pronounced her generous *fiat*: "The Passionists have not wished to receive me, and for all that I wish to be with them, and I shall be so when I am dead." Certainly if God gives me life, and Holy Church in her infallible judgment declares the sanctity of this new servant of God, I hope to see those words of Gemma verified. Then the daughters of St. Paul of the Cross in Lucca will tell positively how the true foundress and patroness of their Convent in that City is the Virgin Gemma Galgani.

CHAPTER 28

St. Gemma's Last Sickness.

ALTHOUGH Gemma had suffered much from spiritual trials, from frequent loss of blood, from the want of necessary food, and from continual and horrible attacks of the devil, she was in spite of such obstacles healthy, well-nourished, of florid complexion, and strong in body. Except for an occasional passing feverishness caused rather by the ardor of those inner spiritual fires than by physical infirmity, no sickness ever troubled her after the miraculous cure of her spinal disease. And this state of robust health lasted until Pentecost of the year 1902. On that solemnity her celestial communications were altogether extraordinary, her recollection more profound, her countenance unusually alight, her bosom heaving as though her heart would burst within.

While undergoing these marvelous spiritual influences she was rapt in an ecstasy that lasted a very long time, and learned that great things were in store for her. She had offered herself to God as a Victim for the salvation of souls, but the victim does not become properly such until immolated. And Gemma had to reach that consummation in order to fulfill her mission of expiation. Our Lord had now come to ask this of her. "I have need," He said to her, "of a great expiation specially for the sins and sacrileges by which ministers of the sanctuary are offending me." And He added: "If it were not for the Angels who assist at My altar, how many of these should I not strike dead!" At these words, at the sight of her Lord angered, the faithful spouse trembled with horror and grief, her face became pale as death, her heart throbbed and her eyes filled with tears. When then our Savior came to ask her if she would accept the expiation of those sins, with an impulse of her whole being she exclaimed: "Dost Thou not know,

O Jesus, that I accept it? Yes, at once, O Jesus. Exhaust Thy vengeance on me and be glorified in this Thy miserable creature."

God accepted the generous offering and Gemma fell dangerously ill. Her stomach ceased to act and she could no longer taste any kind of food. Whatever she was forced to swallow, even the smallest quantity caused internal convulsions and allowed her no rest until she had rejected it. She was barely able to sip a little wine. This was almost her only nourishment for two months, and it was wonderful how she was able to live on so little. No one could say what her sickness was, or what might be the cause of the strange and terrible phenomena that accompanied it. But the victim knew quite well, and one day while in ecstasy she thus addressed Our Lord: "Jesus, we shall shortly be at the end of Thy month (June). "This has been all Thine. Thou knowest that my Jesus. But I shall not be sated. This month ended, I have still many obediences to fulfil. Help me Jesus!"

As I knew the exact state of things and did not want this holy child to get into the hands of doctors, I wrote and told her, under obedience, to ask God to cure her of that terrible malady. She with perfect docility, though doing violence to herself, prayed, and Jesus gave her to understand that, in deference to the obedience, and to show that He was truly the Author of what was happening to her, He would cure her at once, but only for a short time. Gemma suddenly recovered, took her food as before, and from having become a mere skeleton, through about sixty days of absolute starvation, was restored to her full strength and freshness of complexion in a week. The Divine will however had to be accomplished. On the 9th of September, after a respite of about twenty days, she fell sick as before her cure. By the twenty-first of the month fever had set in and she began, as on a former occasion, to throw up pure blood that came with the violent loving throbbings of her heart.

Meanwhile to render the sacrifice of this generous victim of expiation more agonizing, God willed that all at once she should be deprived of all the delights of contemplation, of all those ravishing heart-yearnings, and with few exceptions, of every mysterious manifestation of the supernatural visions, raptures and the like. Thus she was left alone without consolation, being consumed by pure pain as a holocaust to the Lord. The letters that they wrote me from her adopted home at the time move to pity. "Gemma is very ill," they said. "She is reduced to skin and bone, she suffers excruciating torments, and internal pains that terrify. One cannot bear the torment of not knowing what to do to relieve her. Gemma feels great want of you. Come quickly to tell us how to act."

On receiving other pressing requests I determined to go. The poor child evinced the greatest joy when told that I had come, and wished to get up to welcome me. Imagine my grief at finding her in such a state, added to my fear that God this time would act indeed. I blessed her and bade her go back to bed. Then sitting by her side I said: "Well Gemma, what are we to do?" "Go to Jesus father," she answered in a tone of inexpressible joy. "But really?" I added. "Yes father, this time Jesus has told me clearly, so clearly. To heaven, my father, to Jesus with Jesus in heaven!" "But," I rejoined, "our sins, how are we to atone for them? You would make it an easy matter!" "Jesus," she answered, "has thought of that. He will let me suffer so much in the short time I have to live, that, sanctifying my poor pains by the merits of His Passion, He will be satisfied and will take me with Him to Paradise." "But," I said, "I do not wish you to die yet." And she with characteristic vivacity replied: "And should Jesus wish it, what then?"

At this point, I cannot understand why she went into the most minute particulars about her death: how the last sacraments would be administered, how they would clothe her after death, how she should be placed in the bier, carried to the cemetery and buried. She spoke of all these things with an admirable indifference, as she would if it were only a question of changing her room or bed. She listened and answered with brightness and grace. But when we spoke of the place of burial, she became serious, and in an impressive voice said: "Mind, father, attend closely to where they put me. Don't leave Lucca until you have well secured my corpse." I did not see what she was aiming at and asked an explanation. "I mean," she said, "that I wish my body not to be seen or touched by anyone, because it belongs to Jesus." I assured her that it should be as she desired, and she was quieted.

Nothing could exceed her contentment at knowing that her spiritual father was at hand. It seemed to her that she was then quite safe against any attack of Satan, and in her soul she thanked God for giving her this comfort after so much suffering. I heard her confession that evening, and in order to gratify her still more I allowed her to renew her general confession. During this act I could not refrain from tears of consolation at the reassurance of what I already knew, that during the whole twenty-five years of her life, Gemma never committed even one deliberate venial sin, and was taken to heaven unspotted the fair garment of baptismal innocence. It would be impossible to give a just idea of the spiritual refreshment she experienced in this confession. So great was the expression of her joy through ardent words and excessive emotion, that it was feared it might hurt her owing to her state of exhaustion.

I arranged that she should receive the holy viaticum next morning at an early hour, and notwithstanding her burning thirst owing to lung congestion, she wished to pass the whole of the night without any restorative. She was placed in a sitting posture in bed wearing a bridal veil, and having said a few words to her I withdrew to kneel in a corner of the room. She very quickly was rapt in profound ecstasy, with her hands raised and joined, her eyes closed, and became insensible, as on similar occasions, to all exterior influences, even to being burnt by a lighted taper. She seemed an angel in adoration before the majesty of God. The priest soon arrived with the viaticum, and having placed the Pyx on the little altar he turned towards the sick girl; but as she appeared to him to send forth rays and light from her countenance, he stood still, filled with religious awe. I encouraged him to go forward with the sacred particle, assuring him that although in ecstasy she would do the right thing, and so it was. On the approach of her Jesus she opened her eyes full of tears, put forth her tongue, received Him and at once returned into ecstasy. When the devout ceremony was over and the Blessed Sacrament taken back to the church, the priest returned immediately to Gemma's room and kneeling by her bedside he remained praying and weeping while her thanksgiving lasted. I too could not restrain my tears although accustomed to such transfigurations of the favored soul. I shall never forget that day, that room, that Communion.

The malady continued its ravages with occasional vicissitudes. Her faintings were frequent and alarming. Hence it was necessary to remain with her day and night, always ready with oxygen to restore breathing and hinder suffocation, and I waited to give her the last absolution. However as some days passed I said to her: "Gemma, how long shall we be? I must be going." And she answered: "If you wish, father, you can go, as I shall not die now. This illness will certainly finish me, but not yet; at least, this is what Jesus has told me." I blessed that angel for the last time, as I was not to see her again in this world, and I left her.

Before leaving I wished to make sure that the children of that good family should not be exposed to danger. The majority of the doctors had declared that Gemma's disease was tuberculosis while others, in the absence of any microscopic proof, stated that, in their opinion, her malady was a new and mysterious one. All however admitted the possibility of contagious infection and the need of separation. In effecting this I met with incredible difficulties. "What?" they all, old and young, exclaimed, "that we should let Gemma leave us? God has brought her to us, and shall we now allow her to go? Never! If she is to die we will assist her to the last." "And what would become of us," said the eldest son, a University student, "if Gemma were to leave us? God has always protected and helped our family through the merits of our holy guest. You will see, you will see what will happen." It was the same with all the others, who so opposed Gemma's removal, that four months had elapsed after my visit and they could not even then make up their minds to the separation.

At last wise counsels prevailed and a middle course was agreed to. One of Gemma's Aunts rented a small apartment close by with the windows facing her adopted home, and on the evening of the 24th of January, 1903, she was taken there. Little or nothing was charged with regard to her service and attendance. Her affectionate benefactors were constantly at the bedside of their sick treasure, and in spite of all the doctors' warnings, even the little ones, managing in turns to elude every vigilance, ran after their Aunt to see Gemma, from whom they could not bear to be separated. The poor invalid herself felt the separation most acutely; for in her turn she tenderly loved that affectionate family, but most of all her whom she called her second Mama. Therefore, on leaving their house she said as she wept: "This is the second time I lose Mama. But Jesus remains for ever! I alone with only Jesus!" She wrote to her spiritual father on the 6th of February as follows:

> *"My good father, Jesus always! These are my words every moment of the day. Jesus mine for ever! He has given me such great strength and courage that I ought to keep thanking Him without ceasing. I have made my sacrifice so easily that I have not even noticed it. I have understood, dear father, that now it is time not to be any longer a baby. Strength and courage! But you must help me by often giving me a little sermon, that does me so much good. Be contented as I am in the midst of affliction. Bless me always and with a big blessing. Every morning, indeed every moment I pray for you, that you may have patience with me a little longer. I am poor Gemma."*

Soon after she was settled in her new quarters she wrote her last letter to the Queen of Heaven. It was her custom to write to the Blessed Virgin on her principal feasts and when some special need called for it. She enclosed this last one to Our Lady in her last letter to me. I cannot tell her reason for this as she never did so before. Assuredly the good child could not have left me a more precious keepsake, for in this letter she set forth her whole spirit. Here are its principal expressions:

"Mother, my frail existence here drags on; always fighting, but I am contented, and between fear and hope I abandon myself to God. 'If I am all thine,' Jesus said to me this morning, 'who can overcome thee?' Dear Mother I am not at all well, thou knowest it. My life burns down and is day by day consumed. But the spirit? O my God! I cry out, I call aloud in the midst of much suffering. I turn to Jesus promising Him love, but Jesus is hidden. He no longer seems to love me, or very little. Patience! But you away from me, no, no, no! I will intone my nunc dimittis at my last moments. O Mother, 'Viva Gesú!' Jesus very soon and divinely will be avenged, through His love for the most ungrateful of His creatures. O Mother, pray for me. Tell Jesus that I will be good and obedient. But I want to go soon to paradise if He wills it. Bless me, I am poor Gemma."

Thus over the most furious waves of the tempest the calm faith of this holy girl was seen to ride triumphant. Thus the sweet expansiveness of her love in the depths of bitterest agony; thus the serenity of her hope and her longing for Heaven while facing the terrors of death. Blessed they who imitating Gemma have learned how to train their hearts to such sublime sentiments.

Chapter 29

Last Sufferings And Heroic Virtues Of The Dying Servant Of God.

IT was to be expected that a life wholly spent with Jesus Crucified would end on the Cross with Him. Gemma had participated one by one in all the sufferings of the Man God—in His agony of soul and external torturings; in His Sweat of blood; His scourging and His wounds; in the piercing of the Crown of Thorns; the dislocation of His bones and the lacerating of His flesh by the nails. In order to perfect the life-likeness to Jesus there only remained to be accomplished the last agony and death in an ocean of pain, and He would not deprive her of this. As Gemma's delicate body was certainly not capable of so much pain, He compensated for its intensity by its duration, keeping her on the Cross for several long months. We have seen something of the progress of this Martyrdom, now let us see its Consummation.

Although Gemma's state was most serious, she managed for a time to rise early every morning and drag herself with great difficulty to a Church close by for Holy Communion. Her faithful adopted mother came every day to take her, bring her back, and put her to bed, there to make her thanksgiving. The joy that this angelic girl found in the Bread of Life was too great, and its invigorating powers too energizing, so she had to forego it. In less than two months increased fever prevented her moving. Then she bowed her head and said: "Jesus, so be it!" Her corporal food now consisted only of a little nourishing liquid, which her stomach very soon refused, and, for some time at least, she could not take it, but she rejoiced in her inability. Her whole system was breaking up by degrees, and had reached such a stage that there was not a sound spot left in her body, nor one that was not tortured by some special pain. "Poor Martyr!" they wrote to me from Lucca, "poor victim of Jesus! She suffers without cessation and feels as if her bones were being disjointed. It is evident that she is tortured in every part of her body, and is being dissolved in hopeless agony. For the last twenty days she has lost her eyesight. Her voice has become so weak that she can scarcely articulate, so that it is impossible to catch what she says. She is a living skeleton that seems to waste more and more, and to behold her is to be filled with pain and dismay."

And yet all these sufferings so great in themselves were a mere nothing compared with those inflicted on the poor patient by the powers of hell. The Holy Spirit has said that in our last moments Satan will use desperate efforts in tempting us, knowing that little time is left him to effect our ruin. Imagine then his last hellish assaults on Gemma against whom during her whole life he had nurtured a hatred so deadly and waged such a relentless war. I read of other Saints who at the end of their days had to sustain fiendish assaults that were more or less lengthened and fierce, but they were intermittent. With Gemma the siege was continuous with only momentary intervals. The mention of these particulars makes me shudder, but they are true, for all those who were on the spot during the seven months of her last illness are unanimous in their statements of what happened.

The evil spirits disturbed her imagination with every sort of fantasy apt to excite anxiety, sadness, disgust and fear, in order thereby to drive her to despair. He pictured to her the whole scene of her life of trials in its blackest aspects—her family reverses, her privations of every kind, and even the appearance of the public officer who on the death of her father came with his creditors to seize what remained in their home. Then he said to her: "That is what you have had for so much done in the service of God." And profiting by the profound desolation of spirit in which our Lord, for her greater sanctification, allowed her to remain, he strove by every artifice to persuade her that she was entirely abandoned by God, and would to a certainty be lost for having taken the wrong course. Even the heroic virtues she had practiced and the exalted favors that she had received from Heaven were made by the astute tempter to appear as hypocrisy and deceit. This temptation was the most terrible of all and lasted longest. The poor child was crushed by it, but still, hoping to be saved, she resolved to remedy her state as far as possible by making a general confession.

In the midst of this agitation of mind and the confusion of ideas that beset her, she wrote a long history of her life, declaring that she deserved a thousand hells for having with diabolical malice succeeded in deceiving Confessors, directors and herself. Then descending to particulars she went through all the Commandments, the deadly sins, and the duties of her state, making herself out to be guilty of the greatest crimes. This document, having first been read at her request by a third person, was sent by her to a priest of holy life well known to her, with an entreaty that he would come and absolve her from all those sins. He came, heard her confession and reassured her. But the enemy did not on this account desist. He disturbed the irascible part of her nature with violent impulses to anger and impatience, in order that thus at least she might lose the reputation of sanctity in which she was deservedly held by all who knew her.

That which more than all agonized this angel were the violent efforts of the enemy to tarnish her purity. This spirit of uncleanness knew very well with what love and care she had guarded this treasure during her whole life and with what heroism she had always fought and defeated him in her determination to defend it. Now his aim was, if not to gain a victory which he knew was impossible, to be at least avenged against her by embittering the last days of her spotless life; seductive thoughts and imaginations were out of the question, for she could not be influenced in that way. So he had recourse to apparitions in ever-changing forms and to open violence. "Father, father," she wrote to me from her bed of pain, "this torment is more than I can bear. Ask Jesus to change it for me into any other one. Send an Anathema and an exorcism from where you are that will expel this contemptible demon, or tell your Angel guardian to come drive him from here."

But when one battle was over another began immediately. There was no respite. Hence one who was nursing the sufferer and often wrote to me said: "That abominable beast will be the end of our dear Gemma—deafening blows, forms of ferocious animals, etc. I came away from her in tears because the demon is wearing her out, and there is no remedy for what the wretch will surely do to her. We help her by sprinkling holy water in the room. Then the disturbance ceases, but only to begin soon again worse than before." From tormenting her soul he passed to torturing her body. Who could enumerate his artifices for this purpose? Her difficulty to take food had somewhat lessened, so they began to give her a little nourishment; but in vain. No sooner was it put before her than the fiend caused it to appear covered with disgusting insects and with the most repulsive things imaginable. As a natural consequence her stomach sickened immediately so that everything had to be taken away. Horrible and fetid animals, whether real or imaginary, came into her bed, crept over her limbs and tormented her in various ways so that the dear child had no means of relief. More than once, full of terror, she said to the Sister in attendance that she felt a serpent winding around her from head to foot and striving to crush her. In order to be relieved she repeatedly asked with great earnestness to be exorcised; but it was not thought well to gratify her. Then she tried to repeat the exorcism herself, and turning towards the enemy with animation and in a resolute voice she said: "Wicked spirit, I command you to depart from here to the place that is destined for you. If not I will accuse you before my God." Then turning to the heavenly Mother she exclaimed: "O Mother, I am in the hands of the devil who labors, strikes, torments me in order to drag me from the hands of Jesus. No, no, Jesus! do not abandon me, Mother, I will be good. Pray to Jesus for me. I am alone at night, full of terror, oppressed, and as it were tied in all the powers of my soul and powerless in all my bodily senses. Jesus my life for Eternity!"

From time to time our loving Lord came to encourage and reassure her, and, allowing her to feel His presence He spoke Divine words to her: "Why my child instead of being intimidated by those attacks of thine enemy, dost thou not increase thy hope in Me? Humble thyself beneath My potent hand and let not temptation weary thee. Resist always, never yield and if the temptation lasts, continue thy resistance; and thus the battle will lead thee to victory." On other occasions it was her Angel guardian who came to comfort her, and, as she herself wrote to me, these visits reanimated her, but only for short moments. Her soul returned into darkness, and the tempter presented himself anew with greater fury than before. The poor sufferer passed days, weeks, and months in this way giving us an example of heroic patience, and motives for salutary fear of what may happen to us, who have not Gemma's merits, at the terrible hour of death.

This saintly girl did not even bestow a thought on all that concerned the bodily pains and discomforts of her malady. She never showed that she was annoyed or weary, nor displayed the least sadness of countenance, but was always smiling and contented. She never seemed alarmed at the many varied crises in her sickness; nor did she ever allow those groans or sighs to escape her that excessive pain forces from the bravest sufferers even without their knowing it. She never asked for any restoratives, not even to be lifted or moved in bed although it was noticed that she was often in the most uncomfortable positions. The assistance given her, she said, was all that could be desired, although it sometimes happened that she was left whole nights alone when she stood most in need of aid.

To avoid such a recurrence recourse was had to the good nursing Sisters of St. Camillus de Lellis, and these with their usual charity took every care of the invalid and remained with her to the end. This is how one of these Sisters speaks of the extraordinary patience of the Servant of God: "During all the time that I had the consolation of assisting dear Gemma in her last illness I never heard her complain. I only heard her at first repeat occasionally this ejaculation: 'My Jesus, it is more than I can bear.' And when I had reminded her that with the grace of God everything is possible, she never again used those words. But when any of her visitors moved to pity happened to say: 'Poor child, it is more than she can bear,' she instantly replied: 'O yes I can still bear a little more.' And yet, continues the Sister, what I saw Gemma undergo was so much and so excessive that I believe one could not suffer more in Purgatory." All who used to visit this heavenly child during her long sickness speak in the same way of her patience and other virtues.

Notwithstanding so many obstacles–in the midst of so many torments and such fierce battles–Gemma found time to treat with God familiarly, and with the same serenity and serene unruffled spirit as during moments of the greatest consolation. "O where art Thou Jesus?" she used to be heard saying after her battles with the infernal enemy, "do not believe that I am trifling with Thee. Thou knowest all O Jesus, Thou seest my heart." She repeated these and similar words with open arms, her eyes raised to heaven, and in accents of ineffable tenderness. Then turning to the Blessed Virgin: "Mother, my own Mother," she continued, "you must tell Jesus that I will keep my word with Him, that I will be faithful to Him." And with the same affectionate abandonment, on feeling herself again suddenly attacked with greater violence by the enemy, she called aloud: "O Jesus, if it is pleasing to Thee give me a little respite! I feel myself growing faint. A little respite, Jesus!"

These aspirations, either outspoken, or mental, were incessant. "Dost Thou not know, Jesus," she would say, "that I am all Thine? Yes, all Thine, soul and body. Suffering yes, but I wish to be Thine. I want to go to Paradise to Thee." Once on hearing such expressions the Sister attendant said to her: "And if Jesus were to give you your choice what would it be–to go at once to Paradise and cease to suffer, or remain here to suffer when this would give greater glory to God?"

She answered with animation: "Better to suffer than to go to Heaven when the pain is for Jesus and to give Him glory." She asked the Sisters to repeat prayers and ejaculations during the long night hours, saying that she found great consolation in them. "Come Sister, come, let us pray, and not think of anything else. Jesus only!" Those good Religious were full of joy at finding so much fervor in a poor child already half dead, and they vied with one another to be with her, because, as they said, their souls profited by being near her, and it gave their bodies comfort and strength so that they did not feel either fatigue or its effects. They will themselves tell us what they felt: "The impression that young girl made on me," says Sister Camilla in her attestations, "is that she was a union of all virtues. During the whole time I was with her, it was a continual scene of edification. I noticed in her a profound knowledge of spiritual and mystical things. While talking with her, and we never spoke except on Holy subjects, I felt my soul greatly consoled and seemed to listen to an Angel. Her words were so lucid, so exact and impressive that one could not expect better from a Doctor of the Church. When I reminded her of the example of Jesus to encourage her to bear her pain patiently her whole countenance lit up. She smiled charmingly and her suffering seemed to cease, such was the effect on her whole being of the ravishing thought of Jesus."

The sentiments to which this saintly child gave vent most freely were those of compunction. Indeed witnesses say that she was often seen to tremble at the thought of her sins, and during the whole course of her sickness this thought seemed specially to terrify her. The words she used to express what she felt in her soul were so ardent and moving that listeners could not refrain from tears. "O Jesus, oh how many sins! Oh dost Thou not see them, Jesus. But Thy Mercy is infinite. Thou hast pardoned mine so many times. O forgive them now once more." And turning to the Madonna: "Mother," she said with tearful eyes, "when I shall be in the presence of thy Son, tell Him how to deal with me mercifully." Her most frequent ejaculation, day and night was, "My Jesus Mercy!" so that one of the same Infirmarian Sisters was able to say in evidence: "That which was most resplendent in Gemma during her last sickness, and affected me more than anything else, was her great humility."

Her prayer, in a word, was continuous. And usually seeing none around her but familiars she prayed aloud, turning alternately to a large crucifix, that she had caused to be hung on the side wall of her room, and to an image of the Blessed Virgin that she had opposite her bed. When tired by the repetition of words, it was still evident from the expression of her countenance that she was continuing her prayers with unabated fervor. "Monsignor," she said to me, "has told me, when unable to use my lips, to pray with my mind and heart and I do that." Before losing her sight she used to read occasionally. Once her Aunt seeing a book in her hand asked: "What are you reading, Gemma?" "I am reading, Aunt, the preparation for death. O Aunt, why don't you also read it, for you are old? At all events I am preparing for death!" And she performed this devout exercise every evening during the whole course of her malady. "But tell me, Gemma," continued her Aunt, "do you regret to die?" "Oh no," she answered, "I have no longer any attachment to anything in this world."

Not only did this child of heaven in the midst of her greatest sufferings find time to converse with God, she did the same also with creatures. And when she was not in actual combat or prayer, paying no attention to her corporal troubles, she gave herself up to those around her, edifying them as we have seen by all that she said, and trying to turn their thoughts from the sorrow they evinced at her pitiable state. To her Aunt who was moving about her bed in tears she said: "Aunt, I know your disposition, you are too sensitive. You fret at seeing me suffer. You must go away, go now. Yes, take her away, she grieves too much about me. Don't let her come any more by my bed." She answered all questions, and knew even how to mix witty words in her conversation, replying to the pleasant things they said to cheer her in terms equally agreeable or else with charming laughter. When her benefactors' little children came to see her she caressed them most lovingly, and gave them comfits and pastry, brought her by others, and carefully put aside for the little ones.

Her only surviving sister came to visit her, and on seeing her such a wreck, gave way to intense grief and tears. And Gemma, trying to soothe her said: "Don't cry, Angiolina, be calm, for it is nothing. And listen, Angiolina, I want to ask your forgiveness if I have ever shown you bad example." This speech increased her sister's grief, and she in turn asked pardon. Gemma's rejoinder was: "Don't think any more about all this, Angiolina, but strive only to be good, I beg of you." Then they parted. She showed the greater deference and gratitude to the good nursing Sisters, and although owing to her frank and simple disposition she could not pay compliments, it became quite evident in her eyes that she was full of recognition. She happened once to hear her adopted mother saying to the Superior of the good Sisters: "I shall not forget my duty in recompense for all you have done for her," whereupon with earnest looks she called out: "No, no, I will see to the Sisters with Jesus." Likewise to anyone who did her the least service she used to say: "Be good, and be assured I will remember you. When in the presence of Jesus I will not forget what you do for me now."

In the last stage of her illness, owing to extreme weakness, she fainted very often and became delirious. The devil availed himself of this loss of strength and impossibility of action in order to torment her the more with phantoms and fear. But the result was only to increase the merits of the helpless victim, who even in that state of prostration was able to intone her usual exclamations of defiance: *"Viva Gesú!* All for Jesus. Jesus only!" And thus she repelled the wicked suggestions. It was further noticed that even while in the greatest delirium, no sooner was she spoken to of God, than she instantly returned to herself and answered intelligently as if her mind had been perfectly undisturbed. The same thing happened when of her own accord, moved by divine impulse, she raised her mind to some exalted thought of God. Then the lower at once gave way to the superior sense, and from the delirium there was an immediate transition to words of the sublimest Mysticism. Thus on one occasion being deprived of her senses in a severe fit of coughing, that seemed as if it would either choke her or burst her breast, she spoke some incoherent words, and then all of a sudden, noticing one of the family who was holding a basin and looking at her compassionately, she returned her gaze and said: "Learn, Euphemia, how Jesus wishes to be loved." The child to whom Gemma spoke was her favorite and the confidante of all her secrets. She was her assiduous attendant during the whole time of her illness. She was present at her death, and received the precious inheritance of her spirit. But we have yet to see this saintly Virgin on her Cross and learn how Saints die.

CHAPTER 30
St. Gemma's Holy Death.

THE cruel malady has run its course. Gemma has nothing more left than a breath of life. Her whole body is in agony, the pallor of death is depicted on her countenance, she is stretched motionless on her bed in aspect so pitiable that one sees in her an image of Jesus expiring on the Cross. Four or five days before she died she became so heavy that three strong persons, even the workmen of the establishment, could scarcely lift her although reduced to skin and bone, and so slight in figure that a baby might have moved her. "We have managed," said the Sister, "a great many sick people, but never have we met anything like this." They expressed their wonder to Gemma herself, and she being in a position to know, candidly replied: "It is not I, you know, that weigh so." One is forced to believe that the devil had something to do with it for some malignant end, probably to increase the torments of the poor victim. And it was noticed that she had no sooner expired than she returned to her natural weight.

We have come to Wednesday in Holy Week. Gemma seems in ecstasy, she raises her eyes from time to time and fixing her gaze on Heaven, cries with an expression of intense yearning: "Jesus! Jesus!" Then at a given hour she is rapt in ecstasy just as happened so often during her life, but only for a short time. On coming to herself the Sister asked her if during those moments Jesus had consoled her, and she without hesitation answered: "Oh! if you, Sister, could see an atom of what Jesus has shown me, what joy it would cause you!" And the good Sister declares that in saying these words Gemma seemed to be totally transfigured. On the same day she received the Viaticum with sentiments of the greatest devotion, but, as had always been her custom, without any extraordinary outward manifestation of fervor. (From the 23rd of March when last she went to Church she had not received Holy Communion.) On the following day, Holy Thursday, a day so divinely solemnized in her heart, she asked to receive Our Lord, and as the priest made some difficulty about giving her Communion again as Viaticum she said that rather than be deprived of so much she would willingly bear the burning thirst and acted accordingly. "She seemed a Saint," says a witness, "sitting in bed with her hands joined and downcast eyes, her face all radiant and smiling in spite of the relentless malady that was consuming her." Having received Holy Communion she remained absorbed in deep recollection which after two hours became ecstatic, not however so as to hinder her answering persons who now and then spoke to her of spiritual things. During this ecstasy she seemed to behold a Crown of Thorns and said: "Before Thou art finished, oh how much more has to be gone through!" And turning to the Sister she added: "What a day tomorrow (Good Friday) will be!"

And that Friday came. Towards ten o'clock in the morning the lady friend who was with her, feeling that she herself was growing faint from fatigue and loss of sleep, resolved to go to her house close by to rest a little, but Gemma said to her: "Don't leave me until I am nailed to the Cross. I have to be crucified with Jesus. He has said to me that His children have to be crucified." She remained and, behold, soon after the suffering child entered into full ecstasy, opened her arms by degrees and remained thus until nearly half-past one. Her appearance was a mixture of grief, love, desolation, and tranquillity. She never spoke, but yet her silence was most eloquent. She was in agony with Jesus Crucified. The bystanders in astonishment gazed at her with insatiable earnestness. One of them wrote to me as follows: "Look at Jesus dying on the Cross, that was the appearance of Gemma in those moments." She continued to suffer the agony of death during the whole of that day, the following night and Saturday morning. It seemed as if she would expire from moment to moment, submerged in an ocean of excruciating torments in her body, and much more so in her soul. About eight o'clock on Holy Saturday morning she received Extreme Unction in the full exercise of all her faculties, following all the prayers of the sacred rite with singular devotion, and striving her best, though with weak voice, to repeat the answers.

The greatest suffering of Our Lord in His Agony on the Cross was, according to the Saints, His apparent abandonment by His Eternal Father. Add that abandonment, too truly real, by men. Of all this He Himself complained from the Cross, and Gemma in this also had to be like Him. It would naturally be asked with some surprise, why our dying Saint in her moments of greatest need was abandoned by her confessors and directors, and spiritual guides, and that only a few pious women stood by her moved rather by charitable sympathy at the sight of so much suffering than by the desire to be of assistance to her. But it was so, because God so willed in order to put a climax to the martyrdom and merits of His faithful Servant. The priest of a Church near at hand brought her the Viaticum and disappeared. The Curate of the parish anointed her and went his way, returning only at the last moment to read the recommendation of her soul. The extraordinary confessor, called expressly by her, heard her confession in a few moments, and withdrew. Her ordinary confessor who alone having directed her from her infancy, knew thoroughly all the mysteries of her life, and would have been able to help and console her in the midst of such pains, temptations and battles, only showed himself for a few moments, although the poor Soul had asked him several times to come and see her. I myself being at a great distance, knowing nothing of her imminent danger and great need, neither thought of going or of writing a consoling letter to her. Thus Gemma was left alone to suffer with Jesus only. As soon as her last sickness had taken a violent form she asked to have me called by telegram. But on its being made known to her in spirit that God asked this additional sacrifice at her hands, she said no more about it. And when others reminded her of me, having shown by a modest smile that she bore me in her mind, she replied: "I seek for nothing more. I have made the sacrifice of everything and of everyone to God. Now I prepare to die." God, in His turn, withdrew and allowed not a ray of light to enter His Martyr's mind nor a spark of consolation to move her heart.

In fine wasted by the violence of her disease, crushed under the weight of immense desolation, tormented in all her faculties of soul and body by the ministers of hell, without comfort from Heaven or earth, this innocent soul raised her feeble voice and said: "Now it is indeed true that nothing more remains to me, Jesus. I recommend my poor soul to Thee, Jesus!" It was the *Consummatum est* and the *In manus tuas* of Our Savior dying on the Cross. These were Gemma's last words.

The victim was offered, and nothing now remained but to breathe her last breath in completion of her sacrifice. Another half-hour passed. Gemma is seated on her bed, her head resting on the shoulder of one of her benefactresses. Her youthful friend Euphemia, kneeling before her, like Magdalene at the feet of the dying Christ, with head bowed down is holding her hand pressed to her own breast. The nursing Sister and all the members of the family are standing around contemplating the affecting scene. Gemma seems absorbed in peaceful thought. Then quite suddenly, while all eyes are fixed on her angelic face still beautiful despite the ravages of such a sickness, she smiled a heavenly smile, and letting her head drop on one side ceased to live—just as the Gospel tells of Our Redeemer on the Cross: *Et inclinato capite tradidit Spiritum.*

No one perceived that she was really dead, for besides having no specific agony, she underwent no muscular strain in breathing her last. There was no sigh of oppression or suffocation. Her last movement was like a smile of salutation and nothing more, a bidding farewell to her innocent body. In a word, her death was truly the "sleep of the just," her birth to eternal life.

This blessed death happened an hour after midday on Holy Saturday, the 11th of April, 1903. Gemma had once said to her Aunt:

"I have asked Jesus to let me die on a great solemnity. What a delightful thing to die on a great Feast!"

Yes, what a charming thing to die on the Solemnity of Our Lord's Resurrection, after having kept Good Friday on the Cross with Him, sharing in all His agony! After Gemma's death the Sisters took charge of her body, and at the suggestion of one who well knew her old longings to be a Passionist, they clothed her in brown, with on her breast the badge of the Passion, which is the distinctive mark of that Institute. They put a crown of flowers on her head, her beads around her neck, and joined her hands on her breast as she used to hold them when in ecstasy. The charming smile that played on her lips as she expired remained there. Her whole body was so composed and at ease, breathing something indescribably celestial, that it appeared to be the body of a living person who either was asleep or in ecstatic communion with God. Those present remained riveted in ceaseless admiration.

At the announcement of her death numbers ran to pray by her remains. Even the little children of the family that had made their home hers, ran also, and seemed not to wish to leave her. The very youngest of them, two or three years old, wished to kiss her hands and kept saying "Gemma, Gemma!" The old priest of the family, already spoken of, who more than others venerated and loved the angelic girl, betook himself to her room, and remained there all Easter Sunday in prayer and tears, until her blessed remains were taken away. Among others present was the worthy priest to whom, as we have seen, Gemma wished to make a general confession. He was filled with such reverence at seeing her that, throwing himself on his knees, he said aloud: "O Gemma, thou hast at thy feet a great sinner, pray to Jesus for me!" The concourse continued all Easter Sunday until her body was removed. Some took flowers from her Crown, some touched their objects of devotion to her hands and feet, others tried to get some of her hair, and so indiscreet were they that they would have taken it all if the nursing Sisters had not stopped them. One of the priests withdrew to pray in her room after her body had been removed and was heard to say: "I feel that I am in a Sanctuary, of which that bed is the altar. How well one can pray here! I would gladly remain here." When he had left the room he returned again saying: "Blessed Gemma who knew how to live as an angel, and die a Saint." Again a third time he came back to look at the room.

On Easter Sunday, a little before the Ave Maria, the body was removed to the Cemetery. The venerable Company of the Rose (Church of Saint Rose) carried out the ceremony with great solemnity; but the eldest son of the family in which Gemma had lived, a student at the University, wished to share the privilege of carrying the precious treasure on his shoulders. He did so with one other of the family and two of the Confraternity. The hallowed remains were put in a wooden coffin in which was placed a crystal tube containing the following inscription on parchment by the Reverend D. Robert Andreuccetti, official of the above-named Church of Saint Rose:

> *"Gemma Galgani, born in Camigliano of Lucca on the twelfth of March, 1878, of Henry Galgani and Aurelia Landi. Of spotless life and singular piety, she gave admirable proofs of all Christian Virtues. Tried from her childhood by serious domestic misfortunes, purified by long and painful infirmities borne with edifying resignation, she found her only comfort in constant devotion to Jesus Crucified to Whom she ardently desired to consecrate herself in the Institute of Saint Paul of the Cross. Ripe for heaven she winged her flight thither on Holy Saturday, eleventh of April, 1903. Live thou with the angels, holy soul, and pray for us."* March 12, 1878 — April 11, 1903

25 yrs.

When all was in order and the coffin placed on a rich bier adorned with flowers and borne by pious persons, the reverent procession, in which the clergy and a crowd of devout people took part, proceeded to the cemetery. All wish to go the whole of the long distance on foot. The Easter Solemnity always contrasts strongly with a funeral ceremony. This time the contrast was most exceptional and most eloquent. The procession was like the return from a nuptial Feast. The soul of the departed Virgin had gone with the angels to celebrate Our Lord's Resurrection in Heaven, and now men were taking back those put-off garments, to bury them until that day when she would want to use them again. She was buried in the open, in a privileged tomb over which was placed the following inscription:

GEMMA GALGANI Lucensis Virgo Innocentissima

Quae

Divini Amoris Aestu Magis Quam Vi Morbi Absumpta

Quinto Aetatis Lustro Vix Emenso Ad Coelestis Sponsi

Nuptias Evolavit Die xi M. Aprilis A. MCMIII

Pervigilia

Dominicae Resurrectionis

Anima Dulcis Te In Pace Cum Angelis.

When translated thus it says: *"Gemma Galgani of Lucca, a most innocent virgin, who in her twenty-fifth year, consumed rather by the fire of Divine Love than by the violence of disease, flew into the arms of her Heavenly Spouse on Holy Saturday the eleventh of April, 1903. Peace be to thee, O sweet soul, in company with the angels."*

The intense grief that overwhelmed the family at Gemma's death, and the shock it caused them all made them forget what was previously agreed upon, namely, that in the event of her death they would have her heart examined in hopes of finding some extraordinary marks. After the burial they remembered this and resolved to put it into execution at once. Many days however were spent in taking the legal steps before the civil authorities. Then when all was ready on Friday the 24th of April, the twelfth day after the death of the Servant of

April 24, 1903

God, they proceeded to exhume her body. It was found just as when placed in the coffin, but not without signs of incipient decomposition. It was uncovered and the heart removed. This heart showed no sign of decomposition, but, on the contrary, was fresh, healthy, flexible, ruddy and full of blood, precisely as in a living person. This greatly surprised the professional men deputed to make the autopsy. The shape of the heart too was singular; for, contrary to the usual form, both faces were very much flattened, and the sides greatly widened, so that the width was greater than the length. But what was not their astonishment when on opening the heart it was found that the blood in both ventricles and in the orifices was still fresh and red and ran freely over the marble slab on which they were operating? Everyone knows as a matter of fact that immediately after death, on the body becoming cold, all the blood contained in the heart leaves it, or else, if the becoming-cold is rapid, it congeals and loses its vivid color. How much more likely should not this be thirteen days after death, and death from an infectious disease?

That heart that was a furnace of celestial fire. It so beat with pure love of God, that, unable to contain itself in its natural cavity, it raised and greatly curved three ribs. Its fire burned the exterior corresponding part of the pectoral region and whatever touched it. That heart could not die! It was a mistake that it should have been cut open by the hand of man. But God permitted that so it should happen in order to manifest a prodigy that otherwise would have passed unobserved. As regards the abnormal shape of this wonderful heart, the only possible explanation of it would seem to be the violence of Divine Love with which it was on fire, of which we have already had proof. It must be noted that Gemma never showed any symptom of heart disease that could account for such a strange effect. Her heart was always healthy and robust and, except during the time of ecstasy and of her mystical spiritual martyrdom, never manifested the least irregularity. Hence, on the cessation of those ecstatic emotions it returned in an instant to its normal state. She was rather anemic during the last months of her life, but who would dare to say that a short period of anemia could distort the organ of life to such a degree? Worse still if this phenomenon were attributed to the decomposition of the tissues during those thirteen days in the grave; for the decomposition of a member together with freshness of the blood contained in it would be a manifest contradiction. Likewise the destruction of the tissues and the vivid freshness of their color are things that cannot co-exist. Despite the incredulous then, let us acknowledge the miracle and bless its Divine Author Who is always wonderful in His Saints.

Having brought this Life of Gemma to an end, I implore of Thee, Divine Master, that these pages may make known to all how good Thou art, and how sweet it is to serve and love Thee only, as did Thy faithful Servant Gemma Galgani.

Nov. 2, 03
Sunday, all Soul

CHAPTER 31

Extraordinary Devotion Of The Faithful To St. Gemma.

IT did not seem likely that Gemma Galgani after her death would be held in remembrance by the Faithful in general. Her life had been so hidden that she was scarcely known outside her adopted home. But our Lord has said that He will exalt the humble, and His words cannot fail. When Gemma and the wonderful happenings of her life seemed to have lapsed into oblivion, the report of her sanctity spread abroad. And while in her lifetime no one seemed to notice her, now on all sides one heard loud praise of her great virtues. Many have chosen her as a particular advocate before God, and invoke her protection in their spiritual and temporal needs. They come in pilgrimage from Rome and other distant provinces to pray at her tomb in the cemetery of Lucca, and the graces that many declare they have received through her intercession strengthen more and more their confidence in her. The result is, that as the reports of these graces received spread abroad earnest requests came from all parts for some little thing which once had belonged to the Servant of God, to be used as a remedy for infirmities of soul and body, just as is done with the relics of Saints. On this account, before closing the story of this Servant of God's Life, it remains to treat of two things: First, of the devotion of the Faithful to Gemma's memory, and Second, of the marvelous graces that God is pleased to bestow on many through her intercession.

Among the Saints that are held in honor by the Church we know of very few who immediately after their death were so venerated by the Faithful far and near as the humble Virgin of Lucca. Persons who had not known her while living, or had no opportunity of hearing her mentioned, came to know her through reading the first edition of her life published late in 1907. This Life, though written in unpretending style and by an inexperienced hand, attracted attention, was eagerly sought for, and in about two months the first edition was out of print. The second edition, three times more voluminous than the first, was impatiently awaited. Within two years a sixth edition was printed and over 23,000 copies have been disposed of. Most certainly God has willed through those roughly drawn lines to inspire readers with an affection for His faithful Servant;for it is noticeable that almost all who have read Gemma Galgani's Life cease not to bless God for having adorned His Church with such a precious gem in these calamitous times. Her fame has spread far and wide, and requests are continually coming to the Editor from all parts of the world for permission to translate and publish her life. I will quote the words of a few among many authoritative persons who have written to me on the subject.

And first of all, the reigning Pontiff Pius X, having read this Life deputed the Cardinal Secretary of State to write to the Author as follows:

> *"The Holy Father has charged me to make known to you the great pleasure he derived from reading the book in which you (display a deep knowledge of mystic Theology and)[1] describe the riches of extraordinary graces that our Lord poured so abundantly into the soul of that innocent maiden. The August Pontiff trusts that by reading this Life hearts may become more inflamed with that love of the supernatural which the enemies of the Faith strive to obliterate."*

—CARDINAL MERRY DEL VAL

Still more emphatic words of admiration of the humble Gemma were written to me by many Cardinals, Bishops and exalted Prelates among the Secular and Regular Clergy, as well as by distinguished laymen–and this particularly from Rome where the merit of things is so carefully weighed. But outside Rome, similar expressions have come from Florence, Genoa, Turin, Milan, and almost every Province in the Peninsula. Those letters, each dictated by the desire to manifest its writer's sentiments of devotion to the Servant of God, were like the voices of many in one harmonious choir. The much-regretted Bishop of Fiesole in Tuscany, Mgr. Camilli, wrote thus:

"I have just finished the Biography of the young Servant of God Gemma Galgani, and I don't know how to tell you what I have thought and experienced in my poor heart while reading it. That angelic figure has appeared to me in all her splendor. Her profound humility, her rare and generous obedience, her dove-like simplicity, her ardent charity towards God and towards her neighbor in general, and towards sinners in particular; her ineffable pains, her martyrdom of soul and body, all, in a word, have illuminated my mind, all has gone down into my heart, and in tears I have thanked our Lord, that a lily so beautiful and so sweet has grown and flowered in our midst. Oh! may Jesus Crucified soon glorify on the earth His Angelic Spouse who wished to die with Him on the Cross. I have begun to invoke her, but I beg of you, Father, help me to obtain her protection, and send me, if you can, something of hers for my devotion."

Another reverend holy Prelate of the Florentine Province wrote as follows:

"You cannot imagine with what great spiritual joy I am reading the biography of the holy Virgin of Lucca, Gemma Galgani. I desire to make the dear Saint known here. Send me therefore thirty copies of her Life. Since I began to read it I have begun to entertain a strong hope that through her intercession I shall obtain from Jesus more abundant graces for the sanctification of my soul and the fulfillment of my duties."

A most worthy Priest of Lucca who had the consolation of knowing Gemma intimately writes in his turn:

"The Biography of Gemma Galgani is a treasure for me. You can imagine with what desire and devotion I read it, seeing again as I do so in my presence that admirable girl whom our God in His Infinite

Mercy has given to the people of Lucca. Oh that God would grant me the grace to join my poor voice with those who will have the enviable lot of preaching Gemma's panegyric when she is raised to the Altar!"

"What a fragrant air of Paradise one breathes," wrote another Priest who was Gemma's Confessor in her childhood, "while reading the precious Life of Gemma in the midst of the deadly atmosphere of this perverse world! How many charming and treasured memories it recalls to my mind, of the time when she and her family lived in my parish, when for a short time I was her spiritual director as well as her saintly mother's. I believe that this Life written so conscientiously will do great good, specially to devout souls."

One of the most illustrious preachers in Italy expressed the inmost feelings of his heart towards Gemma in an affecting but rather long letter. I feel sure however that my readers will be glad to read his very words. "Some very spiritual persons," he says, "spoke to me with enthusiasm of Gemma Galgani whose Life they were reading, and marvelled that I did not know of it. Distracted by other thoughts I paid little attention to what they said, and did not care to obtain it. Three months later I saw the book in the hands of a Priest who spoke in the same enthusiastic terms of the heroine of Lucca. Then, whether through curiosity or for other motives, I resolved to look through the Life. On reading the first pages, I, who hitherto had never found any pleasure in reading the lives of the Saints, began to experience an unusual heartfelt emotion. Contrary to my natural habit when reading any book, as soon as the noble figure of Gemma came before me in a picture drawn in simple and attractive lines, I felt a need to hasten and devour, as it were, in one effort what I held in my hands. And thus hastening and devouring what was before me I reached the end, but only to be inspired with a still greater desire to read it again. The whole world seemed to have gone out of my mind. I saw nothing but the unsullied soul of that Angel in human form, covered with the wounds of Jesus Crucified, adorned with supernatural and celestial gifts that are seen distributed among other Saints. I heard the voice of a child speaking with her Angel Guardian, with the Blessed Virgin, with Jesus, in the same way that a little girl would speak to her brother, to her loving mother, to her affectionate father. In reading the lives of the Saints repeated quotations and long passages from their letters had always produced in me a sense of distaste and weariness. In this Life of Gemma on the contrary I should have been glad if she had been always allowed to speak, and if the Author, instead of making an apology, had given her discourse in full. And not finding in this book as much as I wanted, I sought out those who had known the Servant of God and asked them to tell me something more about her.

And if others wish to know whence comes this, my ardent devotion to Gemma, I answer candidly that it springs from the salutary effects that my soul has experienced through her. God has willed to make use of Gemma to crown His Divine Mercies in my regard, arousing me from my tepidity, detaching me from all and everything, enabling me to work for Him and in Him only. In a word, on the appearance of this virgin before my eyes, a real transformation has been wrought in my soul. And I should be ungrateful if I did not confess it openly. Every hour of the day, in all my occupations, I see before me this child of Heaven encouraging, advising, and reproving me who am an unworthy Priest. And when I am wanting, how ashamed I feel to find myself before her! 'Pardon, pardon, O Gemma. Enable me, I beseech thee, to correspond to the mission that God has given thee, for the salvation of my poor soul.' From these facts and from what I have heard from others, I feel convinced that the holy Virgin of Lucca is destined by Heaven to excite a holy emulation throughout the world, specially among the young, and thus kindle in them the fervor of a truly Christian and perfect life."

"I am thankful to God," writes a Priest from Leghorn, "and glad to tell you that devotion to the Servant of God, Gemma Galgani, has been taken up here with great fervor by all who have come to know of her. Her Life is read in the Refectory of some Monasteries, and I have distributed pictures of her to the clergy of the Cathedral and to the Professors and Students of the Seminary—all have them. Some Parish Priests are asking for copies of her Life and pictures, and are making her known to their parishioners. Very many sick people and others, wanting graces, are anxiously looking for pictures. It is indeed evident that our Lord wills to make known this most humble Virgin of Lucca to all Leghorn."

"On reading Gemma's Life," remarks a worthy Canon of Lucca, "one's soul is certainly moved by soothing and devout impressions and filled with admiration and awe at the revelation of such an existence."

"You cannot imagine," writes another, "how much good is being effected in many souls by this angelic creature. I too am devoted to her. She inspires me with confidence. The mere thought of her comforts me, and she in her turn takes special care of my poor soul."

Our Superior General, when granting my request to reprint this Biography, wrote the following words: "I rejoice beyond measure at hearing so many good things about our Gemma, and feel assured that our Lord wills to glorify her on earth where she always kept hidden. I willingly give leave to publish a second edition of her Life and hope that it will do as much good as the first, that was so well received."

A most eminent Cardinal of Holy Church, not satisfied with having read this Life many times and with having procured copies of it for distribution, after having spoken at length of Gemma's virtues to a friend of mine, said to him: "Tell the Author to come and see me when he is in Rome, to talk to me about this dear Servant of God. Be sure to tell him to come, because I want to hear from his mouth about Gemma. It is a matter in which I am greatly interested.

And as with Ecclesiastics and Religious, so also with the laity of both sexes. The words of one will serve for those of many. "I have just learned," said a father of a family, technical director of a leading artistic firm in Rome, "that your Reverence is about to print the third edition of Gemma Galgani's Biography, and I cannot cease to thank

God for having designed to make known His faithful Servant by the prodigious circulation of this golden Life. I feel I ought to tell you that I attribute the reception of many graces to this dear little Saint. Not only have I experienced very great spiritual consolation while reading about her, but I have felt myself enlightened by grace and encouraged to lead a better life. My Communions are more fervent and my energy greater in facing the battle of life. I attribute this to the intercession of Gemma, to whom all my family and I recommend ourselves continually. God grant that all may be moved to have recourse to her, for I feel quite sure that their hopes will not be disappointed. A great many persons known to me to whom I gave the Life of Gemma to read, suggesting that they should take her as their patron, have told me of graces and favors received since reading her life. They have felt themselves drawn to her and, what is more important, bettered in soul and consoled in their troubles."

A letter reaches me, while giving these pages to be printed, from a distinguished Professor, and President of a College in Rome, from which I add here a few extracts. "Rev. Father," it begins, "I have returned from my pilgrimage to Lucca with the Polish Priest whom you know and another pious person. We prayed a long time at Gemma Galgani's tomb, asking through her intercession for a spark of that Divine Love with which her soul was on fire. At the sight of so many memorials of this angelic girl's life a strange impression came over us, and we felt our souls overflowing with feelings of ineffable peace and consolation in the one thought of God's wonderful manifestation of Himself in His Saint. We had already visited Alvernia, yet the impression made at Lucca was even greater than that which we experienced in the Chapel of the Stigmata on that hallowed mountain. We repeatedly blessed God for having inspired you to write the Life of the dear young Saint, the manifestation of whose singular virtues has done so much good to souls. What a help to recollection and meditation! What a school in the ways of the Spirit! These are not only my own private impressions, they are what I have heard from numberless Priests and Religious as well here in Rome as during my journey through Arezzo, Bibiena, Florence and Lucca. All are of the same mind without having any knowledge of the author of the Life. I even heard one very distinguished person say that such a Life surpassed that of St. Teresa (as indeed it does in some respects), and that it is an unfailing fountain—a true school—of the devout and mystical life. Then the veneration that the Virgin of Lucca excites wherever she is heard of is so great that you would not expect more in the case of a canonized Saint. In my Institute she has inspired a real enthusiasm in the students and in the Professors; and I have found a few passages read from her Biography produce marvelous effects particularly in giving new life to faith."

The Extracts given in this and the next chapter have been taken hastily from hundreds of letters, now in my hands. They would form a large volume. They are written by every class of persons, from all parts of the world, including even China, and continue to come daily. The following expressions of thought and feeling by different persons, which close this chapter, are among the more recent and are very striking.[2]

"The Life of Gemma," writes a Rector of the Jesuits, "has given immense general satisfaction. For my part I confess that I cannot keep from invoking her continually, nor from addressing her as Saint Gemma. You, Reverend Father, by publishing the Biography of this Saint and her letters and ecstasies, have accomplished a Mission for the good of innumerable Souls now and in the future that is worth more than hundreds of our ordinary missions. I have already given discourses on this Saintly Virgin in Retreats to Religious Communities, and I will speak of her all the rest of my life, and cause her to be known and earnestly invoked. Furthermore I have promised in gratitude to contribute to the best of my power, even by obtaining subscriptions, to the Cause of her Beatification. Gemma without doubt will be canonized, and that before long, by the Oracle of the Church, and will be numbered among the greatest Saints that we venerate on the Altars. That is my opinion."

Gemma's picture is to be found everywhere, and her relics are worn by many who confidently implore her intercession in all their needs. Over a hundred thousand of these relics have already been eagerly sought and distributed.

Many have chosen this Virgin as Patron of the Catholic works directed by them. Among this number is the Pious Union of the Roman Priests, who, under the protection of Gemma, are striving to promote in Rome the decorum of the House of God and the good of Souls. In their frequent meetings one of their chief practices is to read some passages from the Life of this Servant of God, accompanied by observations that edify and move to the imitation of her virtues.

A writer from Acqui say: "On simply reading this Life one feels as it were dazzled, and I must say for myself, that never in my life have I been so moved by reading any book or found in it so much to edify me."

A stranger called at our Retreat of SS. John and Paul in Rome and asked to see me. On my coming to him he requested to see me privately, and when we were alone he said: "I have been sent to you by Gemma Galgani, who, drawing me from the abyss of sin in which I was involved, spoke the following words to my ear as well as to my heart: 'Go to Rome, seek at the Monastery of SS. John and Paul a certain Fr. Germanus, and settle with him the affairs of your soul without delay, otherwise Jesus will strike you." This and with tears in his eyes, he threw himself at my feet, saying: "Father, hear my Confession." I also shed tears of emotion, heard his Confession, and absolved him. Then, after mutual kind words, he, like one risen from death to life, thanked me and left for the railway station to return to the town whence he had come.

"I cannot tell you in words," writes an illustrious Professor of Mondovi, "how much and in what way I have fallen in love with this charming creature Gemma Galgani. She was to me a revelation. I read her life in tears. I took her for my advocate. I keep her always in mind and when I think of her I find that she corrects and encourages me. One of the Oratorian Fathers here desires me to tell you that he looks on Gemma as the Saint of our day, and as an Apostle specially sent by God in order to awaken new fervor and zeal in the hearts of the Priesthood."

Another person makes the following observation: "I should have wonderful things to tell you. I should be able to show how the name of Gemma alone carries with it an indescribable sweetness, attraction and fascination; and this without describing the still more wonderful effect produced in hearts, more particularly of young people, when they come to know her. As a Missionary I can give clear proof of this statement."

Reading the Biography of Gemma," writes another correspondent, "produces sweet and fervent impressions in the Soul, and the reader remains filled with grateful wonder at the revelation of such a marvelous existence. One could scarcely believe the amount of good that is being wrought in thousands of minds by this Angelic Creature."

A Priest from the Province of Potenza says: "I read those pages," he writes, "with intense avidity and interest, and know not how to express what I felt while reading. It was a mixture of adverse sentiments; of joy at God having raised such a favored Soul to promote His Glory while confounding the wise ones of this world; of grief at not having known how to correspond as she did with Divine Grace; of love for her because of the example of Virtue she has left us, and of abhorrence of our times which no longer know how to value the gifts of God. I have felt such emotion while reading this Life, that I have been frequently obliged to lay aside the book."

"I am reading," writes another, "for the second time the Life of this Most amiable and spotless Gemma, and in so doing am often moved to tears. I don't know how to put it, that in this Life there is a something mysterious that attracts, conquers, and carries away the mind and the heart–feelings I have never experienced in reading the lives of other saints. In these bad and wicked times–oh! what great reason is there not to be comforted–for the good who weep and are consoled–for the tepid who are thus moved to a new life in the flames of so much Divine Love, and for poor blind sinners who, with such an object before them, are almost forced to repentance."

One of the Canons of Fano also writes: "I have read the Life of the holy maiden Gemma Galgani, and to say that I have been bewildered in my astonishment would not be all, nor enough to express the depth of the impression that it has made upon me. One really feels here face to face with a supernatural marvel of the Infinite Goodness of God. It is not possible here to lose sight of Gemma's holy figure, nor to remain indifferent to it. Her story is a continuous miracle, and her words largely quoted, but never enough to satisfy the reader, touch with a sweetness and force that ravish one. I who am so cold and so hard, that I believe I never dropped a tear at reading the life of any Saint, have been repeatedly moved and have found tears rushing to my eyes. Judging by myself I should say that the life of this heavenly Creature is destined to make the deepest impression everywhere."

Father Lewis Fontava, Barnabite, writing from Naples says: "I caused a picture of Gemma to be put under the pillow of a dying Freemason who refused to be reconciled to the Church. That was on Tuesday evening in Holy week. The next day, Wednesday, of his own accord he asked for the Sacraments."

From the few quotations I have given–chosen among hundreds–it is easy to see that the admiration in which the faithful hold this seraphic virgin, and the religious spirit that through her means is being gradually propagated, are not sterile but truly fruitful sentiments. They fill the soul with emotion and move it to imitation. They create a desire to be detached from earthly things in order to love only those of Heaven. They help one to put off the old man so as to be clothed in the New.

After listening to such a concert of praise from every class of persons, and beholding God's merciful working in souls through the humblest means, let us not heed those idle talkers who, without having seen or read or examined anything, make assertions that are contrary to facts!

• • • • • • • • • • • • • • • • • • •

[1] The words in parenthesis are in the original letter from the Cardinal Secretary of State, but were left out through humility by Fr. Germanus in the Editions published while he lived.

[2] These passages from letters received by the Author not long before his death were destined by him to appear in this Edition, and therefore we add them here. We have found among his papers six hundred and thirty such letters, besides countless post cards and words accompanying P.O. orders, all expressing devotion and gratitude to the Servant of God.

Nov. 8, 03, Sat.

CHAPTER 32
Graces And Miracles Obtained
Through St. Gemma's Intercession.

THE strongest argument in favor of the sanctity of a Servant of God is that of miracles. By their means our Divine Savior and, after Him, the Apostles, proved their mission in this world to be from above. And the Church bases her proofs of holiness on miracles before decreeing the honors of the Altar to her Saints. Now, if it is true that miracles are the fruit of the faith, and if the ardor of this faith in seeking the advocacy of Gemma Galgani with God is seen to be great in every class of persons, it follows that a great number of graces or miracles must be obtained through her means. It is not my intention to give particulars of all of them here. I wish to wait until they have been attested by sworn witnesses in the examinations (processi) that are going on in view of the Beatification and Canonization of the Servant of God. I will speak of them in general for the edification of the faithful, and only relate particulars of a few of which I am sure, having had them from persons most worthy of belief. But the acceptance of these also remain subject to the decision of the Ecclesiastical Authority, whose duty it is to judge and pronounce as to whether they are to be considered simple graces or true miracles.

Philomena Bini of Pisa, aged seventy-two, suffered for a long time from malignant stomach disease, pronounced by several eminent physicians to be a cancerous ulceration of the worst kind. Various prescriptions were tried, more with the object of lessening pain than with hope of cure. Finally, it was openly declared that any further attempts to cure such a disease in a woman of her age, reduced to such a state, was loss of time, and so medical attendance was discontinued. Meanwhile, the Parish Priest visited her daily for months and administered to her the last Sacraments. In this extremity, a good lady of the City, hearing of Gemma, felt inspired to implore her intercession. Having procured a relic, she hastened to the bedside of the dying woman. She made all present kneel, said some prayers to the Blessed Trinity in honor of the Servant of God, and applied the relic to the patient. Almost immediately the sick woman, who for a long time had not closed her eyes, owing to the violent pains that tormented her, fell into a placid sleep that lasted the whole night. In the morning, on awakening, she found herself perfectly cured without the least remnant of the pains that had tormented her for five years. She asked for food and ate with appetite four times that day, taking broth, meat, biscuits, milk, and eggs. Imagine the astonishment of the doctor when Philomena Bini, whom he believed dying, presented herself to him in robust health. Not trusting to what he saw, he wished to examine her with electric rays, and finding that all disease had gone, he exclaimed: "This is a miracle wrought by God!" Many months have passed since that miracle, and Philomena Bini continues to be in good health, such as she had not previously enjoyed since the days of her youth.

Maria Menicucci of Vitorchiano, Province of Rome, was suffering from acute pain in the knee, which she took to be rheumatism and treated accordingly, but in vain. Later she was examined by surgeons and pronounced to be a very bad and far-advanced case of artrosinovite. In their opinion, the malady might be arrested, but they gave no hope of a complete cure. The patient came to stay with some relatives in Pistoja in May, 1907, when everyone was talking of Gemma of Lucca. "Oh!" thought a certain lady, "could not this new servant of God work this miracle?" She procured a relic, applied it to the bad knee, and began a novena. On the ninth day the bandages were taken off and the knee found to be perfectly cured! The favored one then wrote to a friend as follows: "Gemma has heard my prayer. I am cured, as you can see from the medical certificate that I enclose. I am beside myself with joy." The Doctor, Chelucci, of Pistoja, in the certificate referred to, described with precision the nature of the disease and his final examination of the knee, concluding with these words: "This lady, Signora Marianna Menicucci, is now restored to perfect health."

Marianna Angelini, a Roman, twenty years ago had to undergo an operation on her breast. Fifteen years later, in August, 1903, the operation had to be repeated in St. James' Hospital, Rome. It seemed a success, but, after the lapse of four years, a fresh tumor appeared, and a third operation was advised. The poor sufferer was undergoing excruciating torments night and day, which rendered her right arm powerless. Almost in despair, she appealed to all the Saints, until, hearing of Gemma of Lucca, she turned to her with confidence. She applied a relic and a picture of the Servant of God to the part affected, and, having begun a triduum of prayers, although up to that time she had not been able to get any rest, she fell into a tranquil sleep. This lady's child of four years, as soon as her mother awoke, told her that a beautiful girl had come to her and assured her of mamma's recovery. It was so, for the invalid, having slept well all that night, felt perfectly free from pain, and, on his return, the surgeon found that there was no longer any need of an operation. In token of their gratitude, this lady and her husband gave a sum of money, more than proportionate to their means, towards the cause of the Beatification of their benefactress.

In the city of Lucca a pious woman, whose name I do not give, was afflicted with an abscess on her head, which showed all the symptoms of cancer. At least the doctors feared this, and thought that an operation would be necessary. The poor woman finding her ailment grow worse, became terrified, but turned her prayers in time to Gemma, whom she had known. She applied her picture to the diseased part and stopped all the remedies prescribed by the Doctors. A few days were enough. The ailment disappeared, not to return, and this good woman never ceases to thank God and her holy advocate, Gemma.

Isolina Serafini of Vicopelago, near Lucca, was suffering for about ten months from acute meningitis, that tormented her night and day, without her deriving any benefit from the remedies ordered by her medical attendants. From December, 1906, to October, 1907, she was unable to sleep for more than an hour in each twenty-four hours. While in this sad state, she felt inspired to have recourse to Gemma, and invoked her with confidence, saying: "I shall take it as a sign that you are in Paradise and a Saint, if you effect my cure; and I promise to publish it immediately." So saying, she lay down on her bed. The pains left the same moment. Not a vestige remained of the violent and wearing meningitis. She fell asleep, and from that day, the 10th of October, 1907, up to the present, she has not suffered once from her head, and is always able to sleep soundly. "This is the exact truth," she says in the written declaration she sent me, "and I confirm it on oath, I, Isolina Serafini."

These few instances of wonderful cures, taken from among many that are happening continually in Lucca, Rome, and in every part of Italy, as well as in other countries, will be enough for my purpose, which is to edify the faithful and encourage them in their corporal sufferings to apply with lively faith to the powerful advocate given us by Heaven.

But Gemma has shown herself solicitous for others, not only in their bodily infirmities, but in every other necessity of life. We have proofs of this in the prayers that are continually being offered to her by every class of persons, who, instead of increasing in numbers, would be sure to diminish if, at least in the majority of cases, they were not heard. Here too, notwithstanding the quantity of material at my disposal, I will confine myself to a few examples.

Two Passionists, the Provincial and a Consulter of the Province of Mexico, when returning to their country, wished to visit Gemma Galgani's grave, on their way to Genoa where they were to embark for Barcelona. On this voyage they were overtaken by a fearful hurricane that lasted eight hours with imminent danger of the vessel foundering. All the passengers were terror-stricken, and even the Captain was so disheartened that he gave no hope of their being saved. In this extreme the two Religious had recourse to the Virgin of Lucca. "Gemma," they called aloud, "thou alone canst save us. Do not break thy word!" Wonderful to relate! they had no sooner made this prayer than the storm began to lull. In less than an hour there was a perfect calm, and all, as if sailing on a placid lake, reached their destination safely. Immediately on landing, our two Religious wrote to me of the wonderful event, testifying their gratitude to their benefactress, and expressed their desire that all might know this holy soul and see her soon raised upon the Altars.

"A great disaster threatened our family," thus a lady wrote to me from Rome, in June, 1908: "we recommended ourselves to the blessed Gemma, and God, in His infinite Goodness, has vouchsafed to console us. She prayed for us, and we are returning her infinite thanks. My good father, this Servant of God is so dear to me! I have taken her for my special patroness and pray to her always."

A Camaldolese nun in Rome, a certain Mother Romualda of St. Joseph, wrote to me thus: "As soon as I received the relics and pictures of the Virgin Gemma, I offered one to our Venerable Mother Abbess, and she, finding herself in great straits through want of a sum of money that she was called upon to pay, promised the Servant of God that, if she would enable her to find this sum, she would send a good offering for the cause of her Beatification. Two days after her promise, a charitable person sent us an alms, exactly the sum that was needed. The Rev. Mother Abbess, full of gratitude, charged me to ask your Reverence to employ the enclosed money for the desired object." She then added: "I recommend you an unfortunate, obstinate sinner, whose conversion we hope to obtain through the intercession of Gemma."

The reader will remember that, while Gemma lived, she prayed incessantly with many tears for the conversion of sinners. She labored with fervor to this end and brought many back to penance. She offered herself to God for them as a victim of expiation, and, because her offering was acceptable to Him, she died a true Victim in the flower of her youth. Ah! let sinners then hope for their conversion through Gemma now that she is in Heaven; and let all those who take this matter to heart, recommend their own dear ones to her. For the sake of brevity I will only relate three instances of these conversions due to her advocacy. They all happened quite lately.

A certain person, whose name I do not give for obvious reasons, was lying seriously ill in the Lucca hospital in 1907, and having long before lost the life of his soul, was fast approaching the death of his body. He was not only a notorious sinner, but was also well known through the anti-religious principles he proclaimed. The Sisters of the Hospital, however, tried to approach him, were it only to fulfill a duty towards an unfortunate soul. The good Capuchin Fathers in charge of the hospital made a similar attempt. But it was time lost, and they had ere long to desist altogether owing to the Anti-Christian regulations in vogue in the hospitals of our poor Italy. While the hearts of those servants of God were filled with grief at seeing the unfortunate man dying in so hopeless a state, it suddenly flashed across the mind of one of them to call Mgr. Benassini, Prior of the Parish in which the wretched man lived. He came and approached the bed of the dying man, although advised not to do so by those present who knew the patient well and had been witnesses the day before of his impious treatment of the Capuchins and of the Daughters of Charity. The Monsignor spoke quite openly, begged and implored, but in vain. "I have never believed," answered the blasphemer in a burst of envenomed rage, "in these sham terrors of yours, and I don't know who this Christ is of Whom you speak. Soul indeed! Paradise indeed! Hell indeed! Leave me in peace, and let no one come here again to bother me with ridiculous proposals," and with these last words, he made an attempt to spit at the Minister of God. The latter went away greatly afflicted, and, on reaching his house, his eyes fell on the *Life of Gemma*, which he had then only begun to read. At the sight of the book he felt his heart fill with hope, and kneeling down he besought with tears the aid of the Servant of God. Calling his chaplain, he told him to go to the hospital, although it was eleven o'clock at night, and to go in company with a certain woman, an acquaintance of the dying man. It is with great difficulty that any admittance is granted at that hour, and the woman alone was allowed to enter. The Chaplain remained outside in great anxiety, while the Prior at home was praying to Gemma for the successful issue of their mission. The grace was granted! At the sight of the messenger, the poor sinner who, a little before, was so wicked and obstinate, asked that a priest might be sent for without delay. His dispositions were like those of the Penitent Thief and the Prodigal Son of the Gospel, so vivid were the sentiments of compunction with which he made his confession. The Priest, in tears, having lifted his trembling hand to absolve him and give him back to Christ, hastened to fetch the Viaticum and Holy Oils. Finally, the fortunate sinner, strengthened by these two Sacraments, entered into his agony, and, soon after, died quite placidly about four o'clock in the morning, leaving the spectators deeply moved and edified by such an extraordinary conversion and such an enviable death.

The Editor of the second edition of this Biography, having the account of this conversion in his hands, took it to one of the Cardinals of the Roman Curia to read. He did so because he knew that his Eminence was very devout to Gemma, and, therefore, greatly interested in all that concerned the advancement of the cause of her Beatification. "On reading that account," so the Editor wrote to me, "the venerable Cardinal was greatly touched. Then he said to me, 'You are right, you are right, this is the greatest miracle, and greater could not be desired. Assure the Author of the Life that I have this dear little Saint greatly at heart, and ask him to pray to her that I also may advance in the Eucharistic love of Jesus, and in love of Mary.'" A few days later the Holy Father, Pius X, was told of the conversion and was likewise very greatly moved by it, declaring that he also wished to be under the patronage of this dear Servant of God, so as to obtain like graces through her intercession.

There lived in Rome a family totally devoid of religious sentiments, like many others of the present time. The mother of this family had not been to confession for fifty-four years. Her sons were living as though they were not Christians. Her daughters only, three gentle girls, remained good and devout, and, day and night, deplored the sad state of their family, beseeching Heaven to have pity on them. Several influential persons were using all the means at their disposal to bring the old lady to a better state of mind, but it was lost time. God reserved this victory to Gemma. A good Religious, grieved like others at this sad case, had recourse to the Servant of God with sighs and tears. She besought her with triduums and novenas. At length she felt assured of success in her undertaking, and went to see the obdurate old woman. She spoke to her of Gemma and touched her heart by telling her of the wonderful conversions wrought by the little Saint while living. Gemma carried the day! The old woman's heart was softened, she began to cry, and led by the Sister, she went to the Church, made her confession, and received Holy Communion. She felt the consolation and soothing influence of God's grace in the depths of her soul from which it had been absent so many years; and, since that day, she has never omitted going morning and evening to weep and pray in that Church, where she recovered the life of her soul.

The Religious, encouraged by such success, turned all her energies to overcoming, by the use of the same efficacious means, the obduracy of the old lady's sons. "Gemma," she said, "will convert them also." She had hard work with the eldest son. After the first repulse, she returned to Gemma's feet. "And now, Sister," she said to her, "what is to be done. Are you not moving in favor of my sinner? Tomorrow, Saturday, you are to convert him for me."

Heaven granted this request also, and the next evening he asked to go to confession, and received Holy Communion with such joy of soul that, up to this day, he declares that he has never experienced anything like it. A few days later, acting as an Apostle, he brought a friend, a libertine as he had been, to confession, to the same priest at whose feet he himself had acquired happiness. "Now," the same good Sister writes to me, "the youngest brother remains. He has never been to confession and is thirty years of age. He believes nothing and his head is as hard as bronze. I have put him also in Gemma's hands, and she will see to him. I have no doubt of it."

Yes, yes, chosen one of God, see to the conversion of all poor sinners. Say to Jesus, as you often said to Him in ecstasy while here on earth: "I wish all sinners to be saved. Save them for me, O Jesus." And, as for the salvation of sinners, so for every other spiritual and temporal need of thy devout clients, Gemma of Jesus, be not invoked in vain!

Nov. 20, 03, M. S.

The Passionist Sign

The insignia worn by the Passionists is a sign of their devotion to the Passion of Jesus Christ. In the early 1700's, St. Paul of the Cross, the founder of the Passionists, beheld the Sorrowful Mother of Jesus garbed in a black robe with this symbol attached.

The white heart surmounted by a cross signifies the purity of heart that should characterize all those who are devoted to the Passion. The cross over the heart indicates that hearts dedicated to Christ Crucified must expect to be at the foot of the cross and intimately united with it. Within the heart are three words from the Hebrew, Greek and Latin, translated as "Passion of Jesus Christ." The three nails are symbolic reminders of the sufferings of Jesus and of all who are one with Him on Calvary. The black background is a constant reminder of our mourning for the death of Christ. Taken together, the Sign expresses the motto of the Passionists:

May the Passion of Jesus Christ
be always in our hearts.

Tribute to Father Germanus

"I, Gemma, whom with watchful care you confirmed in love for Christ, joyfully grateful for your example that kindled me with ardor of celestial charismas, I have at last received you, Fr. Germano, into this house of peace. This house is yours, since you gave new glory to the name of God as you spread all over the world the graces that Jesus benignly infused into His humble maid."

(Inscribed on the tomb of Fr. Germanus in the Passionist Monastery/Sanctuary of St. Gemma Galgani in Lucca, Italy.)